TWELVE PORTRAITS
OF THE FRENCH REVOLUTION

Robespierre

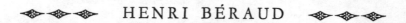

TWELVE PORTRAITS
of the French Revolution

HENRI BÉRAUD

TRANSLATED BY MADELEINE BOYD

WOOD ENGRAVINGS BY BERTRAND ZADIG

Essay Index Reprint Series

BOOKS FOR LIBRARIES PRESS, INC.
FREEPORT, NEW YORK

First Published 1928
Reprinted 1968

LIBRARY OF CONGRESS CATALOG CARD NUMBER:

68-16909

PRINTED IN THE UNITED STATES OF AMERICA

ACKNOWLEDGMENT

The translator wishes to acknowledge the valuable aid given her in the preparation of this translation by Mr. John O'Neal.

CONTENTS

ILLUSTRATIONS

MIRABEAU

June 23, 1789. The royal session had just ended. The king had annulled the decrees of the States-General, commanded the three orders to meet separately and, after making a vague but threatening statement, had withdrawn. The nobles and the clergy had followed him. If the States-General had obeyed, the Revolution would never have been; the privileged would have triumphed. But the deputies remained immovable in their seats and the workmen sent to clear away the hall hesitated to begin their work. The Grand Master of Ceremonies, the Marquis of Dreux-Brézé, came up. "Gentlemen, you have heard the king's orders. His Majesty asks you to disperse." Then, from the seats of the States-General, a deputy rose; his athletic figure, his enormous, pock-marked face, gave him a commanding appearance; his powerful voice thundered in the silence:

"We have heard the king's suggestions and you, sir, who could not represent him in the National Assembly, you, who have no right, no voice, no vote, are in no way competent to remind us of his words. Go and tell those who sent you that we are here by the will of the people and that we shall not leave our places save by the force of bayonets!"

The Marquis of Dreux-Brézé turned on his heel;

3

Louis XVI considered, wanted to act, then yielded; revolution triumphed. That man who with a few phrases decided the course of hesitating destiny, that man was Mirabeau. Posterity always portrays him in that defiant attitude, on that famous day which saw the beginning of his glorious career. But the man is more complex, more varied; he is greater and better than that.

Gabriel Honoré Riquetti, Count Mirabeau, was born in the castle of Bignon, near Montargis (Loiret) on the ninth day of March, 1749. His family, who belonged to the better nobility, had originated in Provence, where they still owned extensive properties. Autocratic, violent, adventurous, the Mirabeaus had all led more or less tumultuous lives. The father of the tribune[1] was not the least extravagant. He was a soldier, a philosopher and a writer celebrated for his work, "The Friend of Men." He had made a stupid marriage: at twenty-eight he had married Mademoiselle de Vassan, daughter of a president of the Paris Chambre des Comptes, who had brought him a small fortune, vulgar manners, an execrable temper and a very passionate temperament. The two ended by quarreling and brought a new cause of disagreement into that wild family. But previously they had had eleven children in eleven years, of whom only five lived.

Son of a passionate, bilious and tyrannical father, who hid his ambition badly under cover of his philosophy, and of a mother so sensual that her conduct

[1] Magistrate chosen by plebeians to protect them against patrician opposition.

was extremely scandalous, Mirabeau, heir to the traits of his race, had all its qualities, good and bad: his nature was all heights and depths, without any moderation.

He was hardly out of boarding school when he went into the army. At eighteen he was in the regiment of Berri-Cavalerie, at Saintes; a year later he ran away after a quarrel with his colonel, and the marquis his father had him confined in the Ile de Ré. He left it to go into the Lorraine infantry, fought a duel, took a brilliant part in the Corsican expedition and fascinated everybody with his quick mind and his charming cleverness. He read, studied, became interested in agronomy, which would to-day be called sociology; quarreled and made up with his father, and finally on June 23, 1772, married a rich heiress from Provence, Mademoiselle de Marignane.

The honeymoon did not last long: Mirabeau was unfaithful to his wife and she to him. A pack of creditors pursued him. His angry father obtained a *lettre de cachet* which confined him in the castle of Mirabeau, then in the small town of Manosque. He was bored and left it for a short escapade, in the course of which he picked a quarrel with a relative and broke the latter's own umbrella over his back. Another scandal! His father was furious and this time had him confined in the Château d'If. On that small island, in the port of Marseilles, distractions were rare; Mirabeau won the heart of the governor and his situation improved, but he made the error of

5

complaining and his father had him transferred to the fortress of Joux, in the heart of the Jura Mountains. He was, as he said, "put among the bears in an owl's nest." And yet he was allowed to hunt and soon he was free to go to Pontarlier, where he read a great deal and attended all the receptions given by the governor.

It was at one of those receptions that he met Sophie de Monnier, a beautiful dark-haired woman, twenty-one years old, wife of the first president of the Chambre des Comptes of Dole, then sixty-nine years old. An idyll sprang up rapidly between the two young people and Mirabeau, who had had innumerable love affairs, knew real love for the first time. So as not to be separated from Sophie, he escaped from the castle of Joux and followed her to Dijon, where she had gone to visit her family. That kindly minister, Malesherbes, allowed Mirabeau to be transferred to the castle of Dijon. But when Mirabeau heard that he was soon to be transferred again to Doullens, in Picardy, he escaped once more and went to Switzerland, where Sophie was to join him. To put the police off the scent, Mirabeau went first to Savoie, met his sister, Madame de Cabris, in Thonon, went from there to Geneva, to Lyons, to Provence, to Piedmont and at last met Sophie at Verrières in Switzerland.

The two lovers went to Holland. Mirabeau had no money and sold his services to the publishers. As the author of an "Essay on Despotism", he contributed to journals, wrote various studies, and especially pamphlets in which he defamed his father. This was a very bad blunder: the old marquis' anger reawakened, the fugitives were arrested, and the States-General of Holland agreed to their extradition.

Mirabeau entered Vincennes prison on June 8, 1777, and remained there three years and a half. Although prisoner, he was not in close confinement: he carried on with Sophie, who was confined first in Paris, then in Gien, a correspondence which, published after his death, clearly owed its popularity to its numerous licentious passages. In vain he piled up memoranda to the ministers and to his father. They were pathetic appeals, but nothing could move the latter. But his great efforts were not to be wasted. It was in those writings that he served his apprenticeship as an orator: he learned how to curb his natural eloquence; his dialectic became firmer and firmer; fiery, commanding, moving, he learned how to use all tones and his prison cell was the first platform to hear his voice.

He suffered from being confined; his prodigious energy was unable to find an outlet in action and he turned to the things of the mind; he read, or rather he devoured, all the books he could get, of all shades and all kinds. He wrote feverishly, as much to use up his unemployed energy as to get practice; he translated, compiled, planned; he wrote obscene works worthy of the closed shelves of any library; he tried the greatest subjects. He wrote his work on *"lettres de cachet* and state prisons" which appeared in 1782, after his liberation, and

7

which brought him a well-deserved renown. Singular state prisons, where one is imprisoned without being guilty, without being given a trial, but where one could write works which were to shake the basis of the social order !

However, the hour of his freedom was near. Mirabeau humbled himself; he appealed to his father, he appealed to his wife. Rebuffed at first, he was not discouraged, and at last the old marquis relented. Mirabeau left his dungeon on the thirteenth of December, 1780; he was free, if one can call free a man who must submit to the troublesome supervision of an easily angered father, and who is always exposed to the danger of further imprisonment.

The first use he made of his recovered freedom was to clear his position before the courts; he had been declared in contempt of court and condemned to death in his absence, for rape and seduction; and, as a matter of fact, the executioner had beheaded him — in effigy. He went to Pontarlier and gave himself up in an effort to have this judgment annulled. As things did not go as he wished, he wrote memorandum after memorandum; finally his adversaries grew tired. A compromise settled the affair. To secure his freedom, Mirabeau gave up Sophie de Monnier who had sacrificed for him her freedom and her love. But she is not the only woman he sacrificed.

Victorious in Franche-Comté, Mirabeau went to Provence to win back his legitimate wife. But

there he encountered a serious opposition: neither
the Countess of Mirabeau, satisfied with her position, nor her father, displeased with his son-in-law,
wished for a reconciliation. Mirabeau pleaded in
vain; then he commanded. His persistency was
answered by a petition for judicial separation.

The scandalous lawsuit was brought in Aix and it
was thought that Mirabeau would come out definitely ruined: his past heavy with evil actions, a
life which counted its years by the prisons where
they had been spent; a dreadful reputation, compromised further by indiscreet letters in which the old
marquis in his anger had accused his son of the
most odious crimes; the judges prejudiced, friends
or allies of his adversaries — everything was against
him. But although he was condemned by the judges,
his reputation was greatly enhanced in the eyes of
the public. His marvelous eloquence, hitherto hidden from all, and perhaps even from himself, had
been revealed: for five hours he had thundered,
howled, roared; dignified, sarcastic, moving, indignant, he had withered his adversaries, crushed
the opposing lawyer, turned the cards in his favor
and provoked the delirious enthusiasm of a public
whose idol he was soon to become. From that day
he was a public man; he needed only favorable circumstances to make the voice of the people articulate
through his powerful oratory.

But in 1784 the time was not ripe. Always short
of money and fearing that his regained freedom
would be short-lived, he went to London, where he

9

published two books. He made the acquaintance of some French refugees, and especially of the journalist, Brissot de Varville, who was to be one of the fathers and one of the victims of the Revolution. But Mirabeau could not stay long in the same place: eight months later, following another rather scandalous lawsuit, he left London and returned to Paris. This time, he sold his services to some bankers and wrote financial pamphlets, the substance of which was furnished him by collaborators more versed than he in those delicate questions; he favored Calonne's policy at first, fell out with that powerful minister and finally left France once more, where it was becoming dangerous for him to remain.

A new Mirabeau was to be revealed: Mirabeau, the diplomat. He directed his steps towards Germany, with Madame de Nehra, a young blond woman, sweet, sensible, who became his mistress and who loved him with absolute disinterestedness, carrying abnegation to the point of effacing herself without complaint when Mirabeau decided to escape from her salutary influence. He went to Leipzig and then to Berlin, made useful acquaintances, saw the great Frederick and his brother, Prince Henry, who enjoyed talking to him. He made use of the information he was able to get to secure an official mission. Thanks to the young Abbé de Perigord, who later became the celebrated Talleyrand, he was given by the French Government the mission of sending a report on the state of Prussia and of all Central Europe. In bad grace with the official

ambassador, Mirabeau, nevertheless, sent remarkable
reports, which show an innate gift for diplomacy
and the vast knowledge accumulated by his encyclopedic brain. He gave a striking picture of the Berlin
court at the beginning of the reign of Frederick
William the Second, that ludicrous sovereign, debauched and mystical, and pronounced upon Prussia's
future judgments that were singularly penetrating.
Not content with being the secret counsellor of the
French Ministry, he dreamt of becoming the mentor
of the new Prussian sovereign, and sent to Frederick
William the Second a long letter full of judicial
advice and absolutely devoid of tact.

In spite of the success of his reports, he tired soon
of a secondary and equivocal position; in vain he
asked for a position worthier of him. Hoping to
find some official post, he seized the occasion of the
Nobles' Assembly and went back to France in January, 1787. Vain hopes! The Ministry would not
give him the post he expected and were willing to
use him only as an officious agent, easy to disown.
His venality and his wild life made people discount
his true worth, and throughout his career these qualities continued to weigh heavily upon his destiny.

Repulsed by Calonne, Mirabeau turned against
him and wrote a violent pamphlet, "A Denunciation
of Stock-Jobbing", in which he advocated a plan of
constitutional government. The success of this pamphlet forced the author to take refuge in Belgium
for a while, and then, after Calonne's fall, he went
back to Germany, where he put the finishing touches

to a work he had been planning for a long time, "On the Prussian Monarchy." The book, in four volumes, appeared in 1788; Mirabeau had required the help of numerous collaborators in its preparation, but it showed traces of his genius.

On his return to France, Mirabeau found himself thrown into the thick of political agitation. Calonne's successor, Brienne, did not succeed any better than his predecessor. Mirabeau kept up a correspondence with M. de Montmorin, Secretary of State for Foreign Affairs. He offered him his services as ambassador but was not wanted. He went into journalism, and published, together with Brissot and the Genevan Clavière, an "Analysis of English Papers" and persisted in demanding a meeting of the States-General for which the greater part of the nation was already clamoring.

At last he triumphed! On the eighth day of August, 1788, Brienne decided to call a meeting of the States-General for the following year. Mirabeau, who a short time before had written, "The day will come when the nation's suffrage will be enough to make a very important man out of a good citizen", felt that his hour had struck.

But to be a deputy he needed money — money was always to be the plague of his life! He begged for a subsidy from Montmorin and when, in spite of his pressing demands, he did not obtain any, he committed a real breach of trust: he published anonymously "The Secret History of the Prussian Court", which was simply a reproduction of the reports which he had sent when he was a diplomatic agent for the French Government. The scandal was enormous: Prussia protested and the book was condemned; Mirabeau denied in vain that he was the author; his reputation, already very bad, received a new injury, which was to hurt his future seriously.

While the storm was breaking in Paris, Mirabeau rushed to Provence, from which district he desired to be elected to the States-General. Through his birth he belonged to the nobility and it was by his peers that he wanted to be nominated. But the hostility towards him did not weaken. If the people saluted him as a triumphant savior, the nobles rejected him. They reproached him with his scandalous life and still more with the audacity of his political views. They desired to exclude him and, for that purpose, decided to admit only those who owned a fief. Mirabeau, thus attacked, replied by a printed manifesto, the peroration of which remains celebrated: "in all countries, in all ages, the aristocrats inevitably pursue the friends of the people, and if through some fortunate combination of circumstances a leader of the people rises from their midst, it is at him especially they strike, so eager are they to inspire terror through their choice of a victim. Thus the last of the Gracchi perished at the hands of the patricians, but, as he was struck with a mortal blow, he threw dust toward the skies, calling on the avenging gods, and from that dust Marius was born, Marius, who owes his greatness less to the extermination of the Cimbri than to his curbing of the power of the Roman nobility."

Rejected by his caste, Mirabeau appealed to the Tiers-Etat, whose idol he had become. He was acclaimed everywhere, bells were tolled in his honor, and he was overwhelmed with speeches. He tried to deserve his popularity — a friend of the people. He did not flatter them. When trouble broke out at Aix and Marseilles, where the inhabitants demanded that bread be sold at a very low price, Mirabeau did not hesitate: he hastened to the spot, organized patrols, harangued, preached, convinced and managed to restore quiet, thanks to his prestige. He was soon to gather the fruit of his efforts; he was elected as Deputy to the States-General by the Commons of both Aix and Marseilles; he decided for Aix. His political life was beginning.

On May 5, 1789, the States-General met. Amongst the crowd of unknown who composed the deputies of the Commons, only Mirabeau stood out. He was celebrated and not only did the people place great faith in him but feared him; his great capacity for work, his extensive knowledge, his impetuous eloquence were guessed at, but the scandals of his private life, his perpetual need for money, the facility with which he sold himself, were well known. So the Assembly was reserved and Mirabeau had to force himself upon it. He never succeeded in imposing himself completely, and the tragedy of his life was his inability to acquire power, openly — he was always obliged to act through tortuous and devious ways.

The principal question which occupied the first

sessions of the States-General was the mode of deliberation. Would they vote as individuals or by separate
Houses? The Commons were in favor of the first
method, which gave them the majority, and they
invited the other orders to join them in a common
attempt to test the powers of the deputies, but the
nobles and the clergy turned a deaf ear to their en-
treaties. The Commons confined themselves in a
"formidable immobility", and Mirabeau approved
that attitude. He had already sparred with the
Ministry. The *Journal des Etats Généraux* which he
founded was suppressed when the second number appeared. What did he care — he published his "Letters
of the Count Mirabeau to his Constituents." No one
could prevent a deputy from writing to his electors !
The Ministry hesitated and gave in. Through his
audacity Mirabeau had obtained the right of the
freedom of the press.

Already the great lines of his political system were
clear in his mind. He wanted the Revolution, but
through the king and not against him. He fought
Necker, "the Idol of the day", but he respected Louis
XVI, and he ceaselessly preached prudence — a dangerous attitude which made him suspected and which even
caused a part of the Assembly to hoot him. But during
the stormy meetings to come, when the Commons and
the privileged protected by the Crown were to oppose
each other, Mirabeau always in the breach, dominating all his colleagues by his magnificent eloquence,
was to appear as the soul of Revolutionary France
itself.

On the twenty-third of June, it was he, as we saw, who crushed with a vibrant reproach M. de Dreux-Brézé, and who brought about the king's capitulation and the union of the orders. But the yielding was not sincere, as foreign troups began to gather all around Versailles and Paris. The Assembly was uneasy and it was Mirabeau who, on the eighth of July, expressed their feelings in proposing a petition to the king, in a speech preserved in the eighteenth letter to his constituents.

"Have the advisers of these measures," he cried, "thought of the consequences they would have for the security of the throne? Have they studied in the history of all people how revolutions begin and how they take place? Have they observed by what disastrous chains of circumstances the wisest minds are thrown out of all bounds of moderation and what terrible impulses cause a frenzied people to commit excesses, even the thought of which would once have made them shudder?" The same prophetic accent dominates the text of the address which his colleagues had asked him to draft:

"The danger, Sire, is pressing, is universal, is beyond all the calculations of human prudence . . . The danger, Sire, threatens the work which is our first duty and which will achieve complete success and a real permanence only if the people regard themselves as entirely free. Moreover, there is a contagion in violent disturbances; we are all too human; our self-distrust, the fear of appearing weak, may cause us to overshoot the mark; we will be beset by violent, irrational counsel, and calm reason, quiet wisdom do not thrive in the midst of tumultuous disorders and factious scenes. The danger, Sire, is very real. You may judge of its extent by the alarms which bring us before you. Many great revolutions have had much less striking cause; more than one action fatal to a nation has revealed itself in a less sinister and formidable manner.''

His efforts were vain: the king was stubborn but did not know what action to take. The uprising took place in Paris and, on the fourteenth of July, the Bastille was taken. The cause of liberty triumphed; but already Mirabeau had foreseen the danger: the intervention of an armed mob, which would drive the Revolution further and further along the path of violence. On the fourteenth of July, the king had escaped Paris; on the fifth and sixth of October, Paris was to capture the king and hold him prisoner.

Between those dates, Mirabeau was active. Logical with himself, whatever some historians may have thought, he tried to have the king given the right of absolute veto to allow him to be opposed to the measures voted by the Assembly; he wanted to establish a constitution and destroy despotism; but he never thought of suppressing the royal prerogatives. On the whole, the king's tyranny appeared to him less unbearable than that of the deputies. He failed in his attempt, but only half failed, for he succeeded in having the king granted the suspensive veto for the duration of two legislatures.

But all discussions stopped because of a very obvious

danger: the financial situation was suddenly found to be very grave, if not desperate. The meeting of the States-General had not restored confidence. Moreover, since the taxes had been proclaimed unjust, they were no longer being paid, and the resources of the Treasury stopped just when the need grew more pressing. Necker, driven into a corner, asked for the vote of a voluntary and patriotic contribution of a quarter of income. Mirabeau, who up till that time had been his enemy, seconded this proposition. Recriminations! Mirabeau justified himself by showing that the danger was great and that the only solution was to agree to the minister's plan. No one was convinced. To carry with him the hesitating Assembly, Mirabeau went up to the rostrum, and through one of his most sublime improvisations, succeeded in moving the deputies so greatly that they voted unanimously in favor of the measure. He showed them the abyss which the deficit opened before them, and he invited them to fill it up by choosing what French proprietors they wished to sacrifice, — otherwise bankruptcy would overwhelm the whole nation, draw the deputies into the universal ruin and provoke disorders in which all would perish. And in a fiery peroration, Mirabeau, with remarkable power, carried away all the deputies and subjugated them by his genius:

"Beware of asking for time; misfortune never gives time! Gentlemen, apropos of a ridiculous movement at the Palais-Royal, of a laughable insurrection which never had any importance except in the weak imaginations or the perverse designs of some men of bad faith, you recently heard those frantic cries: 'Cataline is at the gates of Rome, and we deliberate!' And there was no Cataline, no danger, no factions, no Rome. But to-day, bankruptcy, fearful bankruptcy, is upon us; it is threatening to devour you, your possessions, your honor, and you are deliberating!''

Some days later, on the fifth and sixth of October, the insurrection was knocking at the gates of the Palace of Versailles; the Assembly, which was invaded first, had, following the king's example, to go to Paris. Mirabeau understood that the most urgent need was not to help the Revolution, henceforth triumphant, but to save what was left of the monarchy. He felt himself ready for that task, but he did not foresee the defiance of the Assembly and the ill will of the Court.

In Paris, Mirabeau tried to approach the king. He had to fight strong prejudices; he had a particularly troublesome and suspicious rival to win over. La Fayette, the head of the National Guards, the real master of the palace since the king's return to Paris, suspected Mirabeau, whom he despised as a man and whose political genius he envied. And these two men, who were working sincerely to steady the monarchy, really overthrew it through their rivalry and their intrigues.

The Necker Ministry seemed to be almost ended; weak, without any prestige, it had outlived itself. What would take its place? Mirabeau wanted the power to apply his political ideas, wanted to be free from all financial worries and to be magnificently reëstablished. But he needed La Fayette's help — and La Fayette hesitated, not daring to involve himself too deeply. He had an embassy offered to Mirabeau, which he refused, and money, which he accepted. At last La Fayette made up his mind and it seemed that in the new ministry, so slowly evolved, Mirabeau would play a predominant part. But all his hopes were to be rudely crushed.

The Assembly had accepted Mirabeau's superiority unwillingly, for it mistrusted him, knowing his past and fearing his mercenary spirit. When the pending negotiations were discovered, a plot was formed against him and on the seventh of November, in the course of a stormy debate, a decree was voted forbidding the king to choose his ministers henceforth from the members of the Assembly, a fatal measure, which was to deepen the abyss between the Crown and the Nation and, by keeping Mirabeau from the responsibilities of power, to throw him into crooked and devious intrigues. He tried to oppose it, but could not mistake the personal attack made by the young deputy, Lanjuinais:

"If an eloquent genius can carry the Assembly with him when he is only one of its members, what couldn't he do if he added to his eloquence the authority of a minister?"

Thwarted, Mirabeau, paralyzed by the Assembly, repulsed by the Court, turned to the Comte de Provence, brother of Louis XVI, the future Louis XVIII. He urged him to become a minister so that he might govern in his name, but the prince was timorous; and after a few hesitating steps, he stopped. Another failure!

Mirabeau became obstinate: he wanted power for himself as well as for France. La Fayette had failed; Monsieur had withdrawn; henceforth he would deal with the king. The intermediary was a friend of his, the Comte de Lamarck, an Austrian gentleman and a protégé of Marie Antoinette, who was in the service of France and a deputy to the States-General; even before those October days, he had hinted discreetly that the Crown would find in Mirabeau a powerful defender; but the queen had said haughtily, "I hope that we shall never sink so low that we shall have to ask for aid from Mirabeau." But misfortunes broke her pride; in April, 1790, it was she who reopened negotiations and, through the Comte de Lamarck, appealed to Mirabeau for advice. He was very eager. A memorandum on the situation pleased the king so much that he did not hesitate to buy the powerful tribune. All his debts were to be paid, he was to receive a monthly subsidy of six thousand francs, and, at the close of the Assembly, if the king were satisfied with his services, the lump sum of a million francs.

Such was the arrangement which attached Mirabeau to the Crown and which brought upon his memory a well-deserved opprobrium. Mirabeau was not a traitor since, as before, he continued to uphold the ideas which were the basis of his political system and tried to make possible an understanding between the king and the Revolution; he struggled against the excesses of both reactionaries and demagogues. But he had fettered himself. It was, perhaps, permissible for him, in imitation of numerous *grands seigneurs*, to allow his debts to be paid and to accept a monthly stipend, — he needed to be free from financial worry and deserved a just salary of his work; but that million francs, that tip to a valet whose services had been satisfactory, is an ineffaceable stain which was to sully Mirabeau's reputation forever. "The child is father to the man" — the moral defects of Mirabeau's youth still remained in his character when he had reached the plenitude of his power, when his political genius was patent to everybody.

A chance soon came for Mirabeau to show the Crown that he was its real defender. In May, 1790, the conflict which brought England and Spain to face each other about Nootka Bay brought to the Assembly's notice the question of the right to make war or peace. The Left desired for the Assembly the right to direct foreign affairs; Mirabeau wanted to leave to the king the direction of diplomacy, subject to the approval of the Assembly. There was an exciting oratorical tilt between Barnave, spokesman for the Left, who attacked the tribune violently and provoked an outburst of enthusiasm by a magnificent speech, and Mirabeau who, facing the hostile deputies, while the threatening mob murmured outside, succeeded with a feverish improvisation in regaining his power over the Assembly. "A few days ago the people wanted to carry me triumphantly through those same streets in which they now shout,

'Mirabeau, the traitor.' I do not need this lesson to know that the distance from the Capitol to the Tarpeian Rock is short; but the man who fights for reason and for his country is not easily vanquished. Let those who have been predicting for the last eight days my opinion without knowing it, let those who now sneer at my speech without understanding it, who accuse me of worshipping powerless idols, just as they are being destroyed, or of being the vile hireling of those I have ceaselessly fought — let them denounce as an enemy of the Revolution him, who has, perhaps, been not altogether useless to it, and who, however stranger to his glory, could find security only there; let them deliver to the fury of a deceived people, the one who for twenty years has been fighting all oppression and who was speaking to the French of freedom, a constitution, resistance, when his vile calumniators were living according to the prevalent prejudices. What do I care? Blows from behind won't stop my career. I only say: Answer me, if you can, and then slander me as much as you like!'

Not only a defender of royalty, he was also its counsellor and mentor. His notes interested the queen who, much more than her weak husband, still represented the royal power, and Mirabeau, desiring to influence her by his power of persuasion, asked for and was granted an interview. It took place in the Castle of Saint-Cloud on July 3, 1790: an unhoped-for revenge for Mirabeau, who had hitherto been a pariah of society. And, as always, his power of seduction succeeded: the queen, at first cold, reserved and almost

23

hostile, was won over little by little by that powerful and redoubtable man, who laid at her feet his strength and his courage; and while she gave Mirabeau her hand to kiss, he cried, if one is to believe Madame Campan, "Madame, the monarchy is saved !"

Generous illusions, but still illusions. Mirabeau's advice had been sought, but the Crown was under no obligation to follow it. From the king and his court came always the same suspicions, the same mistrust, and the same renunciations. Mirabeau, riddling La Fayette with epigrams, was listened to; La Fayette, denouncing Mirabeau's ambition and immorality, was listened to, but most of all the supporters of the Old Régime were listened to. And meanwhile, history was made rapidly, and every day some irreparable step was taken. Once again, Mirabeau thought his hour had come: on the fourth day of September, 1790, Necker sent in his resignation and none of his colleagues had either authority or prestige. Vainly Mirabeau urged the king to get rid of them and to revoke the decree which forbade deputies to become ministers. "To yield without seeming to obey," he said, "must always in time of strife, be the policy of governments." Louis XVI did not follow his advice. Furthermore, Mirabeau's intervention in favor of the tricolor, his oft-repeated advice to conciliate the Jacobins, turned the queen against him and weakened his influence. And we have the tragic spectacle of a man, gifted by nature with political intelligence, diplomatic sense, oratorical power, trying unsuccessfully to use them for the common good. He dominated the Assembly, sometimes carrying it off its feet, but mistrust was always at work. He advised the Crown, wanting to save it, but he was not listened to and was suspected of duplicity. His stormy youth, like Banquo's ghost, was always raised against him.

His popularity was immense. The people of Paris, in spite of some slight misunderstandings, cherished him as one of the fathers of the Revolution. He had a last satisfaction: on January 29, 1791, he was elected president of the Assembly for a fortnight. From the presidential chair he directed the debates with tact and replied with wit and eloquence to the numerous deputations which succeeded each other at the bar.

And once again he was to defy unpopularity to defend those principles of justice which rendered him suspect to both extremist parties of the Assembly.

The departure of Louis XV's daughters, and aunts of the king, who left Paris for Rome, had made the deputies, as well as the people, indignant and extremely uneasy. The people were restless and wished to invade the Tuileries, to destroy the Vincennes Prison, as they had destroyed the Bastille. They were ringleaders prepared to push the Revolution to violence and sedition. In that feverish atmosphere the Assembly met to discuss the passage of some law against emigration. For the Jacobins, an agent of the Duke of Orleans, Choderlos de Laclos, the author of a licentious novel, proposed a measure which went so far as to encourage the assassination of émigrés on foreign soil. More moderate, but still violating the principles of freedom, was the measure put forth by the Constitutional Committee: it decreed that in case of a crisis, the Assembly could entrust to a committee of three members the right to authorize or forbid departure from France.

Mirabeau could not let the debate pass without interfering. He was obliged to do so because of agreement with the Crown and also because he was hostile to dictatorship, on whichever side it appeared.

As soon as the proposed laws had been presented for consideration, he voiced vigorously his disapproval of such exceptional measures and cried, as he turned facing the shouts which came from the Left of the Assembly, "The popularity to which I have aspired, and which I, like any one else, have had the pleasure of enjoying, is not a weak reed; I desire it to be firmly rooted, to plunge my roots in the unshakable base of reason and liberty! If you vote a law against the emigrants, I swear never to obey it!" And as one group, more noisy than numerous, clamored louder, he silenced them contemptuously: "Silence from those thirty voices!"

This was only a curtain raiser: the real drama was to take place in the evening at the Jacobin Society. Mirabeau had not been there for a long time and his influence was no longer what it had been. His adversaries, the Duports, the Barnaves, the Lameths, had become the apparent leaders of the club and had done their best to ruin his popularity. That night the anger against him mounted. Duport, from the rostrum, violently attacked Mirabeau's dictatorship, when Mirabeau appeared in the audience. Not moved

in the least by hostile cries, Mirabeau sat down and
allowed the orator to finish, but as he left the rostrum
in the midst of applause, Mirabeau tried to reach it.
Disdainful of insults, threats, he dominated the
tumult and was able to speak at last, little by little
regaining his hold on the audience. "All went for
him," said a German witness of the scene. In some,
indignation mounted to a furious rage . . . In the
end however his gestures and his voice won . . . He
shook from his chest the arrows of his adversary, who
was far from his equal, and threw rocks at him."

But hatred did not disarm. Alexandre de Lameth
reawoke that threatening passion; he attacked
Mirabeau without reserve, recalling his errors and
his faults, condemning his change of attitude which
had caused him to come to terms with the leaders
of the Right. And again the tempest raged. But
Mirabeau, always more audacious in the face of
danger, once more knew how to dominate the
menacing clamor, and how to impose himself upon an
hostile assembly. What did he say? We have no
record, but we know of the prodigious effect of his
speech. "All the resources of his genius," said the
German we have already quoted, "he used to defeat
his young and nimble adversary. He seized him, as
he did his colleagues, with a hand of fire and iron . . .
He hurled at Society, like thunder bolts, unheard-of
truths. His audacity, his noble mien, petrified his
audience. It was thus that he tamed the furious, and,
even if there were some who did not applaud him, all
admired and respected him."

He came victorious out of that struggle, but mortally wounded: a month later, he was no more.

Mirabeau had never spared himself; he had wasted his extraordinary health, his superabundant energy in all kinds of excesses: of work, of food, of pleasure. He was at the end of his vitality when he took to his bed on the twenty-seventh of March. The great Doctor Cabanis diagnosed an inflammation of the diaphragm and declared him lost. He struggled against death for eight days, preserving through his atrocious sufferings a stoical courage.

Feeling in the town ran high; the people forbade all rejoicings; deputation after deputation went to the small house in the Chaussée d'Antin where the tribune was dying; the Jacobins themselves came to render homage to the one who had done everything in his power to establish liberty. If one is to believe tradition, just before he died, he spoke the following prophetic words, "I am taking with me the mourning of the monarchy; the factious will fight over the remnants."

The people of Paris gave a magnificent funeral to their defender. The Church of Sainte Geneviève, barely completed, was designated as a place of burial for great men, and all along the route of the procession, crowds gathered to bid a last farewell to the great tribune.

The favor of the mob is fickle; the discovery of the secret iron closet in the Tuileries laid bare the proofs of Mirabeau's dealings with the Crown; and at once he became unpopular and his mortal remains were, by order of the Convention, removed from the French Panthéon. Where were they taken? Some claim to Clamart Cemetery, but they were never found.

Was he a cynical adventurer? A great statesman? Posterity is still undecided and the historians disagree. Some see in Mirabeau only a vulgar sensualist, greedy for money and ready to sell himself to get it; others see in him the only force capable of restraining and directing that Revolution which he, to such a great extent, had helped to let loose.

The man is all contrasts, but power is the keynote of his personality. His numerous portraits, his bust by Houdon, the small terra-cotta statue by Suzanne, which is kept in the Jacquemont-André Museum, all give the impression of dynamic force. His wide chest, his powerful neck buried in his shoulders and, most of all, his extraordinary head, strong, massive, pock-marked, with a fat nose, but with two fearless eyes under admirably drawn eyebrows, brightened the whole. That unforgettable head of epic ugliness fascinated his opponents. "When I shake my terrible snout," he used to say, "no one dares interrupt me."

But Mirabeau also possessed an unusual gift of seduction. All who came near him fell under the spell of his charm; and I do not speak of his feminine conquests, although they were many: but even those who had the strongest prejudices against him soon felt his strange magnetism. Did not Marie Antoinette herself confide in him after their only interview, and perhaps she would have followed his advice more docilely if another meeting had taken place. He even fascinated his valet: the Picard Legrain entered his service in 1781 and did not leave him in spite of the quarrels, the scoldings and the unpaid wages; he carried devotion so far as to cut, with a whip, the face of the king's prosecuting attorney who had prosecuted Mirabeau in Pontarlier; he gave his master good advice, made him pay his small debts, accepted his prodigious fortune without astonishment, and looked after him devotedly in his last illness.

Since he could arouse such attachments, Mirabeau could not have been quite devoid of heart, but his mind dominated. Gifted with a powerful and marvellously clear intelligence, capable of comprehending at a glance the affairs of Europe and of unraveling the most complicated intrigues, he loved all the subtleties of secret diplomacy, while at the same time he indulged in the most profound speculations as to the rights of people. Although his political conduct may appear hesitating and contradictory, it shows a real unity. An enemy of despotism, but of anarchy as well, he destroyed the tyrannical power of the king, but tried to substitute a strong and respected power; proclaimed the rights of the whole of humanity, but he also knew that the past cannot be entirely swept away, and that the existing institutions must be used while being improved. In a word, he was a strong realist lost amongst passionate dreamers!

The tragedy of his life was that he was unable to put into practice frankly and freely his moderate policy, equally removed from extreme solutions, without any collusion with the money powers. The fatal decree of November 7, 1789, which kept him from power, condemned him to underhand methods. A paid counsellor to whom no attention was paid, he could not influence events as he would have done if he had been the responsible minister of a great kingdom. He could not be the great rebuilder he had dreamed of being, and as he feared himself, he participated only in a "great wrecking enterprise."

If the statesman could not use all his powers, the orator remains one of the greatest who ever appeared on the public scene. His method of work was extraordinary: very much occupied with his numerous duties as a public man, and it must also be admitted by his pleasures, he never had time to prepare his speeches himself. His cleverly chosen collaborators, Dumont, Pellenc, Reybaz of Geneva and ten others, whom he used occasionally, did the work. He made them study the problems thoroughly, write the speeches, and they had even to plan for the interruptions and the objections, and to prepare his rebuttals. But it was he who indicated the ideas to be brought out, who underlined the main points and, when the speech was at last prepared, looked it over, changing a word here and a sentence there, giving to the whole that touch of eloquence which transformed an honest compilation into a masterpiece; as Raphael or Rubens would give the finishing touches to the work of their pupils and completely change the pictures through the greatness of their genius. And he never was more sublime than in his improvisations, when there was no one to prompt the words which rose to his lips.

Although a brilliant orator, it was by his energy that he subjugated his audience; less correct, less clever perhaps than certain of his rivals, he knew how to hold the Assembly breathless by the power with which he hurled his phrases, by the inner flame which devoured him. He was the magnificent voice of the Revolution at her birth. When he died there was no one to pick up the scepter of eloquence as it slipped from his fingers.

In looking back over his life, it seems inexpressibly sad that so many gifts, so much power, so much effort should have been used for such an incomplete and doubtful result. Mirabeau's stormy youth and his immorality clouded his whole life. It is useless for any one to try to be free from all moral laws or social conventions, for one day they will turn and smother. Mirabeau showed that he felt his foolishness when he regretted that he was not as virtuous as Malesherbes. The suspicion with which he was always greeted filled him with a bitterness from which death alone delivered him.

There exists a drawing of Mirabeau's death mask: the face is calm, the features are relaxed and the mouth appears to be smiling, as if the great agitator had at last found peace in eternal repose.

DANTON

Danton

"IF you could only see the monster!" said a contemporary, speaking of Mirabeau. He could have said the same of Danton, who resembled the famous tribune in more than one way. Was he not called the *Mirabeau of the mob?* Everything about him is indeed phenomenal, monstrous, in the real sense of the word, — his physique, his character and his rôle.

George Jacques Danton, born in 1759 at Arcis-sur-Aube, received a very unusual schooling. Upon the death of his father when he was three years old, he began an adventurous and tramping life. Independent, fearless, quarrelsome, he ran about the country, swam in the river, fought those who wanted to fight, as well as those who didn't. Twenty times he courted death, twenty times he escaped. A bull tore his upper lip with its horns. Danton declared war on bulls, and while trying to avenge himself, he had his nose broken. Another time he attacked a herd of pigs with a whip; they trampled upon him and injured him seriously. He had hardly recovered when he was almost drowned, and shortly after he fell a victim to smallpox, which marked his face permanently.

To stop his escapades, he was entrusted to the care of a schoolmistress who was supposed to be very strict; but he ran away. Finally, in 1773, his family persuaded him to enter high school, and he began to work. Although he did not lead his class, he was one of the better pupils. To all other reading he preferred the authors of "Republican Rome", but enjoyed also the Greek moralists. However, his adventurous spirit had not deserted him. In 1775, the teacher of rhetoric gave his class as a subject the coronation of Louis XVI. Before unmaking kings, Danton wished to see for himself how kings are made. He borrowed a little money from his comrades, walked twenty-eight leagues to Rheims, returned very enthusiastic, and wrote the best essay of the whole class.

His family, and especially his uncle, Barberey's parish priest, wanted him to become a priest but the law attracted him and he went to Paris to study. He worked in the office of a public prosecutor to learn legal procedure, and haunted the Palace of Justice, but he did not neglect physical exercise; he practised fencing and swimming; and he loved the Seine. From the place where he disported himself, Danton could see the towers of the Bastille and frequently he would raise his head like a Triton, in the midst of the astonished bathers and shout in his vibrant voice, "The stronghold suspended above our heads annoys and cramps me. When shall we knock it down? I'll use a pickax that day."

Admitted to the bar in 1785, he married a year later and purchased about the same time the office of lawyer to the King's Council, an excellent preparation for public life. Like his colleague, Vergniaud, he pleaded all kinds of cases, — maritime law, ordinary

law, commercial law, forest law, colonial and nobility law. At that time the lawyer's knowledge
had to be very extensive and this alone proves that
Danton was not as ignorant as some of his detractors
try to make out. It would have been difficult to find a
better school for a future deputy, a future statesman, a
future revolutionary. Danton was in a position to
place his hands upon all the sores of French society.
By 1789 he was ready for the great part he was to play.

As president of his district and its representative
at the Provisional Commune, the founder of the
Cordelier Club, a member of the Jacobin Club, the
administrator of the district, an assistant to the
Prosecutor of the Commune, a minister in and the
real head of the Government of the tenth of August,
a deputy of Paris at the convention sent to the front
to report on the army, a member and head of the
Committee of Public Safety, Danton secured all the
honors, occupied all the positions for which a revolutionary of his ilk could hope, except perhaps that of
dictator. This may have been because, as he said
himself, Nature had given him, in addition to his
remarkable physique, "the bitter physiognomy of
Liberty."

In all his activities Danton proved himself to be an
extraordinary orator and a great statesman. He had
more of the orator's presence than Mirabeau or
Vergniaud. He was enormous; his colossal height
dominated the Assembly; his wide shoulders; his
bull's neck; his pock-marked face; his thick hair
brushed straight back; his high forehead; his piercing

eyes; his large, flat, snout-like nose; the scar, which
he owed to his adventurous youth, and which swept
his face with a sneering grin, — all helped to impress
people, all contributed to his air of insolent audacity,
of threatening, passionate tumult.

His personal appearance also added to the impression
he created. Not that Danton was untidy by affectation
like Marat; on the contrary, his clothes were very
neat, almost luxurious. Robespierre wore his blue
coat and silk breeches like a tidy and well-behaved
bourgeois, but Danton gave to his clothes some of the
tempest which brewed within himself. There was
"a windstorm in the wings of his tie and the lapels
of his coat."

His whole appearance brought an assurance of
strength which his contemporaries tried to embody in
the most diverse phrases: "Gigantic Revolutionary",
"King of the Revolution", "*real* tribune of the people",
"Creator of the Republic", "Cyclops", "Atlas of the
party", "Titan", "Stentor", "Hercules" — such were
the various epithets applied to Danton.

From the platform the giant seemed to crush every
one. One hand gesticulated sweepingly and pictur-
esquely, while the other lay limp at his side in his
usual manner. His voice thundered and his eyes gave
forth sparks so terrible that all feared to gaze upon
him. Like a cyclone he carried everything with him,
and upset everything as he passed. "His voice re-
sounded," said Levasseur in his Memoirs, "like a
warning gun to call the soldiers to the breach."
Danton did not need to open his mouth to overawe

people; his silence was as eloquent as his speech. Once Lesourd dared to accuse him of a Royalist conspiracy with Dumouriez. "Motionless in his seat, Danton raised his head with a scornful expression peculiarly his own. His face showed both contempt and anger. His attitude contrasted with the movements of his face and it was easy to tell from his strange mixture of calm and agitation that he did not interrupt his adversary because it would have been child's play to answer him and he was sure he could crush him."

Most remarkable of all, this amazing orator never wrote a speech; he invariably spoke impromptu. Neither his sentences nor his ideas were settled in his mind when he began to talk; he was really an improviser.

Of course, he must not be regarded as the *vir bonus dicendi peritus*. No rhetoric in his discourses; no division; no plan; no exordium, — an assault. No peroration, — a whirlwind. Nothing combed and careful, but a healthy abundance of metaphors, of high-sounding words, of familiar ones, of insults, of risqué jokes, of melodrama, and even of repetitions. His speeches were a real challenge to rhetoric, but they were eloquence, great eloquence; because in the midst of his jumble, from time to time, Danton would hurl a shaft, a formula which rendered unnecessary those tedious reasonings and empty tirades which he hated. "With Danton," said Thibaudeau, "it was a sudden outburst of his soul, with all the ardor and all the abandon of nature. The effect was prodigious."

And the Girondin Meilhan wrote of him: "Danton had an eloquence all his own, spontaneous, un-methodical. He carried his listeners by his audacity rather than by the logic of his thoughts or the charm of his style." In brief, Danton's speeches did not lead to thought but, better still, to action.

And that is why it is very difficult to separate Danton's words from his deeds, his oratory from his statesmanship. He never spoke for the sake of speaking; his speeches were really his acts. Danton, born in a generation of idealists, was a great realist and a great opportunist, and he proved it at least twice: at the Provisional Executive Council in 1792, and at the Committee of Public Safety in 1793.

To tell the truth, Danton's part in the Provisional Executive Council was relatively small; he was only a minister, but he could not remain in obscurity long, and gave himself the lion's share. As Minister of Justice he showed at once the hungry need for activity which characterized him. The different offices watched in fear and trembling the installation of the "Cyclops." They were right, for the moment he entered the palace of the Maupeous and of the La-moignon, he advised the staff to make use of their "right to ask for their pension", circumstances obliging him to replace them by a staff chosen by public opinion. He removed the fleur-de-lis which ornamented the hand of the clock in his office, evidently wishing to efface all traces of royalty, animate and inanimate. Once installed at his desk, he did not dream of the best means of insuring the people's happiness, — he acted. He signed one hundred and twenty-three decrees in eight days.

But it is not as Minister of Justice that Danton is remembered; it is as the real head of a government, as the Prime Minister of the Revolution. It had been decided that the first member elected by the Assembly to that Executive Council, which was to depose royalty, would have a predominant position. Danton was elected to that place by two hundred and twenty-two votes from an Assembly of two hundred and eighty voters.

The Assembly had been right: Danton was the right man in the right place. "Born a government leader," said Albert Sorel; "from the first day he revealed himself to be a government leader." The chaos he operated in was his right element. He loved plunging into it and finding his way out. It was he who took charge of the affairs of a disorganized and invaded France and who, in spite of intrigues of all kinds and of the urgent financial needs, directed public opinion, war and diplomacy. His programme appeared formidable: to remain calm, first of all; to await the enemy firmly, to unite revolutionary and patriotic France against the enemy, to reorganize the army, — in brief, to fight to the death.

All around him people were despairing, and with reason: the Prussians had occupied Eastern France; Longwy had fallen into their hands; a few days later Verdun was threatened. As Madame Roland wrote: "Even though now we never sleep and show very uncommon activity, it is impossible to repair in a few

hours the effects of four years of betrayal." And yet
Danton did repair. Though everybody thought the
cause was irretrievably lost, he refused to give up the
struggle. "I made my mother, who is seventy, come;
I made my two children come," he cried; "they arrived
yesterday. Before the Prussians enter Paris, I want
France to perish. I want twenty thousand torches to
fire Paris in a moment."

And yet the enemy still advanced. On the night of
September first, it was learned that the surrender of
Verdun was only a question of hours. Danton knew
it. Perhaps in his heart he doubted the efficacy of
resistance, but he did not show it. He generously
reassured and encouraged every one. And from the
tribune he revived their waning hopes. "It is really
satisfying for the ministers of our free country,
Gentlemen," he shouted, "to announce that the
country will be saved. Everything is ready; every
one is longing to fight; and from one end of France to
the other every one is rising. You know that Verdun
is not yet in the hands of the enemy, and that the
garrison has promised to execute the first who speaks
of surrender. Part of the people will guard our
frontiers; part will dig trenches; and still others will
defend our towns with pick-axes."

Thus Danton, though convinced of defeat, found a
way to rouse the country's spirit and to restore
courage to a despairing people. He went on, "Paris
will help. The Commissaries of the Commune will
issue solemnly an invitation to citizens to arm them-

selves and to go to their country's defence . . . The
National Assembly will become a real war committee.
We ask that you should aid in the direction of this
sublime move of the people . . . We ask that any
one who should refuse either to serve France in person
or furnish arms should be punished by death . . . All
over France the tocsin is ringing, not as a signal of
alarm but to sound the charge against all our country's
enemies."

The Assembly burst into applause, and then, with a
superb gesture which remained engraved in the mind
of an eyewitness for forty years, Danton concluded,
"To vanquish the enemy, Gentlemen, we must have au-
dacity, still more audacity, always audacity, — and
France will be saved!"

Immense applause answered him. "The effect upon
the Assembly was indescribable," said Choudieu, a
deputy, "and I seemed to see in him a tribune urging
the Romans from the public forum to defend their
country. He never appeared so magnificent to me as
on that day."

That single speech would suffice to make Danton
immortal. As Jaurès wrote, "He rendered an immense
service to the Revolution and to his country by
crushing with his strong words all thoughts of weakness and by inciting every one to hope and to action.
He restored confidence to the Executive Council, to
the Assembly, and to the Nation. He drowned all
difficulties, all rivalries and all hatreds in the torrent
of action."

Michelet, better than any one else, caught the greatness of the part he played during that terrible period. He wrote:

"In those sublime moments Danton was the voice of the Revolution and of France itself. In him France found the strong heart, the deep chest, the magnificent attitude, which could express her faith. And let no one say that words count for little at such moments. Words and deeds are one. That overwhelming confidence, which strengthens hearts, leads to action as well. Here action is the servant of speech, following docilely, just as at the Creation. God spoke and the world was. With Danton speech was so much an action, so much an heroic thing (sublime and practical at the same time) that there is no comparable case to be found in literature. His words were not only words — they were France's energy made concrete, a cry from the Nation's heart."

And yet Danton knew very well that war was not the only means of vanquishing one's enemies. However great a politician he was, he did not hesitate (although he realized that, if discovered, he would have to pay with his head) to appeal to diplomacy. His plan was to separate Prussia from Austria, — its hereditary enemy, — by negotiations to disorganize the coalition and to make an alliance with England, and thus to pull France out of the net which enmeshed her. Then, later on, when the enemy had retreated, he planned to lift the siege, to reëstablish a normal government, and to found a republic based upon respect for property rights and the sacred principle of equality. He had no time to achieve all his program, but saw France saved at Valmy, and it was with tranquillity that he was able, once elected a deputy to the Convention, to resign as a minister. "I received them," he said, "with the noise of those cannons with which the citizens of the capital were destroying despotism. Now that the armies are mobilised, and their coöperation with the representatives of the people is assured, I owe it to myself to give up my first tasks. I am only a mandatory of the people and it is in this capacity that I shall speak in future."

He was not to remain a mandatory of the people for long. On April 6, 1793, he was elected a member of the Committee of Public Safety. And at once, with that steadfastness of purpose which characterized this great statesman, he formulated his program anew. "I warn you," he asserted, "you'll be unworthy of your mission if you do not keep constantly before your eyes these aims: to vanquish our enemies, reëstablish order in the interior and map out a good constitution. We must do these three things first of all." Again Danton had to defend France, for the victories had not continued, and had been succeeded by great disasters. He reappeared as France's good angel. How was he to save his country? By conquering Holland and humiliating the English aristocracy. "Let us take Holland," he had cried some time before, "and Carthage is destroyed and England can no longer exist for liberty only. Let your emissaries go forth and inspire them with your enthusiasm. Let them depart now, this very night, let them tell our wealthy class either that the aristocracy of Europe must pay our debt or they must pay it. The people has only its blood and it pours it out freely. Pour out your riches. Citizens, grasp the great destiny which is awaiting you. What? With a whole nation as a lever, with reason as a starting point, you have not turned the world topsy-turvy? You who are wearying me with your quarrels, instead of thinking of the safety of the Republic, I repudiate all of you as traitors to your country . . . What do I care about my own reputation? Let France be free and my name dishonored. Let us conquer Holland, let us reanimate the Republican Party in England, let us cause France to march on, and posterity will give us glory. Fulfill your great destiny. No debates, no quarrels, and the country will be saved."

Unhappily the whole of Europe had risen against France and the army was demoralized. The Vendée was up in arms, the Girondine revolt fermenting. Then, once more, Danton proved himself a great realist. He looked cold-bloodedly at the international checkerboard. He wished to separate Prussia from Austria, regain the good will of England and obtain the friendship of the small powers. But to attain this end he must use diplomacy. He had been the first to favor France's natural frontiers, the first to promote political propaganda. But the plans he had made had failed and it was necessary to adopt another policy, a policy of moderation. Danton worked at it. "In a short while you'll know that the league of kings is slowly breaking up. Indeed England seems inclined

to be friendly; Prussia has started negotiations."
Danton thought his aim had been achieved and that
therefore it was unnecessary to behead the queen, and
that at any cost Europe should be prevented from
continuing an unforgivable war.

Unfortunately Danton was forgetting Robespierre,
who opposed him steadily and slyly, until Danton
overruled him and resigned from the Committee of
Public Safety in July, 1793. All his projects had
failed, but he bore no grudge. A simple deputy once
more, he tried to work for the ideas which he believed
best. He still appeared occasionally on the political
stage, — he went assiduously to the sittings, he spoke
about the revolutionary government, about freedom
of religion, about obligatory and free schooling for all.
On the fifth of September, 1793, he had a great success
with his speech on the formation of an army by
levy on districts. Before he even opened his mouth
the plaudits accompanied him to the platform and
delayed his beginning for some minutes. The next
day he was reëlected a member of the Committee of
Public Safety. But he solemnly refused. "I won't be
a member of any committee, but the spur of them all,"
he said. Then he disappeared. The extraordinary
effort he had made had worn out his nerves. As is
often the case with violent people, depression followed
closely upon exaltation. He was actually ill, and not
only from a diplomatic illness. He was extremely
tired; he was, in his own words, "sick of men."
And he left Paris with his young second wife, going
first to Choisy and then to Arcis-sur-Aube.

47

He had not gone secretly; he had asked for the Convention's permission. "I am convalescing from a grave illness," he wrote to the Convention. "And the doctors say that if I wish to hasten my recovery, I must breathe my native air." In Arcis, Danton seemed to have forgotten the feverish agitation of the time, but he was thinking of it continually, although he remained very quiet in his peaceful retreat trying to rest. He was seen at his window or on the doorstep wearing a nightcap. He put on his coat seldom and then only when he wished to acquire some new piece of land which would enlarge his property. He refused to talk politics. He wanted to be only a country squire and was anxious to enjoy the peace and calm of the countryside. One day when he was walking with one of his neighbors, he saw a mutual friend who showed him a newspaper. "Good news," cried the messenger.

"What good news?"

"Look here, read! The Girondins have been condemned and executed."

The tribune grew pale and tears coursed down his cheeks. "Good news," he complained. "You call that good news, scoundrel!"

"Weren't they agitators?"

"Agitators? Aren't we all agitators? We all deserve death as much as they did. We'll all follow them, one after the other."

Danton was right. During his absence tongues had been unloosed, gossip was rife. No one in Paris was inactive and his nephew, Mergez, came to tell him so.

"Your friends," he said to him one day, "urge you to go back to Paris as soon as possible. Robespierre and his friends are uniting against you." Danton would not believe any of those rumors. But Mergez was insistent. "Well!" answered Danton, "tell Robespierre that I'll be in Paris soon enough to crush him and his friends."

Indeed Danton did come back to the capital shortly after, but too late. His conciliating attitude when a member of the first Committee of Public Safety, his policy of concessions to foreign powers, had made the people hate him. His opportunism irritated his enemies. Danton, the realist, was not attuned to his time; he was lost in a world of idealists. He knew that it was impossible to get everything at once, that the Revolution could not establish the principle of equality of property, that it must begin with the equality of all citizens before the law; that everything can't be upset and that a period of transition was indispensable. Danton, for example, believed in "eternal" property, because, according to him, it was impossible to found a "Republic of Visigoths." His attitude toward religion was similar. Danton acted like a free thinker, but did not believe in persecution. He thought the de-Christianization of France was bad, for he believed the old song could still help to alleviate human misery.

He did not hide his profound convictions, but nevertheless did not hesitate to be married in church. And when it seemed to him that the Revolution went too far, that the saturnalias of the Hébertists might

49

destroy France with fire and sword, Danton deliberately decided to be reactionary. It was then, under his inspiration, that Camille Desmoulins founded the *Vieux Cordelier*. Now that France was victorious, Danton asked for clemency. The Terror, in his opinion, had no reason for existence, now that the enemies of France were vanquished. "I shall break that damned guillotine before long," he cried, "or I shall fall under it." He did not know how truly he was speaking.

Without doubt, Danton for the moment had not much to fear, because Robespierre was still afraid of him. "Your levity astonishes me," Thibeaudeau told him, on March 24, 1794; "don't you see that Robespierre is planning your fall? Won't you do anything to prevent it?"

And Danton answered, "If I believed he even thought of it, I would eat his entrails." "They won't dare," he always repeated, speaking of his enemies. "Don't be afraid, children," he asserted again to his friends on the eighth of *Germinal*. "You see my head, — is it not well set upon my shoulders?" However, the danger was real. His own circle urged him to act. They even advised him to flee, but the "Titan" did not want to hide. "Can I carry my country upon the soles of my feet?" was his indignant retort to those who begged him to run away.

Meanwhile, Robespierre was busy accumulating documents and patiently gathering the material for the report which Saint-Just would present. When everything was ready he decided to act. On the evening of the ninth of *Germinal*, the Committee of Public Safety had Danton's house surrounded. He was arrested that same night and reached the Luxembourg Palace at six in the morning on the tenth of *Germinal*.

In prison Danton found all his friends: Desmoulins, Delacroix, Philippeau, and Hérault de Séchelles. They were accused, as he was, of fomenting a conspiracy for the reëstablishment of the monarchy, for the destruction of national representation and of the republican government. But Fabre d'Eglantine and some others were also there. They were accused of *degrading* national representation and of *destroying through corruption* the republican government. Political prisoners and criminals had been mixed, so that the latter should dishonor the former.

On the thirteenth the accused were transferred to the Conciergerie and their trial began. The public flocked to this choice spectacle, anxious to see the "chained monster", to hear the roars of the beast at bay. Danton had a tense and hostile face; pride, anger, contempt, all were mirrored in it. The famous "grin" seemed more terrible than ever. Suberbielle, who had been his friend and was now his judge, admitted that he was afraid to look at him. When his name was called, Danton answered in a clear voice, and when asked his place of residence, he replied, "Soon my dwelling place will be in nothingness and my name in the Pantheon of history, whatever may be said about me now."

The first session was short. Danton was not allowed to speak, but he counted upon the second

session, and it was full of incidents. When Danton
interrupted Herman, the president reminded the
prisoners of their duty. "And I, Mr. President,"
cried Danton, "I remind you of justice. We have the
right to speak here." Herman rang his bell franti-
cally to obtain silence. "Don't you hear my bell,"
he shrieked to Danton, who yelled back, "A man who
is defending his life mocks at a bell and howls."
He did not succeed any better than the day before in
having his defence heard, but at last, on the fourteenth
of *Germinal*, he was allowed to speak. Unfortunately
we have not the complete text of his speech, for the
Bulletin of the Revolutionary Criminal Court reproduced it very much altered, but the parts which
have been preserved are enough to prove the energy
shown by the "Titan", and to show the parody of
justice of which he was the victim.

"Danton," the president said to him, when the
accused was protesting violently, "audacity belongs
to crime and calm to innocence. Without doubt, you
have a right to defend yourself, but your defence
must keep within the bounds of decency and moderation, and show respect to all, even to your accusers."

"Doubtless," answered Danton, "audacity is reprehensible, when used to further one's own ends. No
one can accuse me of that, — but that audacity for
the national cause which I have shown so often,
which has often enabled me to help my country, that
kind of audacity is permissible and I am proud that
I have it.

"When I see myself so gravely and so unjustly

accused, how can I master that indignation which makes me rise against my detractors? Do you expect from such a strongly opinionated revolutionary as I, a coldly reasoned answer?

"I sell myself? Men such as I can't be bought, for upon their foreheads is stamped in indelible characters the seal of liberty, of the republic. And I am accused of having crawled to vile despots, of having always opposed the party of freedom! Of having conspired with Mirabeau and Dumouriez! And it is I who am being asked to answer to inevitable and inexorable justice!"

"And you, Saint-Just, you will be responsible to posterity for the defamation you have hurled at the best friend the people has, at its most ardent defender. When I think of that list of horrors of which I am accused, I tremble in every fiber of my body."

Danton was continuing in that tone, but the president once again told him that he was insulting national representation, the tribunal and the sovereign people. Then the accused deigned "to lower himself so far as to justify himself." He explained his relations with Lameth, his journey to England, his flight to Arcis, his relations with Dumouriez, but he was unable to restrain his anger. "I am fully aware of what I am doing," he cried, "when I challenge my accusers, when I ask them to face me. Produce them and I will plunge them back into that void from which they should never have emerged . . . Come forth, vile imposters, and I shall tear away the masks which hide you from public vengeance!"

Danton spoke for an hour. A citizen who witnessed the trial said that he made judges and jurors tremble and drowned the president's bell with his voice. Outside the rumor spread that he was confounding his dismayed accusers. The president was afraid that the crowd might take the prisoner's part. Suddenly he adjourned the session, with the excuse that Danton must be tired.

The next day Danton's friends were allowed in their turn to say a few words. Public opinion was against the accusation. From the debate, it seemed clear that the indictment did not hold water, and moreover, by a singular abuse of the laws, the defence was not permitted to produce witnesses. Danton, when he came to the aid of his friend Delacroix, pointed out the iniquity of a trial where the defence was not allowed to speak. The situation was becoming ticklish. Fouquier-Tinville, the public prosecutor, angry, confused and crushed, saw that things were shaping badly for his side. Then the Convention was warned and a decree of outlawry was torn from it under the pretext that the accused were insulting the tribunal. "That decree," Danton thundered, "is an infernal machination to ruin us. I am Danton till I die. To-morrow, I am sure fame awaits me in death."

On the sixteenth of *Germinal*, after the last protestations of the accused, the jurors retired to debate. Their discussion lasted a long time and without doubt they did not escape the maneuvers made to influence them. At last the jury came back. Their verdict was "guilty." It meant death. The sentence was put into execution that very day. Danton kept all his gayety; he jeered, he joked, he consoled Camille, he had lost none of his truculency. Fabre d'Eglantine complained, fearing lest one of his manuscripts which contained, according to him, such beautiful verses, would be seized. "Verses!" said Danton. "In a week you'll be making worms, not verses."

The tumbrils left the Conciergerie at four o'clock, "three carts painted in red, drawn by two horses, escorted by five or six gendarmes," — and drove slowly through "an immense and silent crowd", which "showed no joy and did not dare to show its horror."

Danton, the cynosure of all eyes, held his "enormous round head" high and "stared proudly" at that "stupid crowd." In front of the Duplay's house, in the Rue Saint Honoré, where Robespierre lived, he turned around. "You will follow me," he cried; "your house will be razed and salt will be spilt upon the ground where it stands."

They reached the square and the condemned climbed down. Danton's calm was the calm of contempt. Samson, the executioner, seemed to be in a hurry, for when Hérault de Séchelles started to kiss Danton, he separated them. "Idiot," said Danton, "will you keep our heads from kissing each other in the basket?"

"The day was ending," wrote the poet Arnault. "At the foot of the humble statue silhouetted against the sky, I saw a great shadow — Danton's shadow;

the tribune in the glow of the setting sun seemed as much like one emerging from the tomb as like one ready to enter it. Nothing as audacious as the countenance of that athlete, nothing as formidable as that profile, which defied the ax, as that head, which although ready to fall, still seemed to be dictating laws."

Danton mounted the scaffold last. He was alone in the midst of a crowd silent with horror. At the thought of leaving his wife, whom he loved tenderly, he had a moment of weakness. "My beloved one," he said with a sob, "I shall never see you again." Then regaining control of himself, he said, "No weakness, Danton!" and turning to the executioner, "Show my head to the people; it is worth it."

In a moment his head fell into the basket. At the age of thirty-four and a half, George Jacques Danton was no more.

More than any other famous man, Danton has paid the price for his celebrity. He has not escaped that sad privilege of public men, of having his life searched, carefully examined with a magnifying glass, and sifted mercilessly by historians, self-appointed censors. Alive, he knew the gravest reproaches. Dead, he has been the victim of more precise accusations. Archives and papers have replaced gossip and speeches. As in his own time, men are divided in their opinions; some praise, some blame. M. Mathiez accuses, M. Aulard defends, and in reality it is very difficult to tell which is the most ruthless, the public prosecutor or the defender.

Did Danton sell himself? All his magnificent speeches, all his noble thoughts, all the grand gestures, — were they only a hypocritical justification of the price which he had been paid? Danton sold to England, to the Duke of Orleans, to the Crown even! Danton meddling with secret funds, prevaricating in Belgium — that is more than enough to astonish and grieve us. Alas, the contemporary testimonies of La Fayette, Mirabeau and Brissot are very clear. This is not the place to separate the truth in their statements from their exaggerations and their passions. Let us say that if they do not absolutely convince us of the venality of the tribune, they leave room for the gravest doubts. Recent discoveries have added more disturbing arguments. Let us be content with an interrogation mark.

Was Danton the debauched man Robespierre accused him of being when he was still alive? Yes, if by debauched one means an admirer of Rabelais, of Diderot, a lover of life, and *gauloiserie*. The colossus adored life and enjoyed all the sensuality it could give. But there his debauchery stopped. Robespierre's puritanism was bound to be shocked by Danton's epicureanism. The conflict between the two friends who became enemies was much more of temperament than of ideas. Robespierre indeed lacked "in his style that spontaneous obscenity which Danton regretted he could not bequeath to him." Well, Danton needed *women*, as he shouted one day, but all his private life showed that he meant "one woman." Danton was not a eunuch. What harm was there in that? He adored his first wife and he adored his second, and his two "small Dantons." And that brings us to the most salient point in the character of the "Titan." The kind colossus loved to love. He never abandoned his friends. Hatred was foreign to his nature; he did not need it.

In short, this corrupt, this debauched man was a happy-go-lucky person, amiable and fond of life. *Homo sum* he could have cried rightly, *humani nil a me alienum puto*. He was not a saint, but a man, and more than a man, he was a genius. If ordinary mortals have their weaknesses, why not a colossus? And in spite of his faults and his errors, we must not forget that once, when all appeared lost, he saved France and, remembering that, we should be indulgent.

ROBESPIERRE

THERE is an element of the miraculous in the life of Maximilien Robespierre. He was a small lawyer, an austere man of letters, quite honest without doubt, but without any apparent greatness, who found himself one day whirled to the topmost rung of the ladder "much higher than any throne", "placed upon a pedestal." Astonishing legend! An astonishing problem, the life of that man who despite his relatively mediocre gifts, acquired an enormous power, an almost theocratic authority, and who, although neither his origin nor his abilities appeared to qualify him for an extraordinary fate, became the idol of a whole people, only to fall so tragically on a day in *Thermidor*.

Very shy, gentle and studious, young Robespierre was a model school boy at the college Louis-le-Grand. Under the direction of his Jesuit masters and with Camille Desmoulins, as a fellow student, he studied the *Conciones*, Plutarch and Rousseau. His professor of rhetoric, the Abbé Hérivaux was enthusiastic about him. There was no college competition in which his name did not appear at the top of the list. He was, at that time a rather frail child, and always serious. Very sensitive and tender, and when he gave the birds he had been raising with so much love to his maternal grandfather, he found consolation in his successes and his passion for the philosophers. Nothing pleased his budding pride so much as the nickname "romain" which the Abbé Hérivaux bestowed upon him; nothing gratified him more than the visit he paid as a young man to his favorite master Rousseau, under the shady trees of Ermenonville.

Nourished by the philosophers and by antiquity, he seemed better fitted for generalities and abstractions than for quibbling subtleties. However, once he had finished his studies, he made for himself an enviable position at the bar of his native town, Arras. Not at once, it is true; because if the new lawyer spoke easily he expressed himself without poetry, in a tone of cold logic, and with an exaggerated use of paraphrase and abstractions.

"He speaks easily," some one said of him, "but he is neither eloquent nor emotional." However, a very much talked-of suit, the "lightning conductor" case, brought him notoriety. A farcical verdict of the aldermen of Saint-Omer had decreed that Sieur de Vissery of Bois-Valé should remove the lightning conductor which he had placed upon his roof. Robespierre pleaded for him and won his case. "Monsieur de Robespierre," said the paper *Mercure de France*, "is a young lawyer of rare merit, and he showed in this affair, in which all science was on trial, an eloquence and a wisdom which give a very high opinion of his knowledge."

Like many of his contemporaries, and like Vergniaud in particular, the young provincial lawyer did not devote himself entirely to the study of law, for he had literary pretensions; and he became a member of the poetical and pastoral society of the *Rosati*. He wrote gallant and Bacchic verses in the fashion of the day, and became first a member, then director of the Academy of Arras.

In 1789, Robespierre was thirty years of age. If he were beginning to be known in the provinces he had no prospects which would indicate that he was destined for any great fate. He did not seem, in any case, destined for politics. It was an address to the Artesian people which brought him the votes of his compatriots at the time of the summoning of the States-General. He was made a commissary for the district of the Cahiers and became first a deputy of the Tiers-État to the States-General, and then to the Constituante.

To say that he shone immediately in his new task would be an exaggeration. He did not always have the ear of the Assembly. His person and his theories were often laughed at. Once when he obstinately insisted on speaking about a question which had been settled and which was of no importance, his colleagues refused to listen to him and Maury obtained a facile success by asking ironically if Monsieur de Robespierre's speech should be printed. He was regarded generally as a very capable provincial lawyer and a serious worker but without breadth or solidity. Tirelessly, letting nothing discourage him, Robespierre pursued his ideal. He was opposed to the *bourgeois* solutions of the Barnaves and Lameths which were really democratic. He protested against the distinction between active and passive citizens, because it unfortunately divided the French people into two hostile classes. He denounced the eligibility qualification, the stated income which qualified a person to be elected a member of the Assembly, the gold stamp which gave political power only to landowners. He pleaded the cause of the colored people and never missed an opportunity to compare the prejudices of the *bourgeoisie* with the principles of the Declaration of Rights. Impervious to all jests and insults, the young deputy walked straight and resolutely in the path he had mapped out for himself.

And little by little he lost his shyness, he faced everything and everybody. "I am not discouraged by those who interrupt me," he cried one day; "I even propose to tell other truths which will excite a lot of discussion." Many of his contemporaries were beginning to see that they had to do with *some one*. Mirabeau, the all-powerful Mirabeau, predicted a great future for him. "He'll go far," he said, "because he believes everything he says." There, indeed, lay the secret of his influence. He did not evade questions, he went straight to the point, sacrificing nothing to sincerity. In the year 1790 he delivered almost eighty speeches in the Assembly, besides those he made to the Jacobins. And it is in his plodding, his capacity for work that, as much as in his political probity, his austerity, his assiduousness and his perseverance, that we must seek the causes of the moral authority he was able to acquire.

After Mirabeau's death, and Barnave's betrayal he

was really the recognized chief of the popular party at the Constituante. All his speeches were effective, — his appeal to the Constituantes to forbid their own reëlection to the next legislature, his answer to the Abbé Raynal, who criticized the work of the Constituante, his speech of the fourteenth of July, 1791, against royal inviolability. Under the Legislative his influence grew all the time — he had, it is true, left the Assembly but he had made the Jacobin Club his headquarters. There he fought Brissot and Guadet. "His speeches," said Carra, "are full of the most sublime eloquence." Even in 1792 his popularity was such that Guadet accused him of having become the "idol of the people."

But up to this time Robespierre had been only the chief of a party at the Convention where he headed the Paris delegation. According to one of his apologists, he would soon represent France and take its measure. It was his terrific speech which decided the death of the king. "Where can you find eloquence and talent," said Camille Desmoulins of that harangue, "if not in that admirable discourse where I found throughout Socrates and the subtlety of the *Provinciales*, with two or three passages comparable to the most beautiful of Demosthenes?"

Robespierre's real success dates from that moment. The fall of the Girondins only increased the considerable authority he was enjoying: his situation as the real head of the Jacobin societies gave him great prestige. He began to be feared, and with the aid of no other title than that of deputy, he became little

by little the *Dictator of Public Opinion*. When he
entered the Committee of Public Safety, in July, 1793,
after Danton's fall, his position was given official
sanction; for a year Robespierre governed France.

And yet, according to the remarkably just portrait
of Lamartine, Robespierre's exterior had nothing
more to recommend him to the attention of his fellow
men than his birth or his genius. "His features had
no distinctive qualities to make him stand out from
the great mass of people; there was nothing in his
physique to indicate the power within; he was the
last word of the Revolution but no one could read it.

"Robespierre was small of stature; his limbs were
puny and angular, his walk jerky, his attitudes
affected; his rather harsh voice sought for oratorical
effects; his forehead was rather fine, but small, and
bulging above the temples, as if the weight and the
slow movement of his thoughts had enlarged it
through his own efforts. His eyes, very much veiled
by his eyelids, and very piercing, were deeply em-
bedded in their sockets; they had a bluish look,
rather soft but vague, like steel gleaming in a bright
light. His small and narrow nose was dilated by very
wide nostrils; his mouth was big, his lips thin and
disagreeably contracted at the corners, his chin short
and pointed, his complexion of a deadly yellow, like
that of a sick man, or one exhausted by night watches
and meditations. The habitual expression of his face
was a superficial serenity, against a grave background, and his indecisive smile hovered between
sarcasm and grace. There was sweetness, but a

sinister sweetness. His whole face was dominated by the prodigious and continual tension of his eyes, his forehead, his mouth, and of all his facial muscles. His face, like his soul, concentrated without distraction upon one point with such power that none of the will power in him was lost, — he always seemed to know beforehand what he wanted to accomplish, as if it were in reality under his eyes. . . He belonged to no party, but he was of all the parties which served in turn his revolutionary ideal. There resided his strength, because when the parties stopped, he did not."

And there indeed was his greatest strength, but he had many others, — even his mode of life, simple and modest, which could not but impress the mob favorably. Until 1791 Robespierre lived in a small lodging in the Rue de Saintonge; he walked, spent thirty sous for his meals, and of his salary as a deputy (eighteen francs a day) he gave part to his sister Charlotte, who lived in Arras, and another part to a woman who was dear to him. He had no great needs; his greatest luxury was his dress. This philosopher, this Spartan, was extremely well groomed, even elegant in his dress. His portraits show him with his hair well powdered, immaculate in a nankeen or blue or brown coat and a chamois waistcoat, his neck smothered in a huge pleated bow tie tied with great care. He was elegant without doubt, but with a sober and tasteful elegance! Later, after the massacre of the Champ-de-Mars, fearing for his safety, an honest and enthusiastic Jacobin, the carpenter Duplay, took him to his house, in the Rue St. Honoré. In that small house of well-to-do *bourgeois*, he continued his simple and quiet life, surrounded by the admiration and affection of his hosts. Robespierre had a very clean room under the roof, with a blue-and-white bed and some good chairs. Upon the walls were some new shelves for his books, and here and there, portraits of the "great man." Wherever he looked, he could not avoid seeing himself, — on the right, on the left, Robespierre, still Robespierre, Robespierre everywhere. "That theatrical, that fantastic maniac Marat knocked about in his cave, as variable in his speech as in his clothes, but here there was no caprice; everything was regulated, honest and serious. One felt moved, and tempted to believe that here, for the first time in this world, was the house of virtue. Such neat, clean, modest, *bourgeois* surroundings were what the *Incorruptible* needed.

The care they took of him made his sister Charlotte very jealous. M. and Mme. Duplay were kind and honest people who had reached, by hard work, the class of the *petite bourgeoisie*, with the four daughters who sometimes amused Robespierre by playing the harpsichord. Thus Rousseau's admirer lived, following the theories of his master, following "Emile" as closely as he could, and realized practically the book which he always imitated in his speeches. However, he did not allow the delights of family life to make him grow soft, or even his predilection for Eleanor, the eldest of the Duplay sisters, who was called Cornélie and whom Danton teased by calling her Cornélie Copeau. In his pleasant room under the roof, while Madame Duplay and her daughters looked after the house, Robespierre ceaselessly prepared his discourses and his articles.

He really *prepared* them, painstakingly, not always, as has been said, like a studious schoolboy under the Duplay's lamp, but by thinking them over carefully. At first, it is true, he polished his sentences and was careful of his style, but when he became a member of the Committee of Public Safety, he did not have enough leisure for that. He contented himself by jotting down on paper some hasty notes, his outline, and on the platform, he improvised from those notes. Nothing can give a better idea of his method than a comparison of the notes taken for his speech on April 24, 1793, upon the rights of property, with the text itself as reproduced by the *Moniteur*. Here is the beginning of his draft:

"Property rights:

Dealer in human flesh, vessel where Negroes are piled up, those are my properties.

Noble. Land and vassals, those are, etc. . . . .

Dynasty of Capet. Its hereditary right to oppress, ruin, bleed dry twenty million men.

A scandal for centuries."

and here is the text of his speech:

"Let us consider in good faith the principles of property rights. It is very necessary, because the prejudices and the vices of men have surrounded no problem with thicker clouds.

"Ask the dealer in human flesh what property is.

He'll tell you by showing that long coffin which he calls a ship, where he has piled up and confined men who seem to be alive: these are my property, I bought them for so much a head!

"Ask the gentleman who had lands and vassals and who believed the universe upset since he has lost them. He will give you ideas of the same kind about property.

"Ask the august members of the Capetian dynasty, and they will tell you that positively the most sacred of properties is the hereditary right they have enjoyed throughout the ages, to oppress, to humiliate and to legally and monarchically have under their good pleasure the twenty-five million men who inhabit France's territory . . . "

This is the great and imaginative language in which Robespierre clothed the few phrases which he had hastily jotted down upon paper. At the tribune, of course, to utter them, he did not have the powerful means of a Vergniaud, a Mirabeau, but ingenuity compensated for natural ability.

"He knew," said one of his adversaries, in a portrait which appeared after his death, "how to soften artistically his naturally loud and piercing voice and how to give grace to his Artesian accent . . . He knew the power of declamation and he possessed the art of it up to a certain point. He handled himself well; antithesis characterized his speeches and he often used irony. His diction was sometimes harmoniously modelled and sometimes rough. In other words, Robespierre knew how to use the inflections of

his voice and thus he avoided the monotony a less
clever orator could not have escaped.

"But what assured his success was that he put his
whole being into his discourse. He did not flatter his
audience, he did not adapt himself to the currents
which animated the assembly, he went straight on
his way and occasionally knew how to resist the
most violent opposition. He spoke against the war,
against the de-Christianization; he defended the
seventy-three deputies who had protested against the
execution of the Girondins. "He never spread himself
out in public," in the words of Roederer. In short,
the secret of his oratorical success lay in his sincerity.
In spite of his remaining rather limited and academic,
in spite of glacial appearance, and his rather dry
manner, — his inner flame flared up and gave to his
words a convincing and persuasive tone. Each of his
speeches was "the story of his spirit since the last
time he had taken the floor."

Robespierre's ideas and their sources were evident.
Imbued with Rousseau's doctrines, he wanted most
of all to fight egoism and to make virtue easy. "We
wish," he asserted once, "to substitute morality for
selfishness, probity for honor, principles for habit,
duty for manners, the reign of reason for the tyranny
of fashion, the contempt of vice for the contempt of
misfortune, the love of glory for the love of money,
merit for intrigue, a magnanimous people, powerful,
happy, for an amiable people, frivolous and miserable;
that is to say, all the virtues and all the miracles of
the Republic for all the vices and all the follies of the

monarchy." A vague and chimerical ideal, but certainly a very high one. And elsewhere Robespierre expressed himself more clearly still. He desired an order of things where distinctions arise only from equality, where the citizen is responsible to the magistrate, the magistrate to the people and the people to justice, where the State looks out for the welfare of the individual. The State, according to him, must exercise a close supervision over the individual and must know, when necessary, how to "force man to be free." It must even impose a religion upon him: the religion of the *Vicaire Savoyard*. Robespierre indeed hated atheism, a word with which he designated all the philosophy of the Encyclopedists. "You who regret a virtuous friend," he cried, "you who love to think that the best part of himself will escape death! You who cry over the coffin of a son or a spouse, are you to be consoled by him who tells you that nothing remains of them but vile dust? You who die under the blows of an assassin, your last breath is a call to eternal justice! The innocent man upon the scaffold makes the tyrant in his triumphal chariot grow pale. Could he do so if the oppressor and the oppressed were not equal before death? Poor sophists! What right have you to take away from innocence the scepter of reason, to give it into criminal hands, and to sadden virtue and lower humanity?"

If he attacked atheism, it was less as a philosopher than as a politician. "In the eyes of the lawmaker," he said, "all that is useful in the world and good in practice is truth. The idea of the Supreme Being and of the immortality of the soul is a continual call to justice; it is social and republican. And now there is the anathema. Woe upon him who seeks to kill sublime enthusiasm!"

When he said those words, on *Floréal* 18, *An* II, the threat was already half executed. "Woe" had fallen upon the furious ones, those who had tried to de-Christianize France, to render her priestless. In instituting the cult of reason, which was directly opposed to the religious doctrine which had been visible in Robespierre's homilies, Cloots, Hébert, Monmoro, Bouchotte, Ronsin, had gone to the scaffold. Danton and his friends, *Les Indulgents*, had not been long in following them, and then Chaumette, the ex-bishop Gobel, who had been guilty of wanting to efface all idea of the divinity.

Robespierre remained alone. To tell the truth since he had become a member of the Committee of Public Safety, with those called the "high-handed", Couthon and Saint-Just, he dominated everybody. He reigned as a master of the triumvirate. All the departments of the government were full of his creatures. If he did not have the title of tyrant, he acted as one. Freed from his adversaries, he became bolder: all the branches of service were "Robespierrized" and then the pontiff was able at last to work toward establishing his partly political, partly religious system.

On the eighteenth of *Floréal*, a decree instituted the cult of the Supreme Being. "The French people," it said, "recognize the existence of the Supreme

Being and the immortality of the soul." Numerous days of rejoicings were set aside to glorify the Supreme Being, nature, freedom, love of country, truth, justice, decency, conjugal love, etc., etc.

The first of those fêtes took place some days later, on the twentieth of *Prairial*. The programme had been thought out in detail by the painter David. Robespierre, then president of the Convention, officiated at the ceremonies. Wearing a light blue coat and nankeen knickers, he led the procession from the Tuileries to the Champ-de-Mars, and delivered two sermons, while the choirs sang a hymn to the "Father of the Universe, the Supreme Intelligence." While they were on their way to the Champ-de-Mars, chance or "maliciousness" caused a disagreement between the Convention and its president. "As the latter," said Fiévée, "walked twenty paces in front of the members of the Convention and of the summoned authorities, very well dressed but looking none the nobler on that account, holding in his hand a bouquet composed of ears of corn and flowers, the effort he made to smother his pride was plainly noticeable. But when the actors of the Paris theaters, dressed in Greek costume, sang the last verse of a so-called hymn for the Supreme Being, which ended with those lines that they actually spoke to Robespierre in the name of the French people: 'If he blushed to obey kings, he is proud of you for a master,' at that moment, all his suppressed ambition was written upon his face. He thought himself both king and God."

And why not, indeed, with the formidable popularity which he enjoyed and which grew greater every day? "Robespierre," the People's Society of Caen, had already written to him in 1792, "that name which is your glory, that name which frightens the souls of tyrants, will be the rallying cry with which to fight them." The day after the Fête of the Supreme Being, Boissy d'Anglas compared him to Orpheus teaching man the first principles of morality and civilization. A major wrote to him on the thirtieth of *Prairial, An* II that he considered him to be the Messiah the Supreme Being who had promised to reform all things. But all this was as nothing compared to the praise Robespierre enjoyed from women. His sentimental rhetoric pleased them. "There was always," said Michelet, "a sentimental passage, usually about himself, about the trials of his hard career, about his personal sufferings, in each speech, and so regularly that the passage was expected and handkerchiefs held ready. As soon as his audience was aroused, the well-known piece would come . . . about the dangers to which he was exposed, the hatred of his enemies, the tears that some day would be shed for the blood of the martyr for freedom. But when he reached that point, it was too much and the hearts burst. The women could restrain themselves no longer and they burst into sobs. He pleased them also by his austere virtue; they loved the one whose manners were most dignified, whose probity was the best proven, who had the highest ideal; and it would be wrong to believe that they did not like his severe and grave appearance, because they supposed instinctively that the austere man kept his heart pure for his beloved."

Thus adored, Robespierre seemed invulnerable. After his fall, Fréron explained his popularity very clearly in a speech: "The tyrant who oppressed his colleagues even more than the nation," he confided, "was so much surrounded by the semblance of the most popular virtues; the consideration and confidence of the people, which he had won by five years of uncompromising hypocrisy, built around him such a sacred wall that we would have jeopardized the nation and freedom itself, if we had yielded to our impatience and had done away with the tyrant sooner."

And yet, even on the Fête of the Supreme Being, the "god" had been able to overhear Danton's friends insulting and threatening him. He was so humiliated by these insults in the midst of his triumph that he felt he was lost. Back at the Duplays, it was said, he was heard to murmur, "You won't see me much longer."

Probably it was under the influence of that fear that he put to the vote, two days after his apotheosis, the awful Law of *Prairial*, which allowed judgments to be given on moral grounds, without witnesses or defenders. Then began the Great Terror. In forty-seven days, from the tenth of June (*Prairial* 22) to the twenty-seventh of July (*Thermidor* 9) thirteen hundred and seventy-six heads fell in Paris, more than in the previous fourteen months. And if the Terror had been tolerated while the enemy was at the gates, the victory of Fleurus and others changed public opinion and ruined Robespierre. "Victories pursued Robespierre like furies." By a decision, which, whether he had desired it or not, was at any rate unlucky for him, Robespierre ceased attending the sessions of the Committee of Public Safety and isolated himself. This gave his enemies time to think of means to bring about his downfall. Fear gave them courage. A plot was hatched which the friends of Hébert and Danton joined. The leaders were Fouché, Billaud-Varenne, Barras, Tallien. On the twenty-fifth of July, a Friday, (*Thermidor 7*) Barrère read to the Convention a report in which he attacked those who were in favor of new proscriptions. The Assembly voted the printing of the report and its distribution to all the Communes. The very next day, Robespierre answered with a long and carefully prepared speech, in which he called himself the slave of freedom and the living martyr of the Republic, in which he asked that the committees be cleansed of the "handful of scoundrels" which oppressed them. He had his last applause. The Convention voted the distribution of his speech to the Communes, but at Billaud's request, the decree was cancelled. His first failure! The wind of battle was in the air. All the evening and throughout the night of the twenty-sixth were spent by both parties in preparing for the next day. Robespierre was applauded by the Jacobins, while Tallien, Fouché and the others, more practical, got the Marais on their side.

It was at the session of the ninth of *Thermidor*

(Sunday, July 27) that the fate of the "tyrant" was decided. That day was very hot, with a suffocating stormy heat. The benches were crowded to overflowing. Suddenly the president rang his bell and Saint-Just mounted the platform. "I belong to no party," he said. "I'll fight them all." But he did not speak long, and Tallien, who was waiting for his chance, threw himself into the fray. "I ask permission to speak, for a motion of order," he shouted, "then I want the veil to be torn aside." Billaud went to his aid. Their supporters applauded him furiously.

Robespierre flew to the platform, but Tallien had already reached it by the other stairs. All three were on the platform, rubbing elbows. Robespierre tried to edge in. He was elbowed out. Collot d'Herbois, who was presiding, refused to let him speak. "Down with the tyrant! Down with the tyrant!" was heard on every side.

He went back to the hemicycle and appealed again to the Marais people: "Pure and virtuous citizens," he begged. "I appeal to you and not to those scoundrels." But the Marais remained unmoved. The end was approaching. Robespierre became hoarse. Desperate, he let himself go and lost what strength he had left, in vain cries; pitifully he plunged in and lost his balance.

Vadier, who had succeeded Tallien, joked about Catherine Théot. The crowd was laughing, but Tallien, who was afraid the debate would stray from the point, cut him short. "I want to speak and to bring the debate back to the point."

Robespierre jumped up. "I know how to bring it back," he shrieked.

"Tyrant, you are not allowed to speak."

Maximilien, pale and covered with sweat, insisted. The clamor grew. "Down with the tyrant!"

"For the last time," howled the hunted animal, "President of Murderers, will you allow me to speak?" He was not allowed to go on.

"Danton's blood is choking him," some one shouted.

"If it is he that you want to avenge, cowards, why did you abandon him?" cried Robespierre bitterly. The scene was painful. Was not the farce ended? An obscure member of the Convention, Louchet, spoke the decisive word. "It is admitted that Robespierre has always been dictator. On that count alone, I ask for a decree of outlawry." He was applauded, and shouts of, "Let's put it to the vote."

Then Robespierre, in a rage, climbed the four steps above him, looked at the benches around him and felt he was lost. "And I ask for death," he cried.

"You have deserved it a hundred times," answered André Dumont. Mechanically, as if stupefied, Maximilien repeated, "Death, death."

Then the younger Robespierre took Maximilien's hand. "I shall share my brother's fate." Le Bas did the same. The Convention, moved by this, hesitated for an instant. At last, it decreed that the two Robespierres, Le Bas, Couthon, Saint-Just and Hanriot, the commander of the army, should be arrested.

But it was not the end. The Tribunal was devoted

79

to Robespierre and therefore he had a chance of being acquitted. It was a mistake on the part of his friends which caused his death. The Commons, as soon as they had heard of Robespierre's arrest, had declared itself in a state of insurrection. About eight o'clock in the evening, the prisoner was taken from the Luxembourg and lodged at the Hôtel de Ville, while they prepared to storm the Convention. The Convention answered this move by declaring Robespierre and his friends outlaws. As such, no judgment was needed to execute them. As soon as they were captured, they could be guillotined. All seemed ready for a battle. Robespierre's partisans had concentrated around the Hôtel de Ville, on the Place de Grève, while the Convention had gathered around the Tuileries the gendarmerie and part of the National Guard. But Robespierre was afraid to take the offensive and order an attack, and the weather did the rest. The storm which had been threatening all day broke a little before midnight and dispersed by its deluge the Robespierrists who had been left without orders. When, about two in the morning, the Convention troops came to the Hôtel de Ville they found it perfectly quiet. Without any resistance they arrested Robespierre's friends, the principal members of the Commons and Robespierre himself. A gendarme, it is said, broke his jaw with a shot. Wounded, he was thrown into a cell until evening, so that Fouquier-Tinville could establish the identity of the outlaws. Then the calvary began.

The carts started for the scaffold with Maximilien

tied to the side staves, mute and very erect. He appeared disgusted and contemptuous. From time to time some scoundrels mounted on ladders insulted him. Robespierre shrugged his shoulders and looked straight at them with hard and unseeing eyes. The tumbril advanced slowly, lurching along the paved way. It took a whole long hour to go through the Rue Saint-Honoré. At the windows, furious men and women shouted, "To the guillotine!" They were applauding from the balconies, and the soldiers of the escort mingled their curses with those of the mob. In front of the Duplay's house they halted. The scenario had been written and all was ready. A band of furies who were gathered there, singing and holding each others' hands, surrounded that cart of the condemned in the throes of death. Then a child appeared, carrying a butcher's pail and a broom. He sprinkled the house with fresh blood. Maximilien closed his eyes. But when they reached the ancient Place Louis XV the nightmare of butchery began. Hanriot, first, was covered with blood, but stood erect, his left eye clinging to his cheek. The executioner pulled it out. They had to guillotine Couthon sideways, after trying in vain to force his poor paralyzed body into the usual position. Drunk with cruelty, the mob howled. It was silent however, when Saint-Just's turn came, and he died surrounded with mystery, in haughty silence, without a smile, with cold contempt.

Then they pushed Robespierre on. A deep murmur came from the multitude which filled the square as far as one could see. It was about seven, and a beautiful summer setting sun reddened the foliage. The Seine glided slowly by like a roll of blue silk. The knife was waiting. Suddenly an assistant of the executioner came behind Robespierre and at one swoop tore off the bandage which held his wounded jaw. The mouth opened wide. Some teeth fell. A howl as from a wounded animal filled the square. For one unforgettable moment, that tortured, agonizing face, with its haggard eyes appeared — a man with his arms tied behind his back, bent forward eagerly toward the knife.

The mob held its breath. Then a terrific clamor was heard, for the head of the tyrant had fallen into the basket.

Two chief accusations have been made against Robespierre and have for a long time defamed his memory. He has been held entirely responsible for the Terror and has been accused of being overweeningly ambitious and of aspiring by all means in his power to dictatorship. Doubtless he was a terrorist, but not through any perverse instincts, not through love of blood, but through necessity. He intervened whenever he could to save innocent or misguided victims. He saved from accusation the seventy-three Girondins who had protested against the Second of June, tried to save, but in vain, Louis XVI's sister, Madame Elizabeth, and succeeded in saving the Abbé le Duc, the natural son of Louis XV, as he was about to go to the scaffold. He recalled Carrier from Nantes and Tallien from Bordeaux, and Fréron and Barras

from the south, when he learned of their excesses. Of
course, there is the Law of *Prairial*, but he was not
the only one who voted for it. Billaud and Barrère
approved of it, and the whole Committee favored it.
It is unjust to make Robespierre responsible for all
the exceptional measures which internal and external
war imposed upon the Convention or the Committee
of Public Safety. The responsibility belonged to the
whole revolutionary party, and better still, to circumstances. But he voted for it, it will be said, and
that's too much. Yes, he voted for it; and yet, as
Jaurès has said so well, "his dignity and his self-
esteem had suffered, as well as his pure love for the
Revolution, from the atrocious actions which had
dishonored the revolutionary government from time
to time. He could not forget them. He hated them
the more because he had not been able to prevent them
and because he could be held responsible for them";
and he wanted to end them all at one stroke, to end
the Terror by making a great example, and by removing, once for all, that "handful of scoundrels" whom
he had so often denounced. And besides, at the time
of the Great Terror, Robespierre was no longer
appearing at the sessions of the Committee. One can
even say, however paradoxical it may appear, that
he was absolutely a stranger to it. It was Anatole
France, who, when all is said and done, has uttered
the last word on the affair: "One cannot," he wrote,
"hold Robespierre responsible for all that was done
then, any more than for the manners and the spirit of
the times. The Law of *Prairial*, we are told, is his

crime. Do not let us be hypocrites. We would revolt
to-day against a law which would suppress defenders
and witnesses before the tribunal, of course; testimony, defence for the accused, those are sacred
guarantees, it is agreed; but well we know that during
the Terror those guarantees were only appearances,
that the defender was then the curse of the accused
and that witnesses could not help him. The Law of
Prairial suppressed phantoms."

Robespierre was ambitious? Desirous of being a
dictator? Why? To satisfy his need for luxury? It
was known, and his adversaries admitted it, that he
was perfectly disinterested. Had he the same need
of money as Danton? Did he want to give free rein
to his love of power? Neither. He may have been
carried away for a while by the homage which came
to him, but on the whole, for what purpose did he
want to dominate? In the interest of all and not from
personal motives only. He crushed the Hébertists, the
Dantonists, of course, but not only with the intention
of ridding himself of bothersome enemies; but because he thought their actions hurtful to France.
The first were too "diehards", the second too "de-
featists", if we can use such anachronisms. Robespierre wanted to keep to the golden mean. He
described admirably his policy in a single sentence.
"We must arm ourselves," he said, "not to reach the
Rhine, for that would mean eternal war, but to
dictate peace, peace without victory." Of course,
there was the Supreme Being, there was that slightly
farcical comedy when he appeared as a real pontiff,

but what were the tyrant's aims? He knew very well that a people as deeply Christian as the French, could not break their idols suddenly without a serious loss of balance.

When that which was for them the source of all morality was taken away, it had to be replaced. And the source of Robespierre's action was the reign of morality, of virtue. "From the viewpoint of policy nothing is just, except what is honest, — such was his rule for governing." In sum, he dreamt of making politics morality in action. His great merit is that he believed in what he was saying and doing. We must admire his sincerity and not reproach him with it. He was only wrong in wanting "to force men to be free." Brute force and morality are two very different things. The latter does not use force, but persuasion. One does not make individuals happy in spite of themselves, but by working with them.

SAINT–JUST

AN obscure young man of twenty-five came to the Convention from his native province. He started with a master stroke, asking and getting a king's head. He interfered henceforth on all occasions, successively bringing down the Girondins, the Hébertists, and the Dantonists. He worked at the project for a constitution about which he had dreamed in solitude and retreat. He was not only a dreamer, but he realized his dreams as well. As representative of the Convention to the armies, he showed a savage energy and brought back victory to the French. Ambitious, austere and firm, the future seemed to be his, but he attached himself to Robespierre: he linked his fate with that of his friend, who was his inferior and who probably was jealous of him, and he was caught in his ruin. He died at the age of twenty-seven, contemptuous and haughty. Such is the short and tragic story of Saint-Just.

Louis-Antoine de Saint-Just was born on the twenty-fifth of August, 1767, at Decize, in Nivernais. His father had been a cavalry captain in the company of the Duke of Berry; in spite of the "de" in his name, he did not belong to the nobility, and therefore had always remained a minor officer. His mother, Jeanne-Marie Robinot, belonged to the upper middle class. A short while after his birth his family left the banks of the Loire to go farther north in to the country of the Oise, in the southern extremity of Picardy. At Blérancourt, the old soldier bought near Noyon a little house and some property; he died in 1777, leaving behind him, beside his ten-year-old son, two daughters of a tender age. Young Saint-Just grew up in that country of Blérancourt, which he left only to study at Soissons, in the college of Saint-Nicolas directed by the Oratorian Fathers; he was a good pupil, rather proud and sensitive, if we are to believe a not altogether dependable tradition.

When he left college, he studied law at Rheims and then returned to Blérancourt. He was doubtless bored there and dreamed of Paris, aim of all the ambitious, because, one night, he ran away with some of the family silver which he sold to a dealer in the capital. He tried vainly to deceive his good mother by having an accomplice write a letter of justification: if he had stolen, it was to pay a doctor who had cured him of a very severe headache, and the so-called doctor needed two more louis to buy a certain anti-hemorrhage powder to finish the cure. Such a naïve excuse did not deceive Madame Saint-Just. She had recourse to one of her neighbors, Chevalier d'Evry, Officer of the Guards, and through him, to the Lieutenant of Police. Saint-Just was soon arrested; when questioned, he did not deny his theft, but declared that he was on the point of joining the Guards of the Comte d'Artois. Before that, he had gone to the Oratorians, but had been badly received by them: the ecclesiastic state did not suit him, for he was too energetic, too desirous of enjoying life, and to his young imagination a military career seemed much more brilliant.

Meanwhile, he was put into one of those extraordinary houses, half-prison, and half-pension, where under the Old Régime it was customary to confine children of good family who had misbehaved. This particular one was in Picpus and according to the police books was kept by a Dame Mary. He remained there six months, from October, 1786, to March, 1787, very well treated and cheating boredom by writing a heroic-comic poem in twenty cantos, called "Organt", in which he tried to imitate Voltaire's "Pucelle"; an unreadable work, the dominating feature of which was lubricity, but which showed a keen intelligence and wide reading. At last his mother found a position for him, and he was free. He entered the office of M. Dubois-Descharmes as clerk. M. Dubois-Descharmes was prosecutor in Soissons and brother-in-law of his friend Rigaud; it was not the brilliant life of which the lad had dreamed, but he was poor and had to live.

In Blérancourt, Saint-Just had begun a love affair with Mademoiselle Gellé, the daughter of the royal notary in the district of Goucy-le-Château, but her family married her off to Master Thorin, who had her father's succession. Was she Saint-Just's mistress? It is probable, since on July 25, 1793, without his knowledge, she left her home to join the young Conventional in Paris.

Those youthful escapades had a profound effect

upon Saint-Just's soul. His virtue became rigid; he affected at all times, an implacable asceticism. His natural honesty had been changed by his downfall to puritanism; he was pitiless to himself and to others and was extremely austere.

However, the Revolution burst, and the fiery soul of Saint-Just was carried away by it. He adopted enthusiastically the new ideas, became their propagandist and soon gained a great ascendency over his compatriots. He spoke in the Blérancourt clubs, in the Chauny, the Coucy; he spoke with such fire that he was, in spite of his youth, elected lieutenant colonel of the National Guard of Blérancourt. He loved theatrical attitudes, and beautiful gestures imitated from antiquity: while an anti-revolutionary pamphlet was being burnt, he stretched his hand above the flame and swore "to die for his country and the national assembly and to perish through fire rather than forget his vows." Such a civic enthusiasm brought him the honor in 1790 at the Fête of Federation, of taking to the Champ-de-Mars the federates of Blérancourt. When he came back, he did not forget the interests of his native village, and hearing that Coucy wanted to seize the free markets of Blérancourt, he wrote to Robespierre, then deputy of Arras, a letter so full of admiring fervor that it began a friendship interrupted only by death.

His activity was remarkable, but not disinterested. In the year 1791 the elections were to take place. To be a deputy to the Legislative Assembly — what a dream for an ambitious young man like Saint-Just!

He prepared himself for the part he wished to play by studying, reading and meditating; he wrote under the shadowy foliage of Blérancourt and then published his electoral manifesto, "The Spirit of the Revolution in France and of its Constitution" . . . It was the work of a revolutionary, but of a moderate one. He was satisfied with the result and did not ask for more. "Democracy judges, aristocracy makes laws, and Monarchy governs !" The future proconsul was already in favor of a strong government, as he showed in such sentences as these: "Where the feet think, the arm decides and the head goes forward !" Or "If we judge affairs sanely, the revolutions in our time are only the wars of imprudent slaves, who fight though chained and walk abroad drunk." But to keep alive revolution needs virtue. And Saint-Just looked at himself: "Every man is right in thinking what he thinks, but any one who speaks or writes must account for his virtue to the city." He was already showing all the proud stoicism, the uncompromising puritanism which rendered him hateful to the "rottenbellies" of the Convention and caused his downfall.

Unexpectedly, his ambitions were crushed. Saint-Just had enemies who worked against him, and they succeeded in having his name removed from the list of active citizens; he could not be elector or elected. Good-by to his dreams of fame and ardent life, good-by to Paris and to enthusiastic audiences; he must be content with his small native province and go back to that gray provincial life which weighed so heavily upon this impetuous young man. He had fever, he was sick with frustrated ambition, with jealousy of the lucky ones; all his feelings conflicted in a frenetic letter he wrote but did not send:

"Good-by, I am above happiness. I shall bear everything but I shall tell the truth. You are all cowards and have not appreciated me. My fame will rise however and darken yours. Traitors that you are. I am a scoundrel and a knave because I've no money to give you. Tear my heart out and eat it. I'll become what you are not: great! . . . Oh, God! Is Brutus to languish forgotten, far from Rome! I have decided however: if Brutus does not kill the others, he'll kill himself!"

But, like Saint-Just himself, the country was feverish and events came in rapid succession. Twenty days later, the Crown fell and the Legislative invited the electors to call another assembly, a convention. Unhoped-for luck, this new popular vote, taking place so short a time after the preceding one! Saint-Just tried again, and on the fourth of September he was elected from Soissons; during that time, in Paris bands of murderers emptied the prisons and finished their macabre work. He thought only of the radiant future in store for him. Some days later he was hastening to Paris — to fame!

He was twenty-five, one of the youngest deputies of the Convention; and yet with his first speech, the whole Assembly hung on his words, because this beautiful, calm young man, with regular features, uttered coldly the most violent statements. Louis

XVI had been indicted and one of the deputies had been talking of the inviolability of the king. Without any oratorical preparations, Saint-Just entered into the thick of the debate:

"I wish to prove that the king can be judged; that Morisson's opinion that he is inviolable and the Committee's opinion that he should be treated as an ordinary citizen, are equally false and that he must be judged by principles which are neither one nor the other. A king is not a citizen, he is an enemy; he is not to be judged, but to be opposed. The inviolability the people have conferred upon one of its magistrates can be taken away when it pleases. Some day perhaps men as far from our prejudices as we are from those of the Vandals will be astonished by the barbarism of a century which made of a tyrant's prosecution something of a religious ceremony, whose people, when they brought a tyrant up for judgment, raised him to the rank of citizen before examining his crimes. It will seem astonishing that in the eighteenth century the people were less advanced than in the time of the Caesars; then the tyrant was immolated in the Senate, without any other formality than twenty-two dagger thrusts, without any other law but Rome's freedom." And fighting the feelings of humanity which might still remain in the hearts of the deputies, he concluded: "Some seek to awake pity; tears will soon be bought as in the burial in Rome; everything will be done to appeal to our interests, to corrupt us. People! If the king is absolved, remember that we will never again be worthy of your

faith in us and that you will be able to accuse us of
perfidy."

The effect was more powerful than the aspect of the
speaker who uttered those terrible words — he, a
mere juvenile, and his calm was great. His implacable
and brilliant rhetoric was applauded and the young
Saint-Just was henceforth one of the most remarkable
members of the Assembly. He intervened once more
in the course of the same prosecution to destroy the
impression produced by the clever and moving defence
of De Sèze, Louis XVI's lawyer. He used again his
cold and pressing logic:

"The public safety demands that the king should be
executed without judgment; why hesitate? To hesitate to strike Louis, — is that not to betray the cause
of the people whom he had caused to be massacred?
You must ignore all other considerations but that of
the public good; you must not allow anybody to be
rejected. If those who have spoken against the king
are challenged, we will challenge in the name of the
country those who have said nothing in the country's
favor. Have courage to tell the truth for the truth
burns in the hearts of the people like a lamp in a tomb
. . . I ask that each member of the Assembly should
mount the platform and say "Louis is or is not
guilty." And he motivated his vote by this short
phrase: "Since Louis XVI was the enemy of the
people, of their freedom, of their happiness, I ask
for death."

Saint-Just was then a public prosecutor of royalty
much more than of the king, but his active mind soon

took him to very different subjects. On the twenty-ninth of November, he tackled one of the most difficult technical questions: the one of apportionment of provisions. He fought those who wished to force the peasant by violent measure to give up the corn he was carefully preserving. He still believed in the theory of the physiocrats, that of absolute freedom of commerce; he fought in favor of that doubtful cause with a firmness, a brilliance not to be expected from such a young man. His style was hard, austere, tight, sometimes obscure, as was his personality. "If you want a republic, see that the people have the courage to be virtuous; there are no political virtues without pride; there is no pride when people are in distress. You are asking for order in vain; you must secure order by producing it through good laws."

Already military affairs attracted his attention: On January 20, 1793, he made an important speech upon the organization of the war ministry. He went over the different questions relating to the armies; he wanted a strong military power, but he wanted it subordinated to the civil power; the Convention, emanating from the people, was to have the general direction of operations, the generals the execution of orders. The doctrine of the future representative of the Convention to the armies was already formulated in his mind. He favored a report of Dubois-Crance about the elections in the army and the fusion of the old army corps. "I know," he said, "only one means of resisting Europe: to oppose to her the genius of freedom."

He applied himself also to the primordial question, that of the organization of the government. On April 24, criticizing the project of the Constitution of Condorcet, he gave his own views upon the question and was applauded in spite of the idyllic naïveté of some of his propositions: did he not imagine that the sedition could be stopped by six old men with the tricolor scarf, whose mollifying presence was to calm the infuriated people! But all the young man said was not ridiculous: he wanted a strong and united government, a centralization which he opposed to the federalism of the Girondins, and he came back to that idea in his two speeches of the fifteenth and twenty-fourth of May upon the political division of the Republic and the formation of municipalities; on the thirtieth of May he joined the Committee of Public Safety in preparing the constitutional laws and on the tenth of July he became definitely a member: the clerk from Blérancourt had become one of those who governed France.

In the Committee Saint-Just did not confine his activity to the very precise rôle that was given to him at first: he turned his hand to everything — to military affairs, to food supplies, to the police. On July 8, 1793, he was the spokesman for the committee appointed to strike at the Girondin deputies in prison, or at those who fled since the second of June. The terms he used were moderate, but his conclusions were coldly violent; Saint-Just who had dragged Louis XVI to the scaffold, assassinated the Girondins and it was always in the name of virtue and for reasons of state that he showed himself to be pitiless. "Public safety is the only consideration worthy of moving you. The Republic did not take into account any weakness or sterile passions; everybody is guilty when the country is unhappy . . . Nothing is more like virtue than a great crime; weak souls have been seduced by the ordinary prestige of the truth." Not satisfied with asking that Buzot, Barbaroux, Pétion be outlawed as they had fomented insurrection in the provinces, he asked for the indictment of Vergniaud, Gensonné and Guadet, who had not escaped, but whom he accused of having hoped for the advent of Louis XVII and of having plotted with Valacé the strangling of part of the Convention! Saint-Just was becoming the chief executor of the Committee.

It was he who on the day of Marie Antoinette's execution, tried to justify the murder of the unfortunate queen. "Your Committee thought that the best reprisal against Austria was to have the scaffold and infamy brought into its royal family and to invite the soldiers of the Republic to use their bayonets in the charge." As if the death of a powerless woman could suffice to strike the enemies of France with terror!

Later it was he again who asked for the heads of the Hébertists and Dantonists. The ties uniting him to Robespierre became stronger and stronger: he was the knight who carried Robespierre's sword. Each time Robespierre wanted to strike a heavy blow, he called upon Saint-Just. The young man came back from the armies with the prestige acquired through his services and, with the violent and cold eloquence, whose secret he knew, persuaded the mute and terror-stricken Assembly to agree to the measures they wanted.

On *Ventose* 23, *An* II (March 13, 1794) the "En-raged" were stricken. Robespierre had not forgiven Hébert and his friends their anti-religious masquerades, their demagogical tendencies. Without naming them, Saint-Just drew a violent requisitory against the "conspiracy of the foreigner"; he accused the enemy of having sought to weaken France by corrupting it, and he had those declared traitors to the country who — vague and dreadful accusations — had contributed to the corruption of customs. "The foreigner who has tried to corrupt our talents has tried to dry our hearts . . . The stranger has only one means of ruining us — by denaturing and corrupting us, since a republic rests only upon nature and morals . . . Monarchy is not the king, monarchy itself is the crime; the Republic is not a senate, it is virtue itself, and any one who is indulgent to crime wishes to reinstate monarchy and sacrifice liberty." The next day, the terrible decree was used against the Hébertists, who were incarcerated: ten days later they went to the scaffold.

To ruin Danton was very much harder, but Robespierre persevered. Jealousy, political disagreements, a deep antipathy between the venial and powerful tribune and the mediocre and uncorruptible rhetorician, all led to the conflict which brought these two men face to face, these two pillars of the Montagnards and the Revolution. But Robespierre himself did not fight the decisive battle; he remained in the wings and once more appealed to Saint-Just. The report of *Germinal* 11, *An* II (March 31, 1794) by which Danton was ruined is a work of collaboration: Robespierre gave the data and Saint-Just arranged it. It was Robespierre's patient hatred which cast suspicion upon Danton's conduct during the Constituante, his friendship with Mirabeau, his so-called desertion at Arcis-sur-Aube on the eve of the tenth of August, his supposed dealings with the Girondins and the Federalists, but it was Saint-Just who put all those accusations in a concise and strong form, a hundred times more deadly than the soft phraseology of Robespierre. And, as always, the eternal appeal of virtue *versus* crime was heard: Danton's indictment was passed unanimously by the terrorized Assembly. "The days of crime are passed," had cried Saint-Just. "Woe to those who help it! Its policies are unmasked! Let all those who have been criminal perish! A republic is not created by soft handling, but by rigor, |inflexible rigor, towards all those who betray it."

Four days later, as the accused, brought before the Revolutionary Tribunal, were defending themselves vehemently and apparently impressing the jurymen, it was again Saint-Just who gave them the fatal blow by denouncing them to the Assembly by a short report of unbelievable violence. He accused them of having revolted against the Tribunal and had them voted outlaws — a legal assassination for which Saint-Just never felt the least regret. "They had counted," he said later, "on the idea that no one dared attack celebrated men surrounded by a great illusion; I have left all those weaknesses behind me; I see only truth in the universe and I tell it." Like Robespierre, Saint-Just believed himself to be infallible and he immolated pitilessly all opposed to him. It is easy to understand why a contemporary writer called him "that panther, Saint-Just."

Luckily for his fame, he has other claims to win the admiration of posterity than as a provider of heads to the scaffold. Saint-Just, the terrible, frightening orator; Saint-Just, the commissary to the armies; Saint-Just, the organizer of resistance to the enemies and of victory, fills us with admiration and astonishment. Half of his short political existence he spent with the armies; recalled by his colleagues, he came back like a whirlwind, read a thundering report, and then went back to another battlefield; he did not fight for victory, he made it possible.

It was in *Brumaire*, *An* II (November, 1793) that with Le Bas, his friend and colleague, he was sent to the army of the Rhine. The situation was bad: at the front defeats, in the rear-guard disorder and betrayals. The lines of Wissembourg had been forced, Alsace invaded and Landau blocked; the army was without food, clothes, discipline; the officers were demoralized, filling the theaters and pleasure haunts; the aristocrats were agitating and preparing almost openly for the entrance of the enemy. Such was the state of affairs when the representatives arrived.

And at once, Saint-Just behaved like a master. The

faithful Le Bas, a fine, honest and courageous nature, signed all the acts, but remained in the background. Saint-Just directed and ordered: he exulted in the task before him; he wished to be the savior of Alsace. He affected to ignore the other representatives of the mission and he made the local authorities tremble before him. He galvanized the army with brief and imperative proclamations, the first outlines of the Napoleonic harangues: "We arrive and we swear, in the name of the army, that the enemy will be vanquished. If there are traitors here, or even people indifferent to the cause of the nation, we bring the sword to strike them. Soldiers, we come to avenge you and to give you officers who will lead you to victory!" And he kept his word. He had unswerving discipline enforced everywhere. The guillotine, ornamented with a seal used in his employment, was put up permanently, decorated with ribbons and flowers, on a square in Strasbourg; in reality, it was not used during all the time of his proconsulate, but the military commissions had all the officers who had betrayed their trust shot, as well as the disobedient or even the casual ones; it was forbidden to go to the town, orders were given to sleep in the tents fully dressed, to be ready for surprises: death for the offenders. And a marshal, an adjutant general, commanders, captains, a general administrator, chiefs of transport, were shot. The story is told that Saint-Just, visiting a camp at night, went to the tent where a friend of his youth was resting; he called him and the friend threw himself into his arms without taking time to dress; Saint-Just kissed him tenderly and then had him shot for his disobedience. The story is doubtless apocryphal, but it shows the reputation of pitiless severity with which the young proconsul surrounded himself.

His activity went into all details. He saw to the equipment, through arbitrary requisitionings; he had all the coats and shoes of the rich Strasbourgians requisitioned and obliged them to put two thousand beds at the disposal of wounded or sick soldiers; he levied upon them a forced lien of nine million francs; he disbanded the departmental and municipal administrations suspected of communication with the conspirators; he arrested the ex-priest Euloge Schneider, who had become the *coryphée* of the Terror and the chief of the "Enraged" in the department of the Lower Rhine, he had him exposed on the platform of the scaffold and sent to the Committee of Public Safety. He was not content to repress with an iron hand the exalted Right and Left; he personally saw to everything. Moving ceaselessly, he never remained one whole day in the same place; he inspected the officers unexpectedly, conferred with the generals and harangued the soldiers.

So much effort was not lost. The reorganized army wanted its revenge. Doubtless, in a first attempt, Hoche failed before Kaiserslautern; but Saint-Just did not withdraw his confidence in him. "At Kaiserslautern, you have undertaken another engagement; instead of one victory, we need two . . . The whole line must strike at once and strike ceaselessly, not giving the enemy time to breathe. All those who command the combined movements must be friends. Advance as quickly as you can on Landau; we can't stop for a moment without being down."

The army on the Rhine and on the Moselle were united and placed under Hoche's command, in spite of Saint-Just, who would have preferred Pichegru. On *Nivose* 6, *An* II (December 26, 1793) to the shouts of "Landau or death!" the troops went to the assault, took the heights of Geisberg and pushed back the Austrians, who retreated in disorder, abandoning Lauterburg and Kaiserslautern and lifting the siege of Landau. "Saint-Just," said his colleague, Baudot, "with the scarf of representative, his hat shaded with the tricolor feather, charged at the head of the republican squadrons and threw himself into the battle, in the midst of the grapeshot and bayonets with the carelessness and the fire of a young hussar." When victory had been achieved and Alsace delivered, he went back to Paris.

Not for long, however: on the seventh of *Pluviose* (January 26, 1794), he went to the Army of the North. The situation was very grave, although not as serious as in Alsace. An army which had been victorious, but which was marking time and doing nothing, with weakened discipline, insufficient and spasmodic food supplies, — that is what Saint-Just found when he arrived. He remedied everything with his usual promptness: Jourdan was replaced by Pichegru; food was assured by requisitioning it from the farmers and a number of Englishmen and nobles who had remained in the region were arrested as suspected conspirators.

After taking all those measures, Saint-Just went back to Paris, where he struck his big blows: Hébert, then Danton, fell. Without stopping with the Committee, Saint-Just, provided with unlimited power, went back to the Army of the North. Landrecies had just fallen and the discipline of the troops left much to be desired. Panics were occurring and a general had been murdered by his soldiers. As in Strasbourg, Saint-Just acted with pitiless severity. It was forbidden to leave camp, to keep women of easy virtue; death for all offenders. Once the army was in his hand, he sent it forward. The Sambre had to be crossed to take Charleroi. Five times they attempted to pass and five times they failed in spite of the soldiers' heroism; successes and failures followed, but Saint-Just was not discouraged. He wanted Charleroi; he would get it. He increased his efforts, dismissing the officers who seemed to lack energy or intelligence, ordered an artillery captain shot in the trenches because he had not been able with the means at his disposal to execute an important command. At last he triumphed and the garrison had to surrender unconditionally. But it had hardly capitulated when a rescuing army appeared and the new conquest had to be defended. Then came the battle of Fleurus, the epic struggle of seventy thousand Frenchmen against eighty-six thousand Austrians. In the evening the defeated enemy army fled in all directions: the conquest of Belgium had begun. Saint-Just, who had been unsparing of himself during that glorious day, did not remain long on the battle field. He hurried back, despising the plaudits which greeted him everywhere on his way; he was cold, self-contained, worried; he seemed to fear that military glory would be fatal to freedom.

He reached Paris the night of *Messidor* 10 (June 28, 1794). He would see his armies no more. The last act, the shortest of his short career, was about to begin.

When he reappeared at the Committee of Public Safety the situation had greatly changed. The perfect unanimity of the members no longer existed. A conflict more or less latent, more or less disguised, existed between Billaud-Varennes and Collot d'Herbois on one side, and Robespierre, Couthon and Le Bas on the other. Between the two groups Barrère and Carnot were hesitating. The other members were almost always away on missions and appeared very seldom at the Committee. The virtuous rigorism of Robespierre, his pontifical manners, especially since the Fête of the Supreme Being, his unhidden contempt and hatred for the corrupt men who had stolen and committed crimes while upon missions, worried part of the Montagnards and excited them against him. Fouché, Tallien, Fréron, Barras felt themselves threatened: they had with them the Terrorists of the Committee, Collot and Billaud. Henceforth the struggle was on between the two factions: the triumph of one side meant the death of the other. All studied and watched their adversaries. Robespierre had in his favor his prestige with the nation, his reputation as the incorruptible, the power he had over the Assembly, the help of the Jacobins and the Commune of Paris; the Terrorists were clever at intrigue; and they knew how to excite jealousy of a man on a pinnacle, of whose virtue one grows tired of hearing praised.

When Saint-Just came back, it had already been a fortnight since Robespierre had appeared at the Committee, leaving the field to his adversaries through his own fault. But with Saint-Just there Robespierre was still watching the Committee. The situation became tenser every day. In vain Saint-Just tried to bring back union; he was unable to manage it: during all the attempts at a reconciliation, Robespierre never ceased to harass acrimoniously his opponents, who felt a vague but formidable threat hanging over them. He felt that the storm was ready to burst.

Saint-Just did not abandon his friend, and in trying to save him he showed his courage, because he was compromising his own position. Without his faithfulness his life would not have been exposed; the recent services he had rendered could not have been forgotten: restored discipline, armies fed and victory assured. Saint-Just had shown himself to be a man of action, while Robespierre was above all a rhetorician: it seemed as if Saint-Just's young star might some day eclipse that of his friend's and the latter perhaps harbored some secret jealousy. And yet, without having a lot of deadly enemies, since he was not the head of a party, Saint-Just had nevertheless hurt a great many of his colleagues. His haughty mien, his cold pride, his way of carrying his head "like the Holy Sacrament", according to Camille Desmoulin's phrase, were laughed at. They held against him the contempt he had shown for the other representatives on missions whom he had recalled; his violence and his irascibility. The coolness he showed on all important occasions was not natural, but acquired, and often the committee room had been filled with his outbursts; several times there had been violent altercations with Carnot, and his outbursts were increasing; "Saint-Just often entered an evening session twenty times and spoke only in angry and short sentences." In spite of all that, in those tragic days of *Thermidor*, he was not directly attacked.

The struggle began before the Convention on *Thermidor* 8 (July 26, 1794) when Robespierre wished to decide between him and his opponents on the Committee. He delivered a long speech, unskillful because of its threatening tone, asking for measures against corrupt members, without clearly indicating them. It aided the coalition of all those who had something to fear. And Robespierre, triumphant at first, saw his success compromised by the counterattack of his adversaries: the printing of his speech was approved with enthusiasm, but rejected at the end of the session.

The night which followed was the tragic night. While Robespierre was being acclaimed by the Jacobins and going quietly home, in the Tuileries, in the room of the Committee of Public Safety, Saint-Just was working feverishly at his report on the situation. About midnight, Billaud-Varennes and Collot d' Herbois very angrily entered: they had come from the Jacobins, where they had been hissed, thrown out, perhaps struck. When they saw Saint-Just writing, their anger increased.

"You are getting a report ready," cried Collot; "I know you are doubtless preparing our indictment."

"Yes, you are right, Collot, I am drawing your indictment." Then, turning to Carnot, "I have not forgotten you either and you are treated as you deserve."

That reply brought on a violent altercation, which Saint-Just closed as usual by refusing to communicate his papers to his colleagues. But he promised to show them his report before reading it to the Convention and the storm blew over. He wrote till five, and only then, when the sun was already high in the horizon, did he go out to rest.

"Injustice has closed my heart. I shall open it wide for the Convention." It was with this threateningly short note that at about eleven Saint-Just warned his colleagues that he would not read them his speech before delivering it. And all, eaten with uneasiness, hurried to the hall of sessions where he had already mounted the platform and begun to speak — a clever and moderate speech which tried to minimize the bad impression made the day before by Robespierre. While the latter had worried the whole Assembly by not giving the names of those he was threatening, Saint-Just contented himself by attacking openly

Collot and Billaud, two Terrorists hated by the Right, and did not even ask for their heads, but for a denial of their conduct and their intrigues. The others, reassured, hastened to abandon the scapegoats, and reinforced by so doing Saint-Just and Robespierre's prestige. The exordium was clever:

"I do not belong to any faction. I shall fight them all. They will only disappear when institutions shall produce guarantees, shall lay the cornerstone of authority and shall bend human pride under the yoke of public freedom for the common good of all . . . The confidence of the two committees flattered me, but last night my heart was trampled upon and I only want to appeal to you."

And after trying to eradicate the impression which might be produced in Europe by the dissensions he had exposed, he passed to his attack on Collot and Billaud.

But he was unable to deliver his speech. From the first words there were murmurs. Tallien, one of the conspirators, rushed to the platform, and pushing Saint-Just back, attacked violently the divisions in the Committee of Public Safety. Then the conspirators followed one after the other, with vehement discourses, passionate invectives, while the president's bell relentlessly drowned the voice of Robespierre and his friends. But Saint-Just's calm did not desert him. "He did not leave the platform," said Barras, "in spite of the interruptions which would have driven any one else away. He only came down a few steps, then mounted again, to continue his discourse proudly; he had been unable to add a word to the two which he had uttered first. Motionless, unmoved, he seemed to defy every one with his calm."

When the indictment was passed and an obscure Montagnard, Souchet, had specified clearly that he included Couthon and Saint-Just, he never broke his contemptuous silence. Imprisoned at the Ecossais, he was soon rescued by his friends and joined Robespierre at the Hôtel de Ville. What did he do first? We don't exactly know: he must have advised the energetic measures which Robespierre, the timorous lawmaker, hesitated a long time in approving. When all was ended and the Thermidorians were victorious, he let himself be made prisoner without resisting, wrapping himself in an enigmatic and contemptuous silence. Brought, with his hands tied, into the hall of the Committee of Public Safety, he lifted his eyes to the poster of the Rights of Man covering the wall and murmured bitterly, "And it is I who put that up!" That was all; he never spoke again to the end.

What did he think of during the long hours of waiting, when all was being prepared for their martyrdom and the victors of the day came to insult those they had worshipped a short while back? Was he thinking of those unfinished fragments which were to be published later under the title of "Republican Institutions" and in which he had noted his dreams as a statesman, his Utopian socialism and his desire for a strong government? Was he going over the episodes of his short and glorious career in his mind, this sudden ascent which had placed him above everybody, even above Robespierre? Or rather, as a practical and resolute man, did he not regret the supreme power he had almost achieved, that dictatorship which he had aspired to establish upon a solid basis, the virtuous republic of which he had dreamed? No one will ever know. He did not belie by his conduct the stoic words he had said with pride:

"I despise the dust I am made of and which speaks to you; you can persecute it and kill it, but I defy you to take away from me the independent life I have created for myself in the centuries to come and in heaven!"

On *Thermidor* 10, *An* II (July 28, 1794) about seven in the evening, on the Place de la Revolution, the knife of the guillotine cut down that head which had never been bowed.

MARAT

marat

MARAT, nicknamed "the friend of the people", presents a very strange and very unusual figure. Rarely has a man inspired such diverse passions: praised to the skies and deified by some, he was hated and thrown to the lions by others. The memory of that curious character has suffered badly from the conflict, and he has emerged from it pretty well disfigured. Even his physical appearance has been a subject of polemics which still rage around his personality. Painters and historians, with their brushes and their pens, have retouched the model according to their own ideas and their own times. Read Michelet: his horrible description of "the greasy hair tied in a napkin, the yellow complexion, the frail limbs and the huge batrachian mouth." Look at David's portrait: it is manifestly painted for the apotheosis, like the Napoleon of the "Coronation."

Marat, it must be admitted, is a difficult subject. Probably no one has ever acted a part as successfully as he; he knew how to make up, though he was not always consistent. His mobile face generally assumed the expression which fitted best the rôle he chose to play at the moment.

A type, however, remains, despite his chameleon-like changes, — the one traced by his contemporary,

Fabre d'Eglantine, which differs but little from the one Marat has given us of himself.

One thing is certain: Marat was not handsome. If we are to believe Fabre d'Eglantine, he was very small, barely five feet tall, but very strong, and not fat. He had wide shoulders and a large chest, a small waist, short thighs, bowlegs and strong arms which he moved with agility and grace. On a thick neck he carried a well-shaped head. He had a broad, angular face, an aquiline nose, flat and with very prominent and distended nostrils. His mouth was of medium size and often contracted at one corner; he had thin lips and a wide forehead; his yellowish-gray eyes were witty and alert, yet serene and open, even gracious. He had no eyebrows, a dull and withered complexion, a black beard and brown hair, untidy and neglected. He walked with his head held high, with a rhythmic quickness which made his body roll from side to side. He was constantly folding his arms in a defiant way.

He added to the bizarre impression he created by his untidy dress. Not that he was so dirty as has been said. Madame Roland said that his drawing-room was very clean and rather elegant, and it is probable that Marat desired precisely that uncared-for appearance which characterized him. The handkerchief around his head, the leather breeches, the open shirt, — is the legendary Marat not ready for the stage? It was thus that the fantastic maniac inspired astonishment and repugnance. "When he was pointed out to me for the first time," said Levasseur in his "Memoirs", "speaking violently from the top of one of the Montagne benches, I looked at him with the uneasy curiosity one feels when looking at some hideous insect. His disordered clothes, his pale face, his roving eyes, had something horrible and repulsive which saddened my soul."

His mania to be different at any price is not extraordinary when one knows the man's ambitions. According to his own biography, Marat, born with a sensitive soul, a fiery imagination, an upright mind, and a heart open to all exalted passions, was especially susceptible to the love of glory. "From my infancy," he said, "I have been devoured by the love of glory, a passion which has changed its object during the various periods of my life but which has not left me for an instant. At five, I wanted to be a schoolmaster; at fifteen, a professor; at eighteeen, a writer; at twenty, a creative artist; to-day, my ambition is to sacrifice myself to my country."

A disproportionate longing for celebrity, a colossal vanity; such were the dominating characteristics to which all Marat's actions, good or bad, can be attributed. It is indeed the extraordinary pride which animated that ex-doctor of the Dauphin that made him spend twenty-five years in seclusion, while he read the best works of science and literature and undertook profound anatomical and physiological researches which gave him the opportunity to publish eight volumes of metaphysical studies. That considerable production was not occasioned only by a disinterested desire to add to the sum total of human knowledge, but also by his determination to pull down everything which had been done in the preceding centuries. "Impervious to the pleasures of eating and the joys of life," according to Brissot, "Marat spent all his means upon experiments in physics. Occupied day and night in repeating them, he would have been content with bread and water if he could have the pleasure of humiliating the Academy of Science. It was the *ne plus ultra* of his ambition."

Of course, although he spent his time trying to humiliate others, he did not intend to be humiliated himself, nor even contradicted. He quarreled with Voltaire, who had dared to make some objections to his theories and was answered by a volley of abuse. Because the physician Charles did not entirely agree with Marat, the latter provoked him to a duel. Even in his childhood he had shown the same vain and tyrannical frame of mind. He himself tells, in the portrait he wrote in the *Journal de la République Française*, that one day, after his father had chastised him unjustly, he felt so deeply humiliated that he remained for two days without food and that when, in despair, they shut him up to force him to obedience, he threw himself from the window. With such a temper, Marat was bound to have many quarrels. He was covered with ridicule. He thought he was being persecuted and despised the world. His already bilious and mistrusting disposition grew worse, and he arrived at a point where he could not bear any one. Such was his frame of mind when the Revolution broke out.

He saw in it a unique opportunity to be, at last, justly appreciated. "For the last five years I have been groaning under this cowardly oppression," he wrote, "until the Revolution dawned with the calling of the States-General. I soon saw how affairs would shape and I began to breathe in the hope that humanity would at last attempt to break its chains and thus find a place for me."

He tried at once to take that place, by publishing in September, 1789, his famous paper *L'Ami du Peuple*. Henceforth, as much through this sheet as through his influence at the Club des Cordeliers, or as later, through his mandate as deputy to the Convention, he played a considerable part and had a prodigious influence, but he imposed himself more by his person and his continual agitating than by his theories.

Marat's theories? It is very difficult to gain an idea of them from the contradictions and vagueness of his writings and his speeches. He attacked everything, denounced everything, but did not propose anything. On October 21, 1790, he wrote in *L'Ami du Peuple;* "It is an error to believe that the French Government can be only monarchical, that it even needs to be monarchical to-day." But on February 17, 1791, he did not hesitate to publish this statement: "I do not know whether the counter-revolutionaries will force us to change our form of government or not, but I know well that a very limited monarchy is the government that suits us best. Louis XVI, when all is said and done, is the king we need. We must bless God for having given him to us."

The most precise and recurrent statement that came from his pen was that he was *the friend of the people*, but he could not make up his mind how best to secure the happiness of that people. Sometimes he wanted them to be free, sometimes he saw them led by a dictator, but a chained dictator who would win the general approval. His ideas were very inconsistent.

It was not his theoretical views that made Marat celebrated. What struck his contemporaries most, and what stands out in all his writings and his speeches, is his eternal call to massacre. On the day of the fall of the Bastille, he asked for five hundred heads. A year later, he demanded five or six hundred more, not for vengeance, but for national security. As time went on, he showed more avidity. In August, 1791, he wanted eight hundred gibbets; towards the end of 1791, he insisted upon five thousand, six thousand, twenty thousand, "And," said he, "let us not hesitate for an instant." With the new year, his demands grew: he asked for seventy thousand! His bloodthirstiness grew with the misfortunes of the nation.

Marat did not get all the heads he asked for, but he got many. He had that of Louis XVI, whose death he voted, of course, without reprieve. He had those of the prisoners of September, and also those of the Girondins, for whose death he worked particularly hard.

These continual incitements to murder aroused many to hate him. Marat had to disappear several times and leave his paper, — after October 5 and 6,

in January, 1790, in July, 1791, in May, 1792, etc. He
did not shine by his courage during these enforced
absences. He generally shut himself up in a cellar,
but from his dark retreat he still found the means to
let loose his hatreds and passions. Reacting to the
perpetual hounding of which he was a victim, each
time Marat came out from his refuge his persecution
mania and his delirium were worse, and he was more
sour and more violent. Several times he was accused,
but his power was so great that he always came out
with a personal triumph, as in the famous session of
April 24, 1793, at the Convention, when he was
exonerated amidst the cheers of the crowd and was
carried out in triumph.

Marat had an enormous influence, an unprecedented
popularity, a formidable prestige, as shown by the
attitude of his contemporaries the day after his death.
The infatuation the people had for him, almost to the
point of fetishism, even survived the Terror; Robespierre had already fallen when he was taken to the
Panthéon.

To what did he owe his success? To his appeals to
violence, which pleased some sanguinary temperaments? Perhaps, but not altogether, because sometimes he only succeeded in frightening his audience,
without convincing it; and sometimes his excessive
violence kept him from being taken seriously. If he
captivated his contemporaries, it was rather through
his rectitude, his love of truth and justice. "Truth
and justice," he used to say, "are my two divinities
upon this earth. I only discriminate between men by

their personal qualities. I admire talent, I respect wisdom and I adore virtue."

He was admired, too, for his courage in attacking everything and sparing nothing at the risk of his life. "Fear has no hold on my soul," he cried one day; "I have given myself to my country and I am ready to shed my blood for her." Such devotion was very much in the spirit of the times. Marat pleased by his audacity, by his carelessness, by his sacrifice of all the proprieties and conventions to what he believed to be the salvation of his country, regardless of consequences. His visit to Dumouriez at Talma's house is often cited as an example. It took place on October 15, 1792.

Marat had reminded people several times that the generals should be watched. He did not share the blind enthusiasm of the Republicans for Dumouriez, who had just arrived in Paris. The general had transferred to a fortress two Parisian battalions accused of having massacred in Rethel four Prussian soldiers. Marat saw in that measure a symptom of Dumouriez' hatred of the patriots. "I want to have a clear idea of the affair," he said, "and as long as I have a head on my shoulders, the people won't be strangled with impunity."

He went coldly to Dumouriez to ask him his account of the affair. He did not find him, but as Dumouriez was attending a fête at Talma's, Marat, undaunted, joined him there. He entered the brilliant assembly brusquely, without having taken time to dress for the occasion. He went straight up to the general and, looking at him with fearless eyes, "It is you I seek," he said. Dumouriez, with true military impertinence, turned upon his heels. Marat, not intimidated in the least, grasped his sleeve and pushed him into a corner.

"You approve of the insubordination of soldiers?" said Dumouriez.

"No," answered Marat, "but I hate the treason of officers." And he left as he had come, leaving behind him an uneasiness not hard to understand. In the hall, he found himself face to face with several soldiers, their swords upon their shoulders. "Your master," he said to them with a disdainful smile, "is more afraid of the tip of my pen than I of the tips of your swords."

Such spontaneous sayings, coming straight from the heart, assured his popularity. All found in him a little of what they would have liked to be. They looked at him as in a mirror and they found there a little of themselves amplified, and all were pleased and flattered.

This explains why Marat was not always thought to be only a sanguinary. Even his detractors wonder if, perhaps, he was not more hypersensitive than cruel. Michelet, who did not like him, wrote:

I know by many examples how the feeling for right, indignation and pity for the oppressed, can rouse violent passions and sometimes cruel ones. Who has not seen women a hundred times who, at the sight of a child being beaten or an animal cruelly treated, have given way to the most unrestrained rage? Was Marat bloodthirsty only because of his sensitiveness? It is possible, and perhaps it is because he was a typical product of the exasperation of a time overexcited by internal difficulties and by war, that he was able to find then, as now, some lenient judges.

Marat was also loved for his integrity and the uprightness of his private life. When so many revolutionaries in that troubled period became corrupted and often completely debauched, he lived according to the precepts of Rousseau, according to the rules of nature. We learn from his autobiography that he had escaped "all the vicious habits of childhood which enervate and degrade man", that he had avoided "all the faults of youth", that he had reached "virility without having yielded to passion." In brief, he was a virgin at twenty-one. All his life he kept the habits of his childhood. He lived with a friend, Catherine Evrard, "a divine woman who took pity on his plight," and who, when he was hiding from cellar to cellar, had concealed in her home the friend of the people, given him her fortune and sacrificed her peace. But he had married her "before the sun and nature," and after his death a promise of legal marriage was found in his papers. And if there was ever an incorruptible, it was Marat. Outside of glory, nothing, not even money, counted. We have the testimony even of his enemies as to his honesty. Brissot tells that Marat was very disinterested and never thought about money.

But, in any case, when would Marat have found time to satisfy his vices or even to think of his own interests? His activity was prodigious and left him not a moment to himself. "Of the twenty-four hours in a day, I give only two to sleep, and one to food, dressing and domestic cares. In addition to the time I give to my duties as a deputy of the people, I spend regularly six hours listening to the complaints of a crowd of unfortunates whose defender I am, in helping them with their claims and petitions, in reading and answering a multitude of letters, in seeing through the press a very important work of mine, in taking notes on all the interesting events of the Revolution, in jotting down on paper my observations, in receiving denunciations and assuring myself of their worth; and last, in making up my paper. Those are my daily occupations; no one can accuse me of laziness. It is more than three years since I have had a quarter of an hour respite."

It is certain that, combined with the demoniacal and violent patriotism which animated him, such public and private virtues gave Marat an astounding hold upon the imaginations of his contemporaries. But would they have been enough to give him the influence he had upon the mob? I do not think so. Most of the time the common run of mankind wants something more visible, more tangible, more concrete, more human, less sublime, in a word something nearer to itself and easier to understand. Marat could satisfy this need as well, and it was on the platform that he showed it. Not that he was an orator in the ordinary sense of the word. He had neither the power of a Mirabeau, nor the elegance of a Vergniaud, nor the mastery of both. There was no coördination in his gestures: he was very agitated, as Fabre d'Eglantine pointed out. There was no variety in his delivery. He almost always ended his discourses by a movement of one foot, which he put forward and stamped upon the ground, rising suddenly on tiptoe to increase his small stature. His diction also was not agreeable. Although his sonorous voice was well-pitched, his enunciation was bad; he had an impediment in his speech which made it difficult for him to pronounce certain letters and made his speech appear a little stilted. But his obvious sincerity overawed, his disorderly movements and his ugliness amazed. He seemed to be an oracle, filled with divine fury and possessed of a spirit which uttered indisputable and final judgments. He did not hesitate to speak of himself and risked ridicule to proclaim his superiority, as at that session when, amid laughter and ironical exclamations, he called himself a man of genius.

"I tell you," he cried, "I am above your decrees. No, you can't stop a man of genius from reaching the future. You don't recognize a learned man who knows the world and foresees events. What would your fate have been if I had not prepared public opinion?" . . . "Bursts of laughter" is the comment in the report of the debates.

In spite of the laughter and jeers, Marat was *listened to*. Never, indeed, were his speeches met with indifference. Tragic or comic, his tremendous vanity was never met with apathy. "People shouted, laughed, hissed, but they were alive," and no one was more pleased than the orator, when he could see from the platform a sea of faces drawn with anger, pale with fear, when he heard interruptions clashing like swords, or cries of hatred, or insulting laughter.

The secret of his influence, in fine, is to be found in that famous session of September 25, 1792, when he appeared for the first time on the tribune of the Convention. Accused of wishing for a dictatorship, he had three quarters of the Assembly against him, but he held his own against everybody. It was during that tragic debate that Marat made his greatest speech. After a first interruption, he repeated that he was honored by the writs against him and added: "The people have declared these decrees null and void by calling me to sit among you, because my cause is theirs. If my enemies had secured from you a decree of accusation, I was determined to blow my brains out at the foot of the tribune." And suiting his action to his words, he took a revolver from his pocket and pressed it to his brow. Then, with a contemptuous gesture, he put the weapon back in his pocket and crossed his arms, as if he thought better of it. "Well," he cried, "I shall stay among you to brave your fury!" And he came down.

Fabre d'Eglantine, who reported the high spots of the session, noted very justly the impression he made and which, at bottom, is to a great extent the one which remained in the memories of all after every appearance of his.

I have never seen him — he said — even in the most violent storm, without a rare and constant presence of

mind, in his aims, in their execution, his opinions, his
patriotic hatred. Nothing made him change, nothing
made him bend. It was not through stubbornness,
because he knew how to listen to reason, and knew
how to praise it in other people when it surpassed
his, and with such simplicity that it was homage to
his own superiority rather than to his truthfulness.
In danger, in the most thorny and unexpected attacks,
in the most violent persecutions, his courage, his
intrepidity were worthy of admiration. No reverse
discouraged him, no selfish consideration dominated
him. A special proof of it will be found . . . in the
magnificent victory he won over all his enemies solely
by his own efforts, through the intrepidity of his
mien and the force of his logic, in the terror which he
inspired, contempt upon his lips and a revolver in
his hand.

And yet curiously, that strange man, with the
extraordinary influence, belonged to no party. He
did not want any; to an offer of collaboration from
Camille Desmoulins and Fréron, he answered: "the
eagle flies alone, the turkey goes in flock."

"I defy," wrote the latter, "any one in the Assembly
to name, I won't say *Marat's party*, but one disciple
of Marat . . . Sometimes Marat calls me his son,
his dear son, because Marat is, at bottom, a good man
ınd a much better character than all those underhand
hypocrites full of moderation whom I see in the
Assembly and who would willingly hang, in spite of
the legislative body, the revolutionaries of the tenth
of August. But, although Marat calls me his son,
this relationship does not prevent me from sometimes
keeping at a respectable distance from the said
honorable father, more than four degrees removed,
when one knows relationship stops" . . . And if

Camille Desmoulins was not a Maratist, who could be in the Convention? It is therefore proven that Marat's party, which consists of Marat alone, is a ridiculous bugaboo raised by the intriguers of the Convention and which could only frighten a flock of sparrows or other stupid birds.

It is certain that the halo surrounding the chief of a party would not have been sufficient for Marat's immense ambition. He would have been more contented to see the whole country worshipping him like a god. He would have been satisfied had he been able to follow the events after his death. When Charlotte Corday's dagger had fixed forever upon his yellow face his sardonic grin, everywhere there was an unusual explosion of sorrow. The Convention decreed that it would be present in a body at the funeral. The sections, the popular societies, all Paris was plunged in gloom. The obsequies took place with unusual pomp and display. The section of the Cordeliers asked for his heart to place in their debating room and the ceremony of the transportation of "Marat's heart" gave rise to scenes of real idolatry. Some went so far as to see a resemblance between Marat's heart and Jesus' heart. Later the Convention accorded him the honors of the Panthéon. His ashes were transferred on September 21, 1794, with magnificent pomp, to music by Cherubini and Mehul. It is true that they were removed in disgrace and outraged on *Ventose* 8, *An* III, at the height of the Thermidorian reaction. A bust of the "Friend of the People" was carried around Paris, heaped with all kinds of insults by the youth of the time and thrown into a sewer in the Rue Montmartre !

But an excess of indignity after an excess of honors . . . supreme insult after supreme glory . . . must have made Marat's corpse swell with pride, just as long before, when alone in the tribune, he had faced torrents of abuse.

CAMILLE DESMOULINS

Camille Des

On July 12, 1789, Louis XVI could not bring himself to believe that the Revolution was an accomplished fact. Giving way to the intrigues around him, he had foreign regiments massed around Paris, making all patriotic Frenchmen uneasy, and raising all Paris to a fever pitch of excitement. On Sunday the news that Necker had been dismissed dropped upon Paris like a bomb: Necker, the popular minister, whom everybody had hoped would be able to save France, had been sacrificed to the Court and the aristocrats.

On the stroke of twelve, a young man of twenty-nine ran to the Café de Foy in the square of the Palais Royal. With all the vigor of youth, he jumped upon a table. "Citizens," he cried, "there is not a moment to be lost. I come from Versailles. Necker has been dismissed, and his dismissal is the signal for a Saint-Bartholomew's of all patriots. To-night all the Swiss and German battalions will leave the Champ-de-Mars to kill us. We must secure arms, and wear rosettes, so that we can recognize each other. What color do you want? Green, the color of hope or the blue of Cincinnatus, the color of liberty and democracy?"

"Green! Green!" shouted the crowd. And then this young man, in a resonant voice, shouted, "Friends, the signal is given. I see from here the spies and the stool pigeons who are watching us. At least I won't fall into their hands alive. Let all patriots follow my example." He brandished two revolvers and put a green ribbon in his hat, while the crowd pulled leaves from the trees and made cockades of them.

At the age of twenty-nine, Camille Desmoulins, hitherto unknown, had entered history.

The Revolution had found him ready. While at the Lycée Louis-le-Grand, where he had a scholarship, he had become a friend of Maximilien Robespierre. The republican convictions of the two schoolboys grew stronger as they studied antiquity. "The first Republicans to appear in 1789," he said later, "were young men who, fed upon Cicero in the colleges, were passionately fond of liberty. We were taught at the schools of Rome and Athens and in the pride of the Republic, only to live in the abjection of monarchy and under the reigns of the Claudians and the Vitellians. What a mad government, to think that we could be enthusiastic about the fathers of the Roman Republic, without being horrified at the man-eaters of Versailles, and that we could admire the past without condemning the present: *ulteriora mirari praesentia secutoros.*" In this characteristic passage, Camille showed that from the first he had been an ardent Republican and a fanatical admirer of antiquity.

With the opening of the States-General, the young man's enthusiasm, as shown by his letters to his father, grew to a fever which animated all his acts. He was continually upon the road to Versailles; went to the sessions; applauded Mirabeau; dined with Target, and with the deputies from Dauphiné and Brittany "who all knew him for a patriot and who paid him flattering attention." In Paris, he never missed a political demonstration. He spent his evenings speechifying in the clubs. "The pleasure I feel at hearing the admirable plans of our eager citizens in the clubs and in some cafés carries me away," he wrote, adding, "Many people who hear my speeches are astonished that I have not been made a deputy, a compliment which flatters me inexpressibly." Camille went to a lot of trouble to draw attention to himself. He wrote to Mirabeau, inviting him to become a contributor to the famous *Gazette*, "which reports all forthcoming events to the States-General, to which people are subscribing by the thousand and which will bring, it is said, five thousand francs to its founder."

But all his efforts were futile, for despite his impatience, he was being ignored, until the twelfth of July gave him the spotlight which he had so greatly desired.

Henceforth he was known. He never stopped talking of that famous day, describing it complacently in great detail, boasting of the celebrity it had brought him. "To think that a majority of the Parisians," he wrote to his father, "place me among the principal authors of the Revolution. Many go so far as to say that I am *the* author of it. I have made a name for myself and people now say: A Desmoulins pamphlet, not a pamphlet by an author called Desmoulins. Several women have invited me to their receptions.

But nothing could give me more pleasure than that moment on the twelfth of July, when I was, I shall say, not applauded by ten thousand people, but smothered by their tearful embraces."

But, to tell the truth, his successes did not fill his pockets. He remained a poor barrister without cases and found himself obliged to ask his father for money, which he got, one *louis* at a time. He was already celebrated as a publicist, but he had no home and lived at an inn. His "Lanterne" brought him only fifteen *louis* against forty or fifty to the bookseller and his *France Libre*, his first newspaper, thirty crowns against a thousand to the editor. To crown his misfortune, the stir which those works created brought down upon him all his creditors, who left him penniless.

Here I am—he wrote on October 8, 1789—almost without creditors, but also without money. I beg you, since you are now collecting your income, since the price of corn is keeping up, to please send me six *louis*. At this moment of my fame, I want to buy my own furniture. Would you be so cruel as to refuse me a bed and a pair of sheets? Why do you send me only two *louis* at a time, so that I have never been able to buy furniture and a home? And when I think that if I had only had a permanent place of residence, — that with a domicile, I would now be president, commander of the district, representative to the Commune of Paris, instead of only a distinguished writer. . .

It is surprising to think that for ten years I have been complaining in this way. It has been easier for me to make a revolution, to upset France, than to obtain from my father, once and for all, fifty *louis* to establish myself.

I have a reputation in Paris. People ask my advice about important matters. I am being asked to dinner. The only thing I need is a home. I beg you, help me. Send me six *louis*, or else a bed.

A short time after, on November 28, 1789, appeared the first number of the paper which was to make of Camille Desmoulins one of the greatest, if not the greatest, journalist of the Revolution: the *Revolutions in France and Brabant*. In the first number, Desmoulins began a hymn to the Revolution, which he thought was over.

Consummated, — he cried, — all is consummated; the king is in the Louvre, the National Assembly in the Tuileries. The canals of circulation are becoming navigable, the national treasury is being filled, the mills are turning, the traitors flying, the priesthood is overthrown, aristocracy is expiring, the projects of Mounie and Lally are defeated, the provinces are holding fast to each other and do not want to be separated, the Constitution is being signed, the patriots are victorious. Paris has escaped bankruptcy . . . Paris is to be the queen of cities and the splendor of the capital will equal the greatness and the majesty of the French empire.

After the defeat of Perseus, while Paul Emile was descending from his triumphal chariot and entering the temple of Jupiter, a deputy of the towns addressed the Senate thus:

"Romans, you have no more enemies in the universe and all that is left for you to do is to govern the world and to care for it, like the Gods themselves." We

139

can say the same to the National Assembly: "You have no more enemies, no more contradictors, no more vetoes to fear. All that is left for you to do is to govern France, to make her happy, and to give her such laws that, following your example, all nations will hasten to transplant them and cause them to flourish in their own countries."

Do you think, my dear reader, that I shall continue to make myself breathless with such long tirades? Do not count upon it, for I shall not be spendthrift with great oratory. A number will appear every week. It will be my aim to make each issue interesting and, like the *Mercure*, to go from marvel to marvel. The universe and all its follies will be the province of this hypercritical paper.

Desmoulin's paper had a great success at once. "My first number has been found perfect," he wrote to his father, when sending it to him. "But will I be able to keep it so?" Judging from this remark and from the precautions he took in the first number of the paper, Camille seemed to doubt his own strength a little. He was afraid that he might run short of breath and be unable to reach the goal, but he was proud of his work, — he had found his career. "Now I am a journalist," he remarked, "and it is quite a worthy profession, no longer despicable and mercenary, enslaved by the government. In France to-day, it is the journalist who has the tablets and the album of the censor, who judges the Senate, the the Consuls and the Dictator himself."

Desmoulin's sheet appeared every Saturday, as a pamphlet of at least three octavo sheets. Each number

contained a print, which was almost always a caricature. Those caricatures were not always delicate,
as for example, the one which, in April, 1791, represented very realistically the flogging of the nuns.
(The nuns of Saint-Vincent de Paul had been stripped
and flogged in the public square.) It is true that
Camille declared on several occasions that he had
nothing to do with the drawings, claiming that
although he had the ideas for many of them there
were some against which he had protested.

But if he did not claim the illustrations, he could
not deny the articles which equaled the caricatures in
violence. They are all quotable, but some of them are
particularly remarkable: the one about the flight of
Louis XVI; the one about La Fayette, whom he
accused of having had a baker hung by his agents, so
that he could accuse the patriots of the murder; the
one about the queen, whose charities he condemned
as liberticide. He was especially good at attack,
satire and vituperation. He attacked, among others,
the Abbé Maury, whom he never mentioned without
prefixing his name with the initials J. F. which were
supposed to be those of his given names, but which
really were a gross insult. This man was an easy
mark for the banter of Desmoulins. All his contemporaries agreed upon the Rabelaisianism of the
ecclesiastic's talk and the loose living of the "formidable giant of the Right."

I have tried to cure him, — wrote Camille Desmoulins, — but I see now that he is incurable. He has
the courage of shame, as he himself asserted the other day;

that is to say, for those who do not understand the
academic language, the courage of those who swallow
shame like water. That man with the eight hundred
farms did so much harm at the session of January 13,
that all the senators of the Left, shouted: "Down with
him! Off the platform! Away with him!..."

One can imagine the consternation of the Augustine
Fathers and the rage of J . . . F . . . Maury! J . . .
F . . . Maury, he doubtless had said to himself, go
now and spend your time proposing incendiary or
anti-popular resolutions, be the damned tool of the
aristocrats, spit blood on the platform, lie like a
footman, laugh at slaps and hisses: Vain words!
Vain infamy! The platform is impossible. The
Jacobins are masters. The galley slaves would not
endure J . . . F . . . Maury's company and yet he is
accepted by the National Assembly! It is well known
that Maury's forehead has been sculptured as the
emblem of insolence and when they do him life-size,
he is the symbol of the seven deadly sins.

The *Revolutions in France and Brabant* established
Desmoulins as a great journalist. Was it his violence
or the coarse caricatures accompanying the text which
brought him renown? Perhaps a little of both. It is
quite certain that the mob does not object to caricatures, even if rather coarse. But they would not have
been enough. In the midst of his excesses, he had
developed a refined and literary style which pleased
cultivated and well-read people. Of course his continual allusions to ancient history and his Latin quota-
tions could not be understood by everybody, nor his
fantastic translations, his voluntary anachronisms,
his amusing parodies, as when he made Cato and

Cicero *Girondins*, and Cataline a *Feuillant*. Many were lost in that erudition, but the literary public found it substantial food. As for the ordinary reader, Camille captured him by the tone of his articles. Far from being boring diatribes, grandiloquent and bombastic, they were more like conversations, intimate discourses in which the writer gave free rein to his imagination, which his light and piquant style made palatable. The *Revolutions in France and Brabant* was more of a news supplement than a newspaper, and was really "The Memoirs of the First Two Years of the Republic." Louis Blanc called Desmoulins, very aptly, "a bright schoolboy whose mind was full of Rome and Greece." Another biographer called him "the gamin of journalism." And Michelet, in his turn, saw in him "a talented but naughty boy, given to deadly jokes." His virulent phrases were, indeed, deadly jokes. When he began his *Revolutions in France and Brabant*, Sainte-Beuve added, "Camille was far from foreseeing its consequences. He thought he was setting off fireworks, and little guessed what a fire he had started, a fire in which he was to perish, child that he was, while joyously lighting his fuses."

He little guessed the approach of the fire, because he had abandoned the Revolution after the massacres of the Champ-de-Mars. He had just married and was enjoying a happiness which his waiting had made immeasurable. Several years indeed had passed since the day when Camille had met in the Luxembourg, "the small, adorable blonde," who was to become his wife, Anne Louise Duplessis-Laridon, better known as Lucile. Lucile was small, graceful, coy, a real Greuze. Camille himself was not good looking: he had, like Robespierre, a bilious complexion, a hard, sinister face, more like the falcon's than the eagle's. But though ugly, his unusual ugliness was charming. "In his face," said one of his biographers, "there was something demoniacal, hellishly witty, devilishly beautiful."

No matter why, but the two young people loved each other. Under the indulgent eyes of Lucile's mother — "Mother Melpomene" as she was called, because of her striking beauty — the idyll went on under the shade of the great trees in the old garden. At first the father refused to give his daughter to a man without money, but when he was made a barrister, Camille went joyfully to the father to ask for Lucile! But the latter still thought his income insufficient and refused. Camille was not discouraged. The Revolution came; when, thanks to journalism, he had become an influential man, he thought that no further objection could be made. Lucile's father thought that journalism could not be called a very brilliant profession but, beaten by perseverance and faithfulness, he ended by giving in. Camille's enthusiasm was boundless. Let politics go to the devil!

To-day, — he wrote to his father,— I see myself at the height of felicity. Happiness has been long in coming to me, but it has come at last, and I am as happy as any one can be on this earth. That charming Lucile I have told you about so often is at last being given to me by her parents, and she . . . does not

144

refuse me. You will know her character from one
incident: when her mother gave her to me a moment
ago, she took me to her room and I threw myself at
her feet. Surprised to hear her laugh, I looked up, but
she was as moved as I. She was in tears and yet she
was laughing. I have never seen such a ravishing
spectacle, and I never suspected that character and
emotion could cause such a contrast.

The marriage took place at the end of 1790. Robespierre and Brissot were witnesses. Irony of fate: the
second was to be a victim of Camille, and Camille
himself was to be a victim of the first!

After reëntering politics about the end of 1791,
Desmoulins, while going regularly to the Jacobin
Club, had again taken to the law. At the beginning
of 1792, during a consultation about some legal
business, he was violently attacked by a colleague of
Brissot, who accused him of having defended gambling. It was a bad move, for the fiery journalist,
perhaps egged on by Robespierre, answered at once
by his "Brissot Unmasked," in which he declared him
responsible for the declaration of war, and attacked
him violently. That villainous polemic, made worse
by the publication of the "History of the Brissotins,"
began hostilities between the Girondins and the
Montagne. Later, when the Girondins were condemned to death, Camille was to repent bitterly. It
is said that at the session of the revolutionary tribunal
which pronounced the death sentence, he burst into
sobs. "Ah!" he cried, "It is my 'Brissot Unmasked'
which caused their death!" It was too late.

Shortly afterward, a son was born to him, Horace, whom he had inscribed on the state registers without any religious ceremony, thus setting the example of a republican baptism. To attach him to life, Camille had home, love, money, and yet he was about to court death.

He had been elected to the National Convention but he did not play a great part in it. He was very quickly put out of countenance at the tribune. He stammered, — it took him a long time to get into his stride and he began generally by monosyllables, "Hon! hon!" . . . . Lucile called him laughingly, "Monsieur Hon!" He had none of the physical attributes of the orator; his chest was weak. So he rarely appeared at the tribune. He replied one day to Legendre, who reproached him with his silence, "But my dear Legendre, everyone does not have your lungs!" On the rare occasions when he spoke, he committed blunders which made him ridiculous, and he went back quickly to his first love — journalism.

The *Revolutions* no longer existed, but in December, 1793, he launched a new paper, the *Vieux Cordelier*. That sheet, which was to be his ruin, and was to bring him to the guillotine, was perhaps the most eloquent work produced by the Revolution, and certainly there is nothing comparable to it in journalism, before or since. For several months he had been discussing his idea with Danton. Both thought that the recent victories had saved the Republic and that it was time to put an end to cruelties henceforth useless.

On one of the last nights of January, Lamartine tells, they left the Palais Royal with Souberbielle, a juror of the revolutionary tribunal. The day had been bloody. The three companions were talking about the events, their hearts heavy.

"Do you know," said Danton to Souberbielle, "that if you continue the way you are going, soon no one will be safe?"

"That's true," answered Souberbielle, "but what can I do? I am only an obscure patriot. Ah, if I were Danton!"

"Danton is asleep," answered the first, "he'll awake when it is time. All this blood begins to horrify me. I am a revolutionary, not a murderer. But you, Camille," he added, turning to Desmoulins, who had said nothing, "why are you silent?"

"I am tired of silence," Desmoulins replied. "Mine weighs upon me. Sometimes I'd like to sharpen my pen like a stiletto and stab these scoundrels. Let them take care. My ink is more indelible than their blood; its stain will be immortal."

"Then begin to-morrow," cried Danton; "you started the Revolution. It's up to you to check it."

Camille left them. He sharpened his pen and wrote his last work, the *Vieux Cordelier*, the *Vieux Cordelier*, that is to say, the first *cordelier*, of the great epoch, the real revolutionaries opposed to the new revolutionaries, mad, ultra-violent, excessive — in brief, the Nouveaux Cordeliers who were leading the Revolution into false ways. It is sometimes hard to imagine the ardent, boiling, aggressive Camille being moderate, but nothing is astonishing from that mobile and light mind, rather scatterbrained and inconsequential.

On December 5, the first number of the paper appeared. Like the *Revolutions*, it had a great success, and fifty thousand copies were printed. Robespierre himself was worried, and Camille promised to show him all the following numbers. The influence of the tribune was easily recognizable. Robespierre wanted to ruin the Hébertists who might be dangerous for him, and he used Desmoulins unscrupulously, without the latter suspecting that he was only a tool and that his turn would come. He used all his strength and all his ability in fighting the faction of the "Enraged". To *Père Duchesne* he opposed the memory of the *Ami du Peuple* who, "thanks to his obscure life and his untiring labor, was looked upon as the summit of patriotism" and he stigmatized those who pretended to have inherited his cloak and, by their excesses, were leading the Republic to its ruin.

Camille was sharpening his tool. Beginning with the third number, the workman and his tool were in perfect form and we have his masterpiece in which Camille, under the pretext of translating Tacitus, uttered his famous philippic, with its transparent allusions. It is considered one of his best articles, if not the best.

Under Augustus' successor, — he wrote,— tyranny soon knew no bounds. As soon as speech became a crime against the state, just one step forward, and ordinary glances, sadness, pity, sighs, and even silence, became criminal.

Everything upset the tyrant.

If a citizen were popular, he was a rival of the prince and might start a civil war. *Studia civium in se vertere; et si multi idem audeant, bellum esse.* He was a suspect.

If, on the contrary, he avoided popularity and remained by his fireside, his quiet life drew attention to him. *Quanto metu occultior, tanto famoe adeptus.* He was a suspect.

If he were rich, there was imminent peril that the people would be corrupted through his largesse. *Auri vim atque opes Plauti principi infensas.* He was a suspect.

If he were poor, well, invincible emperor, you must watch that man closely! No one is as enterprising as the one who owns nothing. *Syllam imopem; unde proecipuam audaciam.* He was a suspect.

Etc., etc.

Desmoulins had never yet risen to such heights of sublime inspiration. The effect produced surpassed all his expectations. People fought over that number. There was a queue at the door of the bookseller and the paper was sold and resold. Its price rose to a *louis* for a single copy.

But those who had been attacked under the disguise of the Romans and who had easily recognized themselves, far from trying to reform, would not rest until they had avenged themselves. Camille fell headfirst into the trap and gave them their opportunity by clamoring for the appointment of a Clemency Committee and the release of all suspects. "Do you want me," he cried, "to adore your Constitution and to fall on my knees before it? Release those two hundred thousand citizens whom you call suspects!"

Alas! By defending the suspects, Camille drew suspicion upon himself. The *Vieux Cordelier* was read in the clubs: the Jacobins, the Cordeliers. There were dramatic debates. Robespierre defended Camille with hypocritical elegance, but in such a contemptuous tone! "He is a child," he said, "led astray by bad company."

Desmoulins himself probably saw the effect of his articles. In the sixth number, he tried to defend himself and to retract. A very understandable weakness, but barely noticeable. Indeed, in the seventh, which he was unable to publish, he took the bull by the horns, and faced the terrible Robespierre by branding by name all the members of the Committee of Public Safety and General Security. He scourged all those "Furies, all those new patriots who refused to believe in the Mary Magdelenes and the Saint Augustines of politics and who make a crime of his pity for patriots, for brothers who are a hundred times less wrong than they were." Vouland, secretary of the General Security Committee, "a short while before a Royalist and a member of the famous Feuillants Club"; Jagot, "another terrible member of the Committee, who threw men into prison for the most trivial cause"; Amar, "the least cruel of them, whose music calms the storm of his business but whom the sword does not suit any better than his colleagues"; David, "ruined by his pride, the most violent of all because of his miserable ambition to see his name in all the papers; President David who filled up the prisons, only to cater to the popular mood of the moment, so that he might for a fortnight be the presiding officer of the Convention and sit upon an armchair of green morocco", etc., etc.

This was too much. This number which people mentioned in hushed tones, which the editor refused to publish, but whose contents were well known, was the drop which caused the glass to overflow. Camille, the *Vieux Cordelier*, was dropped from the Club des Cordeliers; his fall followed close upon that of the "madmen." Many, indeed, were not broadminded enough to understand his generous impulse, which appeared to them only inconsequential and treasonable. What? When the Republic, besieged by all of Europe, had been exposed to the anti-Revolutionary intrigues, Camille had prepared the immolation of Cloots, who had given his life and his fortune to the Revolution, and yet now he cried in favor of the enemies of the Revolution? The faction of the moderates was denounced. From faction to conspiracy is only one step; it was soon taken. On the night of the eleventh of *Germinal, An* II (March 31, 1794) Camille Desmoulins was arrested with Danton and their friends.

In his prison, the old Cordelier, although ready for his great trial, had a moment of utter despair. To know this, it is only necessary to read his pitiful letters to his wife. One especially is celebrated:

Kind sleep has put a stop to my misfortune. I do not feel my captivity. Heaven has been kind to me.

Only a short while ago I saw you all in a dream and I kissed you all, one after the other: you, Horace and Durousse, who was in the house. But our little one had lost one eye through some infection which had settled upon it and the sorrow I felt awoke me. I found myself in my cell; there was a little daylight. Your mother and you were speaking to me, but I could neither see nor hear you, and I rose, for I at least might speak to you in writing. But when I opened the windows, the thought of my solitude, of the awful bars, the bolts which separate us, drove away all the strength of my soul. I burst into tears or rather, I sobbed, while shouting from my tomb; "Lucile! Lucile!"

Oh, my dear Lucile, where are you? Good-by, my darling Lolotte, my dear Lou. Say good-by to my father. You see in me a victim of the barbarism and ingratitude of man. My last moments won't dishonor you. You see that my fears had some foundation and that my presentiments were always true. I married a wife made saintly by her virtue. I have been a good husband, a good son, I would have been a good father. I take with me the esteem and regrets of all true Republicans, of all virtuous and free men. I die at thirty-four, — but it is a miracle that during the last five years I should have passed so many precipices of the Revolution without falling over one of them and that I should be alive still, and I lean my head calmly upon the pillow of my writings, too numerous, but which all breathe the same philanthropy, the same desire to make my fellow citizens happy and free, and which the hatchet of the tyrants cannot strike. I see that power intoxicates nearly all men, that they all say, like Denis of Syracuse: "Tyranny is a beautiful epitaph." But console yourself, desolate widow! The epitaph of your poor Camille is more glorious, it is that of the Brutuses and the Catos, the tyrannicides. Forgive me, my dear love, my real life, which I lost when we were separated — I am thinking of my memory, and I ought to try to make you forget it, my Lucile! My good Loulou! My darling! I beg of you, do not remain unhappy. Don't call me, for your cries would tear me apart in the grave. Live for Horace's sake, talk to him about me; you'll tell him what he can't hear, that I would have loved him much! In spite of my martyrdom, believe in God. My blood shall wash out my sins, the weaknesses of man; and what is good in me, my virtue, my love for liberty, shall be rewarded by God. I shall see you again some day, Lucile! Annette! As sensitive as I am, is death, which prevents me from seeing so many crimes, such a great unhappiness? Good-by, Loulou, good-by, my life, my soul, my divinity upon earth! I leave you some good friends, all virtuous and sensitive men. Good-by, Lucile, my very dear Lucile! Good-by, Horace, Annette; good-by, my father! I feel the banks of life rushing past me. I see Lucile still. I see her! My arms press you to my bosom. My tied hands kiss you and my severed head rests upon yours. I am going to die!"

After her husband's arrest, however, Lucile did not remain inactive. She, who had been accused of unfaithfulness, who had been accused of having had a weakness for Fréron, for General Dillon — she had one thought only: to save her husband. She wrote to Robespierre, who had once been fond of her. She recalled to him that he had been a witness to her marriage, that he was their first friend. "You who made vows for our union," she wrote, "who joined our hands in yours, you who smiled upon my son,

whose childish hands have caressed you many times,
can you reject my prayers, despise my tears and
trample justice underfoot? You will kill us both. To
strike him is to kill me.''

No answer to this heart-rending petition, except
that of the Revolutionary Tribunal. Camille was
condemned to death.

In the fatal cart the unhappy man struggled and
harangued the mob. ''People,'' he clamored, ''your
friends are being killed. Who called you to the
Bastille? Who gave you your cockades? I am Camille
Desmoulins . . . ''

Upon the scaffold, however, he recovered his calm.
Looking at the knife which was covered with Hérault
de Séchelles' blood, he cried: ''A worthy reward for
the first apostle of Liberty.'' He died, holding in his
hands a curl of Lucile's hair.

Thus Camille perished.

> *Un accord singulier*
> *De poète et de Cordelier*
> *Pour aimer sans égal,*
> *Sans pareil pour railler*
> *Ame enfantine et mobile et fol,*
> *Oiseau de flamme*
> *Esprit de faune et coeur de femme.*

After her husband was beheaded, Lucile thought
only of joining him. At such a time wishes of that
kind were easily granted. The unhappy woman had
tried to stir up the people to free Desmoulins. She
was denounced by a man named Laflotte, who knew
her plans, and she was arrested in her turn. ''Good-

by, my dear mother," she wrote in her prison, on her return from the tribunal. "A tear falls from my eyes. I shall go to sleep in the calm of innocence." Then she busied herself with her dressing.

She walked quietly to the guillotine. That romantic young girl, only twenty-two, placed her small, adorable blonde head upon the block!

How shall we judge the complex and contradictory mind of Camille Desmoulins? Perhaps we shall have to content ourselves with adopting the judgment of Mirabeau, whom Camille, when an obscure journalist, was so proud to know. "Good-by, beautiful son, you deserve to be loved in spite of your spirited errors!"

There are two dates in Camille's life, two dates which would honor the most glorious lives and which will eternally plead for him: the first, that brilliant and proud dawn of 1789 when, an unknown enthusiast, he harangued the people at the Palais Royal . . . and gave for a color to the rising generation green, the color of hope, which opened the doors of glory; the second, the publication of the *Vieux Cordelier*, which opened the doors of the grave.

VERGNIAUD

During the year 1780, a tall boy returned to his parental roof in Limoges, rather sheepish and ashamed. At twenty-six Pierre Victurnien Vergniaud had no position and no future, in spite of his best endeavors. Not that he could not have found an opportunity to earn his living! He had received a scholarship at the College of Plessis, thanks to Turgot, and had completed studies which had enabled him to enter the seminary, but the ecclesiastical life did not appeal to him and he left it because he did not like it. Then he was placed by M. d'Ailly in the revenue department, but did not remain there either because of "the antipathy he felt for such work."

It must be admitted that he himself regretted those two false starts, and bemoaned the fact that he was a burden to his father. "It is enough," he said, "to be a burden to oneself." But just as he began to despair, a career was found for him, —found for him, of course, because his natural indolence prevented his finding one for himself.

One morning his brother-in-law, M. Alluaud, caught him improvising a speech and was astonished by his flowing eloquence. "Why don't you become an attorney?" he said.

"I don't ask anything better. But how am I to pay my expenses till I can plead?"

"I'll help you," said the other.

That answer decided his future.

After a year's study in Bordeaux, he was admitted to the bar, but despite his new status he still suffered great hardships until he gained the friendship of the Deputy Chief Justice and became his secretary at four hundred francs a month. Thus he secured financial independence and peace of mind. Then he appeared for the defense in two important cases — that of Marie Bérigaud, accused of infanticide, and that of the Curé Labeyrie, accused of illicit paternity, and after obtaining their acquittal, the young lawyer's name emerged from obscurity, and henceforth he never stopped on his way to fame. In a case involving an inheritance of three millions, he was so brilliant that, contrary to all custom, his peroration was received with applause. His reputation was made and he went from one triumph to another. In 1789, in the affair of the nun, he lost, but was applauded nevertheless. A little later, his pleading for Pierre Durieux, whose acquittal he secured, made him famous as a great lawyer.

That last cause prepared him for political life. It was in 1790. The accumulated hatred of centuries against the aristocrats had not had time to cool down, and here and there peasant insurrections were still going on. At Alassac, in Corrèze, on the day when the municipal law was promulgated, after mass, some young men pulled up and burned the aristocrats' and the judges' pew. Martial law was proclaimed; the whole country was in an uproar; the gendarmes charged the peasants, and killed some of them; the National Guard from Brive was called to the rescue. One of them, Pierre Durieux, was astonished that the castle, from which the order to fire upon the crowd had been given, had not been destroyed.

"What," he said, "our brothers have been killed for the sake of some miserable benches, and yet the castle has not been burned!" His appeal found a ready answer; once the National Guard was gone, the peasants pillaged the castle. The provost marshal of Tulle condemned two of them to be hanged and Durieux was arrested. The affair was removed from the provost's jurisdiction and was brought before the tribunal of Bordeaux.

Vergniaud seized the occasion to deliver his first magnificent political plea. He pointed out all the unforeseen consequences of the sudden equality between noble and peasant. "The first shivers with shame, the second becomes familiar or very quickly insolent. Can we reproach him? Of what exactly is Durieux guilty? Of saying that the castle should be burned? Or of not removing his hat in the presence of the lady of Lissac, of saying to the seigneur of Lissac, 'We are all equal. Monsieur is "Lissac" just as I am "Durieux"' . . . Can we condemn these peasants for walking over, in the heat of their indignation, that soil which they have watered so long with their tears and the sweat of their brows? For looking with the deep uneasiness of resentment upon the superb castle where they have so often belittled themselves with shameful obeisance?"

He denounced the anti-patriots who had done more than Durieux and who were enjoying extraordinary immunity, and he advised against a new inquiry. His peroration was full of grandeur and enthusiasm:

"Citizen Magistrate, you know that the reason of nations, as well as that of individuals, is only a weak spark of the divine reason. The noblest passions have their ecstasies; the ecstasy of liberty, which can lead it to sudden wild outbursts. The great revolutions of empires start tumultuous movements whose tremendous oscillations human wisdom cannot regulate." It was not the lawyer speaking, it was really the tribune. Vergniaud was ripe for the revolutionary platform. To tell the truth, he knew it already on a small scale. In 1790, indeed, he had been elected a member of the Department Council, and at the Jacobin Club in Bordeaux, which he frequented, he had had numerous opportunities to speak and write manifestos. He distinguished himself with a magnificent speech praising Mirabeau, as soon as the death of the famous orator was known, and so, when on August 31 the electors of Gironde sent him to the Legislative Assembly, Vergniaud was ready to take the same enviable position there that he had held at the bar.

It would be wrong to assume that at that moment he was entirely preoccupied with his reputation as an orator and cared only for his art. He was also well read and did not despise the pleasures of charming society. He rhymed easy verses. His "*Epitre aux Astronomes*" shows some slight talent:

Messieurs les amants d'Uranie,
Le ciel brille, l'air est serein.
Par deux astres nouveaux la nuit est embellie.
Dépêchez-vous, lorgnette en main.
Pénétrons sous ce vert feuillage.
Aux vieux observateurs laissons le firmament.
Vous savez bien qu'Amour place, le plus souvent
Sur du gazon, dans le bois d'un bocage,
    L'observatoire d'un amant.''

While he idled, he composed "*Adieux aux bois et aux ruisseaux,*" in which he lets his imagination wander deliciously and takes "a delectable pleasure" in looking at the running water. Our provincial lawyer also acted in drawing-room playlets with a certain amount of success. There were two sides to his character, the one amiable, frivolous, indolent, but the other, sincere, warm-hearted and capable of inspiring him to noble deeds.

Such was the new deputy from Gironde when, with his companions, Guadet, Gensonné, Ducos, Fonfrède, he alighted in Paris from the Turgotine coach which had brought him, joltingly, from his distant province. From that time on the story of his life was the story of his eloquence.

Vergniaud's easy-going nature could not be expected to inspire him with very dogmatic opinions and to make of him a man of ideas. Even in politics his nonchalance was remarkable. He has been wrongly represented to be a leader of the Girondins, but he was not made to be head of a party. How could he have directed a faction, that man "who carried really to a too high degree that nonchalance which accompanies talent and which made him walk alone?" He could not be better characterised than in the words of one of his colleagues:

"He was a Demosthenes who could be accused of the same faults with which the Greek orator reproached the Athenians: carelessness, laziness and love of pleasure. He dozed when he was not speaking, while his enemies gained ground, surrounded the Republic and pushed her into the abyss with her defenders.

"I have never known a man less capable of playing a leading part upon the stage of the Revolution. In the imminence of danger, he showed himself more disposed to await death than to carry it into the rank of his enemies . . . "

"Think of a man," added the same colleague, "a man surrounded and beset by other men, who does not look for a means of escape, but who would stay, even if the circle were broken and he were left free to go."

By temperament, then, he was unfitted to be a leader like Robespierre and Danton. He did not have much political sense, and not even troubled to invent a doctrine, — he was a Republican, of course, but without any definite plan. "The most perfect constitution," he said one day, "is the one which will permit society and the individuals which compose it to enjoy the greatest possible happiness." But what was it? He did not say. "He allowed himself to be deluded," wrote M. Aulard, "by a beautiful but

vague dream that could not be made tangible . . .
Like a great actor, he desired the most courageous
part, because it seemed the most beautiful. In reality,
chivalry was his only rule in practical politics.
Don't expect from him the qualities of the good lawmaker; precision, dryness and even, it must be admitted, narrowness of mind. No! Vergniaud needed
the free spaces and the great flights of idealism.
That explains his patriotism. He encouraged war
with all his might. Why? "Because," as he said,
"nature has given to man the love of fame, country
and freedom: sublime passions which double human
energy, exalt courage and give birth to heroic actions
which make men immortal and secure the happiness
of nations wise enough to feed the sacred fire." The
sacred fire was kept alive by Vergniaud. Vergniaud is
the poet of the Revolution.

It was not astonishing, therefore, that his skill as
an orator gained him remarkable successes. In the
Assembly, he was immediately recognized as a remarkable and formidable antagonist, and stood out
in that gathering of young men, crammed with
talent, but where the talkers were too numerous.

It was a speech about emigration which made him
known. Brissot and Condorcet had already spoken.
The Assembly was tired of repetitions and yet, because of the strict order of his language, his clear
dialectic, his irony and especially his enthusiasm, he
was able to command attention. The printing of his
discourse was voted and the next day Brissot said,
speaking of the new orator, "New ideas, well thought

out, a powerful style full of images and of genius. It is Juno, it is majesty decorated by the graces." Five days later, Vergniaud was elected president, but he was not able to preside for his whole fortnight because, "the fatigue of some days spent in the chair had made him unable to do anything for a week."

It was about that time that some deputies of the Gironde began to meet in a small committee. They met at Vergniaud's about three times a week, to speak or to lunch, and sometimes in the Place Vendôme, in the small town house where Chopin had died and where Marie-Joseph Chénier had once lived. Vergniaud did not feel at ease in those discussions; they suited Brissot better, "the great manager." Vergniaud preferred the platform where he could be himself.

The series of his great speeches deserved to be remembered. One of the most celebrated is the one he made against the intrigues of the Court and in which he preached in favor of war. Once again he had to speak after Brissot, which meant that after reason came imagination and feeling. "To arms!" he cried in closing. "To arms! The country's salvation and its honor command us. To arms! To arms!" It was a real "Marseillaise" delivered before the song itself was written.

Some time later, *the country in danger* inspired him with one of the most beautiful of his speeches. "It was a great day," said Louis Blanc, "in the history of eloquence." Vergniaud pointed out that the king was betraying the Revolution in France itself, as well as abroad. "No, no," he exclaimed, addressing himself to the monarch, "though through the generosity of the French you remain untouched, your love for despotism has rendered you immovable; you have failed to carry out the purposes of the Constitution. It may be destroyed but you won't profit by your perjury. You have not been opposed by any formal act to the victories which are gained for Liberty in your name, but you won't enjoy the fruits of those unworthy triumphs. Now you are nothing in that Constitution you have so basely violated, you are nothing to the people you have so basely betrayed."

So, in condemning Louis XVI, Vergniaud made a moral indictment of royalty. He had with him the people, the Assembly, the whole of public opinion. But, after thus roughly handling the king, this irresolute man could not draw the obvious conclusion. He did not dare to ask for the king's deposition.

From that time on he helped Danton in his struggle against the enemy, but between times, he branded the massacres of September as infamous. At this point the second phase of his eloquence begins. He had denounced the factious, and unloosed patriotism. Henceforth, he was to thunder against the popular excesses, against the tyranny of the Commune, and against the Montagne. He had presentiments of what his fate would be. "And my head also is condemned," he threw at his adversaries. "What do I care for daggers and hired assassins? They want to drown my voice, but until it has been silenced by the fatal blow, it will be heard thundering against the bandits." The *Journal des Debats* said of that speech,

"The finest piece of eloquence which has ever been improvised in the Assembly." It was the last of Vergniaud at the Legislative.

Some days later the Convention met. Vergniaud, elected by a strong majority, still sat on the Gironde benches. He persisted more than ever in the work he had begun under the Legislative, struggling against the Montagne and Marat. The man, whose violent diatribe against Louis XVI will be remembered, now tried to save the king's head. It was the aim of his speech for an appeal to the people, on December 31, 1792. He did not succeed, and he gave in and voted for death without reprieve. Unluckily, his complex attitude, superficially inexplicable, gave his enemies a chance to accuse him of duplicity and caused his ruin. They forgot that he had voted death and remembered only his attempt to save the king. The attitude of the tribune during the king's trial opened a merciless struggle between him and the Montagne.

At that time Vergniaud was at the summit of his energy and his oratorical ability. He was no Adonis. In a crowd he would have attracted no attention; his face was expressionless and his mien nonchalant; but when he was in the tribune, he was transformed. His heavy neck and his wide chest, his head, covered with thick hair, were imposing; his thick eyebrows, his bright black eyes; his square jaw, his pock-marked face, all helped to give him an extraordinarily alive and original physiognomy. "He carried his head high," said another biographer. "His black eyes sparkled under their heavy eyebrows, his thick lips seemed made to let the words flow in magnificent phrases. The sound of his voice, full and round, sonorous and melodious, seduced the ear and was very moving." Vergniaud was not good to look at, but it was divine to hear him.

He did not improvise altogether, for a great orator, if he is really great, never does. He did not write his speeches down and did not rehearse them carefully, but he prepared them orally. He spoke them first, to himself or aloud, and then he took a few notes in which the framework of the speech was indicated clearly and sharply. Thus, he could see at a glance the principal points of his oration.

But when speaking, he really improvised, for he had to bring out one by one and explain the ideas he had jotted down. Then Vergniaud's demon egged him on, inspired him, so that even his allusions to antiquity and the salient points of his discourse carefully worked out in advance, seemed effortless. When he occupied the tribune attention was universal; all parties listened to him and the most intrepid speakers found the magic persuasion of his voice irresistible. Thus Vergniaud justified his own words when, in answer to Robespierre, he summed up his talent in a word. "I'll dare to answer him," he cried, "without meditation. I have no need of art as he has; my soul is sufficient."

His soul was sufficient, indeed, as long as his passions were restrained. But there came a time when the soul was not strong enough to dominate his exasperated fury and that time began with the prosecution of Louis XVI. For some time the Gironde had been under suspicion. "Every day," wrote Vergniaud to his brother, "it is attacked in some libel or some paper." Vergniaud and his friends, caught between two fires, the Crown and the people, were unable to escape.

March, 1793: there was bad news from the front, — one defeat after another. It was a magnificent opportunity for the Montagnards to rid themselves of their enemies at home. A first attempt failed on the ninth of March. The Montagne asked for the installation of a revolutionary tribunal. Vergniaud protested. "If you secure the tribunal you are asking for," he said, "I'll consider all those you'll behead to be assassinated." Fatal words, for which he was never forgiven and which cost him his life! But he did not stop fighting for what he thought right.

On March 13 he attacked Marat and flayed "the usurpers of the title of friend of the people." The applause which greeted him gave peace to the Gironde for a while.

Then an attempt at reconciliation between the Girondins and the Dantonists was made; it was possible, because both sides favored opportunism as well as patriotism, but it failed, due to the intransigeance of the Girondins. According to a perhaps legendary scene Danton seized Guadet's hands and said to him, "You want war: you'll get death!"

The Girondins, after Dumouriez' betrayal, exposed to Robespierre's and Marat's hatred, were already lost, and although Vergniaud's miraculous oratory postponed their fall for a while, the conflict remained. There were continuous manifestations of hostility to the Girondins in the Assembly. Nothing was more tragic than the great battle of April 10, when Robespierre and Vergniaud were heard in a duel to the death. Petitioners asked for the most severe examination of Dumouriez' conspiracy and named the Girondins as probable accomplices. Robespierre mounted the platform and, in a carefully thought out, ironical speech, he gave an idea of what would happen.

"I don't dare to say," he ended, "that you ought to reach with the same decree such distinguished patriots as Messieurs Vergniaud, Brissot and others." Without losing a minute, Vergniaud answered. "I am not afraid," he cried, "to answer Monsieur Robespierre's perfidious and artful romancing written in the quietenss of his study." And he spoke. Reducing the accusation to its essential points, he refuted each with mathematical precision, and, in a magnificent outburst of indignation, began that celebrated peroration in which he defended himself from the chief accusation against the Girondins — that they were weak moderates.

"We are moderates. I was not moderate on the tenth of August when you, Robespierre, were hidden in your cellar. Moderate! No, I am not moderate, if you mean that I wish to decrease the national energy. I know that liberty is always active, like the flame which is hidden beneath the perfect calm of slaves . .

"We are moderates! But for whose profit have we shown this great moderation? For the émigrés? We adopted against them all necessary measures, demanded both by justice and the national interest. For the benefit of the conspirators in the provinces? We have never stopped asking for the sword of the law on their heads, but I voted against the law which threatened to banish the innocent, as well as the guilty . . . We, moderates? Let our opponents thank us for that moderation which is brought up against us as a crime! If — when the torches of discord were waved in this tribune and the majority of the representatives of the people were outraged with the most insolent audacity; if, when some have cried with as much fury as imprudence: No more truce, no more peace between us! — we had given way to our feelings of just indignation, if we had accepted the counter-revolutionary challenge presented to us . . . from all the departments you would have seen men feared equally by tyranny and anarchy coming to fight the men of the Second of September. Our accusers and perhaps ourselves as well would have disappeared in a civil war. Our moderation saved the Republic from that awful fate and we have deserved well of the country for our silence!"

Vergniaud left the tribune in the midst of loud applause. The next day the *Patriote Français* summarized thus the quality of that improvisation, which was a real *tour de force:* "Robespierre read a long speech full of recrimination against Vergniaud, Brissot, Guadet and Gensonné. His discourse made far less impression, even on the public, than the eloquently improvised answer of Vergniaud."

The Gironde appeared to triumph momentarily, but

every day a bitter battle had to be fought and won. When Marat was accused at Guadet's instigation, Vergniaud succeeded in postponing the danger. He seized the opportunity to make several speeches, all admirable, and especially the one about the Constitution, of which Jaurès had said that Vergniaud projected "magnificent rays of wealth and art upon the future of the French Republic." But, nevertheless, the drama went on and reached its climax with Isnard's provocation.

In the middle of May the Gironde had succeeded in establishing a committee of twelve members who had authority to inquire into the acts of the Commune and to revise the illegal bills which it had never stopped passing. One of the first measures of the Committee was to imprison Hébert, the General Prosecutor of the Commune. On May 25 the Commune came with numerous men to the Convention to demand Hébert's release. Isnard, then president of the session, refused.

Repeating the sadly celebrated words of Brunswick and paraphrasing them, he dared to threaten Paris with destruction if national representation were interfered with. It was an unfortunate and maladroit move! The Commune answered promptly, on May 31 and June 2. On May 31, during a tragic session in the Convention, Vergniaud had to hold his own against the sections rushing to the bar and their partisans in the Assembly, demanding the trial of the Twenty-two. As Robespierre rambled on interminably, Vergniaud shouted, "Please conclude."

And the other obeyed, saying, "Yes, I shall conclude, and conclude against you . . . My conclusion is for a decree of accusation against all Dumouriez' accomplices and against all those who have been pointed out by the petitionaries."

Vergniaud could not answer, because the tired Assembly put a stop to the discussion, and the Convention voted the suppression of the Committee of Twelve. The fate of the Girondins appeared very much compromised, and yet, on the next day, Vergniaud attempted vainly a last farewell to the tribune. The second of June, with its silence, was to see the beginning of his martyrdom. On that day Vergniaud was only present at the beginning of the session of the Convention. After his departure the Assembly gave way to the threats of the populace and decreed the exclusion of twenty-nine of its members. Late at night, he heard the fatal outcome of the day, and immediately addressed to the Convention a letter full of indisputable nobility, which described him perfectly.

Citizen President, — he wrote, — I left the Assembly yesterday between one and two o'clock, and there was no sign of any trouble near the Convention. Soon some friends came to a house where I was with some of my colleagues to tell me that the citizens in the tribune were watching the passages leading to the hall of our sessions and arresting the representatives of the people whose names were on the proscribed list made by the Paris Commune.

Always ready to obey the law, I thought it my duty not to expose myself to violences which it was no longer in my power to repress. That same night I learned that a decree of arrest in my own house had been brought against me. I surrendered. It has been proposed that, to restore order, the banished deputies should resign. I do not imagine that any one can suspect that I have enjoyed greatly the persecutions I have been subjected to since last September, but I am so sure of the esteem and good will of all my electorate that I am afraid my resignation would cause much more serious troubles in my department than those they want to allay and which could have been so easily avoided.

Paris will soon be very much astonished that it has been kept three days in arms for the sake of besieging a few deputies whose only defense is in the purity of their consciences. May the violence of which I am the victim be fatal only to myself. May the people, whom I am accused of disliking, although there is not one of my opinions which does not render homage to their sovereignty and although my wishes are for their happiness . . . may the people, I say, not have to suffer from the movement to which my persecutors have delivered it. May they themselves save the country, and I'll forgive heartily the harm they have done me and the greater harm they have wanted to do me.

Vergniaud, through love for the people, was ready for the sacrifice. He showed once more that "he had a soul very much greater than his talent," and later he was to show it even more clearly.

A good many Girondins, indeed, had fled but a certain number, Vergniaud among them, had courageously stayed at home, awaiting their fate. They were soon placed under arrest, and Vergniaud, like the others, was watched in his home. During his relatively agreeable captivity, he kept his gayety and corresponded with some feminine admirers who were on his side, perhaps also with Adèle Sauvan, the future wife of Legouvé, whom, it is said, he had wanted to marry and to whom he gave his last thought. He gave dinners to his intimates, went out sometimes, and even to the Opera, accompanied by his "nurse", who was a gendarme. Unluckily that treatment did not last. On July 24, in spite of his protests, he was put in solitary confinement. On the twenty-sixth, he was taken to the Luxembourg and, five days later, to La Force from where he wrote to his judges. He was to wait for two months and a half, an enervating delay which would have depressed the strongest heart, but Vergniaud was undaunted. "In spite of the persecutions," he wrote to his brother, "I am well. It is glorious to suffer for one's country and for Liberty. I am only worried about the public good. Let my persecutors save it. I forgive them all the harm they do me. I am writing to you from La Force, where I am as well as one can be in prison . . . " Thus, like a *leit motiv*, we see reappearing the forgiveness of the great-hearted tribune.

In spite of the confinement he was in, the prisoner had some consolations. His nephew, Francis Alluaud, was allowed to visit him. The interview was very moving. We have Alluaud's own words:

"I arrived in the infirmary. At that moment Vergniaud was having his hair dressed and, as soon as he saw me, he kissed me and said: 'Well, Francis, do your comrades at the boarding school also want me killed? . . . ' When he had finished dressing we went into an adjoining room with whitewashed walls, which was used as a dining room and drawing-room by the poor Girondins. The conversation of eight or ten of Vergniaud's companions was about the misfortune of France and their own unhappy fate. A frugal dinner was served at two o'clock and at the end of the meal they heard that General Custine had been condemned, and they said: 'Service to the country no longer counts. We will suffer the same fate.' The day wore on. My heart, too, was torn by what I had seen and heard. My uncle said good-by to me and I kissed him for the last time."

If we are to believe this picture, life at La Force was relatively easy. It is also known from other sources, that the mornings were spent reading, and that before dinner all the prisoners gathered in an inside court with rows of trees, and that time was spent in conversation about the history of the times and the daily happenings. However, the régime became more severe. At a demand of the Jacobins and the sections, the Terror was voted and Vergniaud left La Force for the Conciergerie, where he spent the seventeen days which separated him from his trial. While there, Vergniaud saw his nephew for the last time and he said, looking him straight in the eyes, through the wicket of the Conciergerie, "Look at your uncle! Some day you can say that you have seen one of the founders of the French Republic!"

In his narrow cell, he did not lose his usual lazy habits. He lay late upon his miserable pallet, reading Seneca, his favorite author. About eleven o'clock he rose, washed himself and took special care of his thick hair, which his servant, Cotton, curled. In the central passage, he walked a little with his faithful friends, Ducos and Fonfrède, all along the wide alley, the three prisoners walking, talking in low tones as they passed in front of the cell they knew to be Marie Antoinette's. Then they came to the women's recreation court, and through the bars they saw, according to the gallant words of their companion in captivity, the Count Beugnot, "a bed of flowers framed in iron", the last salon where, in ignoble promiscuity, prostitutes and criminals rubbed elbows with great ladies. At two o'clock, the Girondins had their meal together, to the accompaniment of songs, patriotic or otherwise, at which Ducos shone particularly. After that, each worked at his defense.

Vergniaud prepared his carefully, drawing up an outline as for his speeches. It was to be an apology divided into five parts. Accused of royalism, federalism, of having wanted civil war, and war with all Europe, of having kept with one faction, he answered point by point and concluded that the Girondins were not guilty, as no decree contrary to the good of the people could be attributed to them. In the course of it, he pleaded generously the cause of his friends, Ducos and Fonfrède, whose only crime was to have loved him. "If the blood of a Girondin is necessary," he said, "let mine suffice. They can help with their

talent and services . . . They are husbands and
fathers. As for me, schooled in misfortune, my death
will make no one unhappy."

Alas! He was not even able to deliver the apology
he had so carefully planned. On October 24, 1793
(*Frimaire* 3, *An* II) the trial began in the Great Room
of the old Parliament, now called the Hall of Liberty.
The place had been arranged to suit the severity and
solemnity of revolutionary taste. Two placards were
on the walls: the text of the Declaration of the Rights
of Man and the text of the Constitution. Some busts,
those of Brutus, Lepelletier and Marat, were the only
ornaments. Twenty-one accused appeared before the
judges. Some were not yet thirty, and most of them
were not over forty; among them Vergniaud, who had
reached forty, five months previously. All the
Girondins were accused of "conspiracy against Liberty
and the safety of the French people." In reality that
vague accusation hid their anger at Vergniaud for
trying to save the king and opposing Marat. In the
minds of the jurors, the great tribune was evidently
an accomplice of Charlotte Corday. Did not one of
them exclaim, "Marat has been assassinated and yet
Vergniaud is still here?" To the testimony, more or
less perfidious, of the witnesses for the State, Vergniaud answered little, but made a famous answer to
Hébert, which he hurled at them during the second
session and which was purposely not reported. The
prosecutor Fouquier-Tinville, was afraid to give
publicity to the defense and still more to Vergniaud's
eloquence, which had already made a deep impression

upon the public. In his speech of an hour and a quarter, he reached sublimity. It was his only great intervention and he had doubtless kept for the end his last arguments and especially those he had noted in his written defence. Neither the Jacobins nor Robespierre gave him a chance to produce them, for they feared his influence upon the crowd, and it was necessary at any cost to find a way of silencing him. According to the Jacobin Club, public opinion did not need any further enlightenment; only its sanction was necessary. Accordingly they proposed to rid the tribunal of forms "which smother conscience and prevent conviction", adding to the rights of the jury the power to declare itself perfectly competent. It was done. The decree, the draft of which had been made by Robespierre, went to the Convention.

The very next evening the jury announced that its conscience was sufficiently enlightened, and they were ready to give their verdict. To write of the deception of the unlucky ones is impossible. Here is how the official report described their attitude:

"At half-past ten at night, the jurors announced their verdict was ready, and they were admitted at once. One by one, they gave, aloud, their answer to the questions submitted to them by the president. When they had finished, the tribunal had the accused, free and without irons, brought in and the verdict of the jurors was read to them. Then the public prosecutor recommended that the law should be applied.

"The president asked the accused if they had anything to say before sentence was passed. At that moment all the accused rose, shouting, some even crying, 'Long Live the Republic!' Their gestures, added to their cries and their number, rendered impossible any deliberation in their presence, and a great many gendarmes were necessary to restrain them. To the shouts of the accused were joined those of the listeners, who manifested their indignation against men whom the sword of the law was punishing for their betrayal and perfidy. It was impossible to debate before the accused who, by their own shouts and gestures, and those of the public who answered them, threw the audience into such disorder that the tribunal was obliged to have the accused withdrawn, in order to deliberate and pass sentence."

Disorder, indeed, had reached its peak. Valazé had fallen from his bench, after running a dagger through his heart. Camille Desmoulins, who was among the spectators, was lamenting.

"My God!" he cried. "It is I who have killed them. My 'Brissot Unmasked.' My God! That's what is killing them!" The tragic scenes were many.

Fonfrède, turning to Ducos, who was behind him, embraced him, crying and said, "My friend, it is I who am causing your death."

"Console yourself," answered Ducos, "we'll die together."

Vergniaud lost none of his grand manner. He thought of killing himself, because he had some poison, but his two friends were also condemned and he did not have enough poison for three. He must die with them. He threw away the poison.

Once the accused were out of the way, the tribunal

deliberated. The president asked for the opinions of all; they were unanimous. It was death for all the accused!

Vergniaud had gone back to the prison with his comrades. It was about midnight. All that awful night the Girondins sang. If they stopped occasionally, it was to speak of their country, sometimes also, to enjoy one of Ducos' sallies, for he had not lost his good humor. It was during that terrible night that the famous "Banquet of the Girondins" took place. Nothing much is known about it but it was, it seems, only a simple meal, for the hearing had lasted too long.

Several of the accused confessed, but Vergniaud was not among them. He was satisfied to examine his conscience and meditate. To whom did his last thoughts go? Without doubt to a woman — a pure young girl for whom, on the gold of his watch, he traced interlaced initials.

About noon the next day, three carts brought the surviving Girondins to the scaffold. Their hands were tied behind their backs and they were shivering in the rain, for the weather was awful. An immense crowd had gathered along the way and it was shouting, "Down with the traitors!" Some Girondins sang, while others answered the cries of "Long Live the Republic!" with the same cry. "But you won't get it," they added. To those who were insulting him, Duchastel answered, with contempt, "Poor Parisians, we leave you in the hands of people who will make you pay dearly for your pleasure of to-day."

It was about one o'clock when the carts reached the Place de la Revolution, to-day the Place de la Concorde. The scaffold was erected in the continuation of the projection of the Jardin des Tuileries. It had been placed in such a way that the heads of the Girondins would fall before the statue of Liberty, which had succeeded the statue of Louis XV, and in the name of which they were deprived of life.

The oldest of the condemned, Brulart de Genlis, ex-Marquis de Silley, went first. The others followed in no order. As they came down from their cart, Ducos and Fonfrède kissed each other.

"There is only one means of saving ourselves," said Ducos.

"What's that?" asked Fonfrède.

"It is," answered the other, "by asking the Convention for a decree of the unity and indivisibility of heads!"

Lehardi shouted, "Long Live the Republic!" Others sang the "Marseillaise."

When Vergniaud's turn arrived, he tried to speak, but the drums prevented him from doing so. In thirty-eight seconds, all was over. With his murdered friends, the great orator was taken to the graveyard of the Madeleine and buried quite near the hole called "The Mirabeau hole."

The great tribune, whose speech was his only reason for existence, did not even have the consolation of using it one last time.

THE KING

WHEN studying the first years of the Revolution, the quick turn of events always seems rather astonishing. France, which in 1789 was deeply royalistic, became almost entirely republican two years later. What had happened? Had a few men been able to radically change public opinion in such a short period? Had the prestige of a Camille Desmoulins, a Danton or a Robespierre created such an upheaval? Or had the country arrived at a stage in its historical evolution when the change was unavoidable? Not at all, but France had the ill luck or the good luck, depending upon the point of view — to be led by a man who, while thinking he was serving his own cause and perhaps his country's, precipitated his own ruin and hastened the advent of modern times. In that sense it is possible to say — however paradoxical the statement may appear — that the first revolutionary, in spite of himself, was Louis XVI. Every one agrees to that, even the Royalists themselves. When enumerating the principal reasons for the fall of the Old Régime, Comte Lally-Tollendal wrote, "The character of the unfortunate Louis XVI, the variance between his virtues and those demanded by circumstances, obviously played such a great part in the triumph of the Revolution that I must present it as a fourth principal cause." In other words, Louis XVI had good qualities, but those he needed were lacking.

When the States-General met, the king was thirty years of age; he was in his prime; his traits were fixed, morally and physically. Although very little inclined to the pleasures of the mind, he had read rather widely; he loved the theater and was especially fond of tragedy (he adored Racine and could recite whole scenes from his plays); music bored him; he did not dislike geography, travel tales and history. He knew Latin and English. Martial, visiting the king's library, found a book very much the worse for wear; it was an English dictionary. "It is so worn," said he, "that it might be a schoolboy's," which proved that it was in daily use.

The king kept in touch with current events and read the "Annales" of Linguet; he was even capable of taking an interest in serious works, and spent a fortnight studying Necker's attack upon Calonne. Even his brother-in-law, the Emperor of Austria, who was not inclined to overestimate his abilities, found him "not absolutely devoid of knowledge." Unluckily he had acquired his knowledge desultorily, by fits and starts, of his own volition, without any direction. The Duc de la Vauguyon, who had been in charge of his education, reared him in the principles of a very narrow devotion, with no thought of developing his mind and without preparing him in any way for his future position. Louis XVI felt this himself, and reminded his tutor's son of it in no uncertain terms. "You know," he said to him one day, "you and I have been very badly brought up."

He had some critical sense, but his mind did not

move quickly, and his slowness of comprehension exposed him to misunderstandings, such as the following: One day a declaration with regard to the wearing of the cockade was submitted to him by the Assembly; he did not understand it, but he signed it nevertheless. When the queen came in and reproached him for doing so, Louis XVI explained that he had refused to sign the first declaration which had seemed bad to him, but that he thought the one he signed to be innocuous. The queen opened his eyes: and he recognized that he had been wrong.

To his slowness of mind must be added his lack of curiosity and initiative. He hardly knew his own surroundings. When the Emperor Joseph II, after a week's stay in Paris, told him that Paris contained the most beautiful monument in Europe, the Dome of the Invalides, Louis XVI admitted naïvely that he had never noticed it.

However, though he had no great intelligence, he was not without a certain store of common sense which allowed him to judge clearly when he had at last understood. "He is not stupid," wrote Joseph II; "he has ideas, he has sense;" and the Austrian Ambassador added, "It seems to me that the Emperor believes him to be more stupid than he actually is." Indeed, the king showed his common sense several times at the beginning of his reign: in rightly mistrusting De Maurepas and in resisting him upon occasion and, later, in 1780, in taking Necker's part against the cabals of the Court. It was that same common sense which made him angry one day when he found that Marie Antoinette had lost one hundred thousand *écus* at gambling. "It was a return game," said the queen, as an excuse. And he answered, "One is easily ruined by such return games."

And also, with prophetic vision, he forbade the production of the "Mariage de Figaro." "It is dreadful," he cried, after reading the manuscript. "It will never be acted. So long as the Bastille stands, a performance of that play would be dangerously imprudent."

The king's principal quality was kindness, for Louis XVI was really kind, and not in words only. Upon his accession to the throne, he wrote to the Comptroller General of Finance, Abbé Terray, "With regard to my personal income, I shall be content to live as simply as I may without compromising any public services, for I wish to lighten the burden of my people, to cut the expenses of my household as much as possible and to keep only what is absolutely indispensable to the dignity of royalty."

Following his natural bent, he helped Turgot at first. "Only you and I," he wrote to him, "really love the people." One day when, although he seldom gambled, he had lost eight hundred *louis* at cards, he remarked, "That's money very badly spent. I would have done better to distribute six *livres* each to thirty-two hundred soldiers; it would have encouraged them."

His adversaries themselves recognized his kindness. Bailly, in his "Memoirs," tells that the first time he saw the king and spoke to him alone he "carried away with him an impression of his natural kindliness."

Unfortunately, this well-read monarch, full of common sense and naturally kind, possessed none of the qualities which give prestige to a king. His appearance did not inspire respect. If we look at the portrait by Duplessis, which hangs at Versailles, we see that the king, although still young, was already fat and heavy. His puffy face shows a benevolence akin to stupidity; his expression is soft, and nothing in his attitude corrects his lack of physical advantages. His walk had no dignity. "He was careless," said Madame Campan; "in spite of his hairdresser's cleverness, his hair was always disheveled." He did not know how to behave in public. Once, when he had to receive the King of Sweden, he dressed in too great a hurry and made his entry with a gold buckle on one shoe and a silver one on the other, with all his decorations wrongly placed and his face very badly powdered on one side only. Another time he mistook a maid for a lady of the court and bowed deeply to her, while the queen and the courtiers burst out laughing. At a very important ceremony, the decoration of the Duc de Berri with the *cordon bleu*, Louis, who sat between his brothers, was extremely bored, and made no attempt to hide his feelings.

Without dignity before the nobles, he could not adopt the necessary attitude towards his inferiors. First of all, he was shy. Two members of his body-guard were half-killed when trying to save the queen at Versailles, and the king received them. "He remained silent," said Madame Campan, who was present, "although his emotion was visible and his eyes were filled with tears. The queen rose and the king went out. Madame Elisabeth followed him, the queen slowed her step, and in the recess of a window she said to me, 'I am sorry I brought the king here. If he had said to those brave people a quarter of what he felt, they would have been delighted, but he can't overcome his shyness.'"

On other occasions, like all shy people, he was very tactless. One of his favorite pastimes was to push the courtiers under the awnings sprinkled with water which covered his balcony, so that their coiffures would be spoiled. He joked with plebeians. Once, when hunting, the king saw a postman looking at a stag which had fallen into the pond, sneaked up behind him, took his letter bag and threw it into the pond, delighted with his joke.

He was, in fine, according to Maria Theresa, his mother-in-law, a boor. The Duc de Saxe-Teschen called him a fat smith, and correctly, for the king had a weakness for manual labor. He helped the workmen of the castle move beams and stones. He was extremely fond of forging and was happy whenever he could get to his workshop without being seen by the queen. "I was quite impressed when I saw his workshop," said the Baroness d'Oberkirch. Imagine a great king so busy over such small things!"

He had nobler distractions apparently, but like everything he touched, they were open to ridicule.

Louis XVI was fond of hunting, but he had no elegance, and his hunts were massacres. In three days, in Compiègne, he killed nine thousand heads. At a battue, he himself killed two hundred swallows.

He came back from such excursions with a dirty face, tired out, desiring only to feed himself copiously and endlessly, for he also loved the pleasures of the table. They cost him 455 *livres*, 11 *sols*, 10 *deniers*, on ordinary days, and 620 *livres*, 5 *sols* on fast days. Not even the gravest events could take away his appetite. During the fighting on August 10, he ate three hundred pounds of peaches, which did not prevent him from dining later with his usual voracity. Ordinarily, it is said, his breakfast consisted of four chops, a fat chicken, six eggs, a slice of ham, and a bottle and a half of champagne. It is not surprising that such gluttony induced in him an irresistible desire to sleep. Once, when the King of Sweden was telling him of his travels, Louis yawned several times in succession. On July 14, 1790, the day of the celebration of the Federation, Louis, during the ceremony, was stretched out lazily in his armchair. The people took for indifference what was only a very comprehensible drowsiness. Frequently after his meal, tired by the open air, and stuffed with food and wine, he had to be helped to bed, as if he had been drunk, and thus the legend of the king's drunkenness spread. At other times, he suffered from acute indigestion which forced him to use purgatives, of which he talked with pleasure.

Even the most private details of his life lent themselves to raillery. The king was a good husband. It is
said that only once was he tempted to unfaithfulness
— at a ball at the Opera — and even then it was only
a fancy. But it is well known that it was a long time
after the ceremony before his marriage was consummated, and clandestinely, the most risqué stories
were told on that subject. The king was accused of
impotency; it was soon learned that his frigidity was
due to an infirmity of which he had not been aware
himself. Joseph II, during one of his visits, had to
teach the King of France and to urge him to submit to
a necessary operation. Of course the Court jeered at
those stories, and little by little the royal dignity
declined.

Nothing can give a better picture of the insufficiency
of Louis XVI — of the poverty of his imagination
and his ideas — than his mania for statistics. He
wrote his diary scrupulously; he noted exactly the
number of his indigestions, his purgations. If he
interested himself in literature, it was only to write:
"On Sunday, August 9th, saw from the terrace a man
writing verses on horseback." He meticulously put
down all his walks. He recapitulated the nights he
had spent in Versailles since his marriage. Another
time, he wrote that he had received "the curtseys of
319 men in the morning, and of 256 women at 6
o'clock." What interested him above all was the
hunt. He always mentioned the number of birds that
he had shot. On days when he was not shooting, he
wrote, "Nothing." Thus: On July 11, 1789, the day

of Necker's dismissal — *nothing;* and, stronger still — July 14, 1789: *nothing.*

Nothing! The right word to fit Louis XVI. The king was ineffective, and his ineffectiveness was sadder than any active wickedness could have been. "His apathy frightens me," wrote a contemporary. "The house is on fire and he does not seem in the least concerned." And the Ambassador Stael-Holstein: "The King is nothing, as usual."

And yet Louis XVI found means to be popular. His great and native kindness pleased his subjects, in spite of all his faults and failings, and in 1789 the people were still ardently Royalist. After the fall of the Bastille, when the king came to the Hôtel de Ville, his hands and his footprints were kissed. After October 5 and 6, the public rushed to greet the royal coach when the Tuileries gates were opened, with respectful curiosity. In February, 1790, the *Journal de Prudhomme* rated him above Henri IV, in the following words:

"Since Louis XVI taught us to know what a good king is like, a king who is an honest man and an honest citizen, it is more and more doubtful if even Henri IV himself was worthy of our devotion."

Later, in June, when the king went to Saint-Cloud, the mob applauded him and shouted, *"Bon Voyage au bon papa."* And on July 14, 1790, at the Champ-de-Mars, he had only to kiss his children to turn the heads of all in the crowd. "They were drunk with love," wrote Stael-Holstein, "and yet the king had neither spoken nor moved." Mirabeau himself was impressed in the same way and could not refrain from saying bitterly, "What can you do with a nation which can do nothing but shout, 'Long live the King!'"

But, gradually, that great love began to hurt the king. He inspired commiseration more than real affection. "Poor man," said a stranger in 1790, "he is loved, but not with the kind of love which a monarch ought to inspire! It is the kind of pity which tender-hearted people feel for convicts on their way to prison." A grenadier did not even hesitate to say to La Fayette, in October, 1789, "Let us go to Versailles; they say the king's an imbecile. We'll put the crown on his son's head."

This reputation had been won for him by the dominating trait of his personality, weakness of character, his perpetual indecision which, in spite of a rather pleasant disposition, made him perpetrate the worst blunders, and even crimes. It was weakness on his part, on August 10, when he ordered the Swiss guards not to shoot!

"The Swiss guards on the tenth, like those of October 6", said one of his intimates, "obeyed heroically the blind and selfish orders given by the king, more intent on saving his enemies' blood than his servants'." It was not an act of kindness or generosity on his part, but a recoil before danger.

"It is inconceivable," wrote the Archduke Leopold, "that at the moment of the attack on Versailles, the king would not rather have been killed than give in and sacrifice those who had defended him. Only

196

blood like water, no backbone and a cowardly soul would cause any one to act that way."

And, on that occasion, it was only his servants he sacrificed; but when he went so far as to betray France, to play Austria's game and even to contemplate an attack by the enemy upon his own kingdom, what can be said to justify him?

Marie Antoinette was more responsible than he, of course, but that's precisely the gravest reproach which can be made against the king: He reigned but did not govern. He was *the husband of his wife*. To use a rather vulgar expression, "he let himself be led by the nose." The queen did not hide the fact, and never missed an opportunity to show how little she cared about her kingly spouse; she even went so far as to humiliate and ridicule him. One day when he entered a drawing-room less awkwardly than usual, Marie Antoinette remarked, "You'll have to agree, Mesdames, that for a badly brought up child, the king has just saluted you very gallantly!" And it was well known that when she wanted to get rid of him, she did not hesitate to advance the hands of the clock to send him earlier to bed.

"The queen's authority is very great!" said Mercy-Argenteau; "nothing can be obtained except through her." "She has absolute power over her husband," added the Swedish Ambassador; and the Swiss Besenval said that "she held her husband in slavish subjection."

It would not have mattered so much if Marie Antoinette had used her authority for the good of her people, but unfortunately she used it at the expense of the interests of France. She also was popular at first; she was very witty, and knew how to find striking phrases which caught the fancy of the people. They were grateful when she tried to be a real French-woman, when she refused to pay court to the DuBarry, when she tried to be good to the poor; and then she was pretty and charming, having unique grace and charm in every fiber of her being. "Marie Antoin-ette," as the Baroness d'Oberkirch said, "won all hearts."

But the enthusiasm with which her marriage to the Dauphin had been greeted did not last, for she had grave faults which were soon evident. She was ignorant and frivolous. Even Maria Theresa, her mother, knew that the Queen of France brought no accomplishments to her throne — neither music nor drawing, nor dancing, painting or any other agreeable art. "She had a very empty head and was incapable of writing and of thinking." "She did not even seek," said Besenval, "the knowledge which society can give; as soon as conversation took a serious turn, boredom showed upon her face and froze all speech. Her conversation was desultory, and she jumped from subject to subject."

Her frivolity made her impudent, and she committed many blunders, to say the least. She adored balls. When she went to them with Louis XVI, she always let him leave first, so that she might be alone and freer. She frequented the balls of the Opera, to which she went incognito and where she found herself,

according to her brother, "in mixed society, and rubbing elbows with all the riffraff of Paris."

If Louis XVI hurt the royal prestige by his nullity,
Marie Antoinette undermined it by her frivolity.
Surreptitiously many pamphlets appeared against her:

> Reine de France en apparence
> Vous l'êtes plus réellement
> Des ministres — de la toilette,
> Des comédiens, des histrions
> Et, bravant en tout l'étiquette,
> Des filles vous avez le ton.

Such jibes spread all over Paris. "One of the
greatest inconveniences at the present time," wrote
Mercy-Largenteau to the Empress Maria Theresa, "is
the Queen's complete forgetfulness of all that ap-
pertains to her dignity." She was worse than
impudent. Very much admired, very much flattered,
she allowed herself shocking audacities. When she
had the measles, she stayed in her apartment with
four nurses,— the Duc de Coigny, the Duc de Guines,
the Comte Esterhazy and Baron de Besenval. The
queen was very intimate with her brother-in-law, and
rumor gave her many lovers, more than she had in
reality. All whispered about her adventures; she was
accused of strange tastes: her exaggerated affection for
Madame de Polignac and the Princess de Lamballe
were joked about.

These scandals were more than enough to discredit
her, and yet the French people, tolerant and gallant, would have forgiven her her faults, for she was

beautiful and a woman, had her private conduct not influenced public affairs and helped to precipitate France into a financial disaster from which good ministers tried in vain to rescue her. When the people were dying with hunger, Marie Antoinette made herself talked about, because of her taste for expensive jewelry, which her mother criticized severely. Madame Bertin, the Court dressmaker, had more prestige than Turgot. The money paid her by her royal client appeared, not without reason, somewhat excessive. Moreover, Marie Antoinette's stables cost two hundred thousand *livres* more than the late queen's. The wife of Louis XVI had very costly fancies, like the Petit Trianon. She spent four hundred thousand *livres* on one ball she gave. The queen gambled furiously; she lost continuously — and who paid? Calonne, the Public Treasurer. And the rumor went around that France had been turned into a gambling den.

Marie Antoinette's friendships were not less costly. The Princess de Lamballe, who only cost one hundred and fifty thousand *livres* at first, ended by getting three hundred thousand, and her brother fifty thousand. The Polignac and her family also replenished their fortune at the expense of the public finances. Mercy calculated that in one year all those people got five hundred thousand *livres* income, besides a hundred thousand *écus* to Madame de Guines and thirty thousand *livres* annual income, beside a domain to the male favorite of the favorite. One day, it was learned that not only was Marie Antoinette wasting the public funds, but she was liberally sending them to Austria. The queen became *Madame Deficit* or the *Austrian*.

The queen also engaged in not very loyal intrigues. She had, according to her own mother, "a crooked mind."

"I'll confess," wrote the latter to Mercy, "that I am uneasy. I have often found her at fault and she is always able to get out very cleverly and to make things seem right even at the expense of truth." Indeed, she understood thoroughly the art of lying and her dissimulation even went as far as duplicity.

So, long before 1789, the French people's common sense had judged their queen. They had seen the unfortunate influence she had on the government. They had seen her welcoming Malesherbes coldly, fighting the honest Turgot, openly pleased with Necker's dismissal, and they did not hesitate to show their discontent publicly. As early as 1787, she was hissed when she went to the Opera. The most repulsive accusations were current about her. She was held responsible for everything, and accused of being the king's evil genius.

It is thus that she appears in history. Without trying arbitrarily to reconstruct the events, it can be said that the Revolution might have turned out differently had it not been for the fatal acts of the queen and her court, and the king's weakness. From 1789 to 1793, the Court, which did not understand, or did not want to understand what was going on, committed a series of blunders which led it to its ruin. The examples are legion. First was the vote of the civil constitution of the clergy. Louis XVI, sincerely Catholic, would, without doubt, have been opposed to this measure if he had followed his own inclinations. But his weak nature made him listen to those, who ill-inspired, advised him to make apparent concessions, a policy of hypocrisy. The king ratified the constitution. Only, for his own religious duties, he refused to have anything to do with constitutional priests. This false and contradictory attitude of his was not forgiven later. The Constitution of 1791 was established and the king gave it his solemn allegiance, but without any sincerity whatsoever; like the queen, he thought it audacious and frightening. It was their intention of wearing this constitution thin which brought the sovereigns to practise the most maladroit and noxious politics, which consisted in helping the extremists against the moderates, to provoke a crisis and thus bring good from an excess of evil.

It soon became known that King Louis XVI was negotiating with the Emperor, that he was calling to his help Catherine the Great, Sweden, Spain and Prussia. Exasperated, the people revolted against the "Austrian committee" which sat in the Tuileries, and which, headed by Marie Antoinette, plotted with the foreigners and the *émigrés* against the nation. It saw with anger the Court rejoicing openly over the Brunswick manifesto. Its anger, too long suppressed, burst forth. Two days: June 20 and August 10; and royalty, so popular a short time before, was swept away.

After the fall of the Tuileries on August 10, 1792,

the Commune decided that the royal family should be confined to the Temple Tower. It was the remains of the citadel which the Templars had owned in Paris, until the destruction of their order by Phillippe le Bel. Nothing was ready to receive the prisoners. For centuries only a porter had lived in the old dungeon, in which, in a very narrow space, were only miserable attics and very dirty old beds. It is true that the Convention immediately tried to render the place habitable, but six rooms for the five members of the royal family and two servants were really small. And the king, sanguine and obese, suffered from the smallness of his prison and the want of air.

This does not mean that the Convention had bargained over the support of the royal family. At first it had voted a credit of five hundred thousand *livres*, and it is well known that the king spent forty thousand *livres* of that in four months. The amount was ample for a time of famine and general poverty. Besides, Louis XVI had three servants and thirteen house stewards to look after him. Every day at dinner he was given "four entrées, two roasts, four puddings, three kinds of stewed fruits, a small carafe of Bordeaux, and one of malmsey or Madeira, which he drank alone. Food was therefore abundant. The only thing against it was its abundance, justifiable for a man accustomed to a great deal of exercise, but much too much for a prisoner who could only take a few steps a few hours a day in a small, bare, and narrow space. In the make-believe garden where the royal family was authorized to take the air with the

Dauphin, in that poor piece of ground with dry grass, hardly enlivened by some stunted trees losing their leaves in the autumnal winds, Marie Antoinette walked back and forth, haughty, irritating, provocative under the jests and insults of their keepers. Her kingly spouse at her side carried sadly his "myopic air", his "vague glances", his "ungainly walk" of a "fat farmer from the Beauce province."

He, at least, was not to suffer imprisonment for long. About the end of November, 1792, with the help of a locksmith who, in former times, had helped the king to build it, a secret wardrobe with iron doors was found. Abundant and irrefutable proofs of the king's betrayal were found there. The prosecution was urgent and inevitable. It began on December 11. The king, attended by his three attorneys, Malesherbes, De Sèze and Tronchet, showed great dignity, but in spite of all the efforts of his lawyers, Louis Capet, as he was called by Desmoulins, was declared guilty of conspiracy against the safety of the State and condemned to death on January 20, 1793, the sentence being passed within the Temple.

Louis XVI received the judgment with calm and fortitude. He slept deeply the night preceding his execution. On the morning of January 21, at eight o'clock, before going to the gallows, he gave his valet, Cléry, his wedding ring, saying, "Give this to my wife and tell her that I part from it very reluctantly." A municipal guard took charge of his will. The king, who wore a brown coat, black breeches, white stockings and waistcoat, climbed, with his confessor, into the carriage which was waiting for him. There were very few people in the streets. At ten minutes past ten the funeral procession came into the square. Louis XVI got out, took his coat and his tie off himself, and, with great reluctance, let his hands be tied by the executioner.

"Sire," said his confessor, "that last outrage is another point of resemblance between Your Majesty and God who will be your reward."

"Do what you will," said the king to the executioner, "I'll drink the cup to the dregs." Then he tried to speak to the people, but a roll of the drum drowned his voice.

"The Widow Capet," less lucky, waited for several months for her destiny to be decided, first in the Temple, then at the Conciergerie, in a small cell, almost a cave, which is still shown. There was no doubt what it would be after the Terror became the order of the day. After a session lasting more than twenty hours, on Wednesday, October 16, 1793, the Revolutionary Tribunal sent to the scaffold "the ferocious beast who devoured a great part of the Republic."

Louis XVI and Marie Antoinette committed all kinds of blunders and were even guilty of the crime of high treason. They are responsible, first for the Revolution, then for the sanguinary turn of events, Marie Antoinette by her frivolity, her intrigues, her falsity; Louis XVI by his stupid Machiavellian methods and his weakness.

"If a king of a firm and decided character had been in Louis XVI's place," said Etienne Dumont, the author of "Souvenirs sur Mirabeau", "the Revolution would not have occurred. All his reign did was to bring it on . . . His indecision, his weakness, his half-measures, his half-hearted advice, his improvidence, lost everything."

However, we cannot forget that the man paid with his blood, not only for his own mistakes, but for those of his predecessors and his Court. The indictment which the historian can prepare against Louis XVI is tempered by the excess of his misfortunes. In the presence of such misfortune, we can only say with the Marquis de Ferrières, "I stop. Louis XVI was unfortunate; I won't go any further. Let us pity him for being born without character, let us pity him for having always been the plaything of his own weaknesses and of external forces which he could not understand."

THE WOMEN

"One of the noblest characteristics of the Revolution," said Michelet, "was love. In every sense of the word," he added; "love of ideas, love of woman, love of country and humanity." How then could woman, whose nature is all feeling and passion, have avoided playing a great part in that period, when enthusiasm carried away the least excitable and most cool-headed people? "Everywhere women, everywhere private and public passions went hand in hand, and sometimes became inextricably mixed." Whether inspired by "devout royalist idolatry" or "republican idealism", at court, in the drawing-rooms, in the street, no matter where, the same religion urged women to the greatest follies and the noblest sacrifices; and it was not only the pure of heart, the irreproachable, but also the least worthy who aspired nobly towards an unselfish ideal, taking "the country as their best friend, eternal rights as their lover."

Although their part was usually discreetly obscured by the complexity of events, women took an active part in the great revolutionary movement of 1789. Sometimes, in the center of the stage, they encouraged the men; sometimes, hidden in the wings, they pushed them forward.

On the celebrated days of October 5 and 6, they went to Versailles to get "the baker, the baker's wife and the little baker." In that mob which walked to the castle, shouting, laughing and jeering, were women of all kinds: shopkeepers, carriers, women of the Halles, of the Faubourg Saint-Antoine and, at their head, a beautiful pure young girl, only eighteen years old, by training a sculptress but forced by unemployment to become a flower girl, — Louison. They all invaded the town of the Roi-Soleil, shouting over and over, "Bread! Bread!" It was not a desire for blood which led them. It was poverty, and also an immense affection for the royal family from whom they expected miracles. At the Assembly, to which the women went first, they surrounded Mounier, the president; they kissed him and would not leave him alone until he agreed to take them to the king. When they reached the king's presence, they thrust forward the most beautiful of them, Louison Chabry; and that young girl, who a moment before, might have been taken for a wild Bacchante, was so moved that she could only stammer two words, "Bread! Bread!" and then fainted. Meanwhile the beautiful Théroigne de Méricourt flirted with the soldiers and turned the heads of a whole Flanders regiment; after many shouts and parleys, the king gave in. With his unusual escort he returned to his capital. The men took the Bastille, but the women took the king.

We see them in the federations, in July 1790, always in the vanguard and in places of honor. At Saint-Jean du Gard, near Alais, Protestants and Catholics, priests and clergymen, kissed each other. The priest began a hymn to freedom, and a man, surrounded by his family, responded enthusiastically. His wife led her children to the altar and declaimed pathetic verses. Elsewhere, it was a young girl, pure and innocent, who, exposing a piece of glass to the sun, lighted the incense upon the altar of patriotism.

Later, we find them again in those fraternal societies whose moving spirit they were. "Homage to the most interesting part of the human race," wrote the *Mercure National*. "Till now women have taken very little part in the Revolution, till now, we have counted very few patriotic women, but at last candor and grace are also with us, and now *ça ira!*" Following the example of Madame Robert-Keralio, Madame Motte of the Academy of Painting, and Madame Roland, many women joined those societies.

Women helped their husbands, and the young unmarried girls swore never to marry aristocrats. Far from being at the beck of men, they were leaders, such as Olympe de Gouges, who founded several groups in the South and who, seized with pity for the king, died on the scaffold; such as Rose Lacombe, the leader of "Revolutionary Women", who played an important part in the fall of the Girondins, who was a real fury, going much further than any of the men, and who ended by selling sugar and gingerbread to the prisoners.

No important event took place with which women were not connected. The flight to Varennes, which showed the real projects of the king, did not leave them indifferent. In Bordeaux, three or four thousand women formed the "Society of the Friends of the

Constitution", and immediately, all dressed in white, with ribbons of the national colors, they took a bouquet of wild flowers to the constitutional bishop, in a huge procession. All women were admitted into that society, born of indignation and enthusiasm; all, with no other proviso than that those whose character was suspicious should be excluded. Their exaltation was so great that when the Carthaginian women were pointed out as an example because they had given their jewels to save their country, they thought that a very ordinary sacrifice. In Tours also, the flight of the king impressed the women very greatly. Six hundred citizenesses took the oath, and one of them proposed a federation of women. It was decided at once that women should have a place in the Champ-de-Mars; that the flag under which they would march would be carried by a young woman, and that the feminine contingent, which would go to the Field of Federation, would walk two by two; that the women on the right should be the mothers; that the headdress for all should be a bow of white gauze with the tricolor cockade; that the hair should be done cavalier-fashion and piled high; that the uniform would be a white blouse and a white skirt, slit on the side and caught by a green ribbon, with a pink slip underneath. And finally, a tricolor ribbon would be used as a belt.

To give a complete picture of the activities of women during that period, it would be necessary to take one by one all the important events of the Revolution. Of course, they have not all remained in history or even in the memories of men, but some among them have left symbolical names which will always live. Who can think of the phases of that great storm without evoking the names of Théroigne de Méricourt, Madame Roland and Charlotte Corday?

Théroigne de Méricourt was the Amazon of the Revolution. And yet no one could have foreseen that she would be called to that rôle. Daughter of a well-to-do farmer in the Belgian Luxembourg, brought up in a convent, she seemed destined to make happy some gentleman from the country around Liège, but her quick and passionate temper decided otherwise. When seventeen she ran away with a young nobleman who soon left her; then she went to England where she had a rather adventurous life, and then to France.

She had hardly reached France when the Revolution burst. Théroigne led a very luxurious life. She received Marat, Sieyès, Danton, Desmoulins, Romme, Pétion; at once she was delighted with the new ideas. Lamartine, with his usual imagination, said that she found in them a way to avenge herself upon the aristocrats who had caused her licentious life, but this is an exaggeration. Théroigne was a woman of the town, but she was not a woman of the streets, as her acquaintances prove. It is truer to say that her lively imagination was struck by the great enthusiasm which surrounded her, and that her naturally ardent nature carried her into the thick of things. She took part in all the fêtes, all the demonstrations, all the processions.

On July 14, she was at the fall of the Bastille, and
on October 5 and 6 she took the mob to Versailles.
Dressed as an Amazon, wearing a Henry IV hat with a
feather, a revolver in her belt, a sword at her side, her
assured air, her piquant beauty, and her natural elegance gave her great power over the mob, which she
had no trouble in leading and which she was able
to keep from the worst excesses. She walked back to
Paris beside the royal carriage. Henceforth, she was
known, she was celebrated. She followed all the
sessions of the Assembly. She became famous as the
beautiful woman of Liège, and patriots called her
the *First Amazon of Liberty*.

A number of the *Vieux Cordelier*, Camille Desmoulins' paper, shows the extent of her popularity.
One day Théroigne de Méricourt came to the Cordeliers during a session, while an orator was speaking.
"The orator was interrupted," reports the *Vieux
Cordelier*, "by a noise at the door, a flattering and
agreeable murmur . . . A young woman entered and
wished to speak. Yes! It was Mademoiselle Théroigne herself, the beautiful Amazon of Liège! There
she stood in her red silk frock coat, with her big
sword of October 5. Enthusiasm was at its height.
'She is the Queen of Sheba,' cried Desmoulins, 'coming
to visit the Solomon of the district!' Quickly she
crossed the Assembly room with her long panther-like
steps; she mounted the platform; her lovely inspired
face sparkled near the somber apocalyptic visages of
Danton and Marat. 'If you are really Solomons,'
said Théroigne, 'you'll prove it. You'll build the

Temple, the Temple of Liberty, a palace for the National Assembly and you'll build it where the Bastille used to stand.'

" 'What? While the executive power is installed in the most beautiful palace in the universe, the Pavillon de Flore and the colonnades of the Louvre, the legislative power is still camping in tents, at the Jeu de Paume, at the Menus, at the Manége . . . like Noah's dove, it has no place to rest. This must not last. The people should be able to learn just by looking at the respective houses of the executive and the legislative where the real sovereign resides. What is a sovereign without a palace? A god without an altar? Who will recognize his cult?

" 'Let us build this altar and let every one contribute. Let all bring their gold, their jewels. Here are mine. Let us build the only real Temple. No other is worthy of God except the one where the Declaration of the Rights of Man is uttered. Paris, guardian of that temple, will be more than a city. It will be a Fatherland for all, the meeting place of the tribunes, their Jerusalem !' "

This leader of both men and women, this prime mover in all popular demonstrations, aroused violent hatreds. The Royalists gibed at her; they mocked her mania for being always present at all the meetings. They spoke ironically of the marriage of Théroigne to the deputy *Populus*. Their sarcasms pursued her to Liège, her own town, to which she had decided to go after it had fallen again under the yoke of Austria. She was arrested and imprisoned, because she had taken part in the events of October 5 and 6. She was taken to Vienna, but the Emperor Leopold, curious to see that extraordinary woman, had her brought before him and ordered her release.

Back in France, she took part in the events of June 20, then in those days of August 10. On that day, walking upon the terrace of the Feuillants with a French guard, she met her deadly enemy, the Royalist Suleau, who ceaselessly insulted her and abused her sarcastically in the *Actes des Apôtres*. He was walking with a small group of Royalists, and when she saw him, she could not restrain herself. In a moment her blood was up; she jumped at him; she spoke against him; the mob rushed upon the group, and the unlucky ones were done for. In the twinkling of an eye, they were strangled.

Nevertheless, Théroigne was not fond of blood. She did not approve of the massacres of September. She did not even hesitate to condemn them. She broke away from the Montagne during its struggle against the Girondins, and this was the cause of her ruin. One day, as she walked in the Tuileries, some women of the Montagne seized her, raised her skirts and spanked her amid the laughter of the mob.

Crushed by this cowardly attack, her reason gave way; and henceforth the beautiful Théroigne, the Amazon of Liberty, was insane almost to the day of her death. For a long time she was haunted by what had happened to her; she would utter terrible howls and strike her head and her body against the walls of her prison; she would also throw iced water upon herself to wash away the insult to which she had been submitted, and which she remembered perfectly, despite her madness.

By dint of constant and patient care, she appeared to recover some lucidity, but she died miserably in 1817, at the age of fifty-five.

If Théroigne de Méricourt was the slightly dishevelled Amazon of the Revolution, Madame Roland was its calm and staid philosopher, in the real etymological sense of the word. Because of her moral strength, her virile love for ideas, Madame Roland seems less like an enthusiastic but weak heroine of a novel than like one of Plutarch's great men.

At the age when young girls are usually dreaming of a handsome knight or a Prince Charming, Manon Philipon was reading Voltaire and Diderot, as proved by the correspondence she kept up with the Cannet sisters on that subject. These young people were much more interested in Helvetius and Descartes than in their suitors, or, if they wrote about them, it was only to mock them. Reason had triumphed over youth, philosophy over love. The great sorrow she felt at her mother's death increased still more her natural bent for reading and studying. She immersed herself in Rousseau. She used to say, "Plutarch had inclined me to republicanism; he had awakened in me that strength and pride which are his characteristics; he had inspired in me a real enthusiasm for public virtues and liberty; but Rousseau showed me the domestic happiness to which I could aspire, and the delights I could enjoy.'' She enjoyed those delights first in her father's house, and then with her husband, Roland de la Platière; because although Manon Philipon did not play at love, she nevertheless thought about marriage in an entirely original fashion; it never seemed to occur to her that marriage was anything but a purely spiritual relationship. ''From fourteen till sixteen,'' she wrote in her Memoirs, ''I wanted a polite man; from sixteen to eighteen, a witty man; ever since I was eighteen, a philosopher.'' There was no mention of love in her aspirations.

Manon found exactly the man she desired when she married Roland, for her suitor was ''more respectable than enticing, and their five years of courtship were unusual. Their conversations were about the Greeks and the Romans, about Montesquieu, about political economy, etc. etc. . . Until it ended in February, 1780, when Roland was forty-eight and Manon Philipon twenty-six.

Was she ugly and badly endowed by Nature, that young girl, who took refuge in the arms of an old philosopher? Not at all. If we are to believe the interested party herself, she had, at first sight, ''good-looking legs, well-shod feet, well-formed hips, large, and ample bosom, narrow shoulders, a firm and graceful carriage, a light and quick walk.'' Looking closer, one found she had a great freshness of face, a tender, a seductive smile, a bright complexion, lovely colors, a soft skin, charming hands, fine teeth — in brief, a lot of ''treasures.''

Those details, which are unexpectedly given to us

by Madame Roland without coquetry, were confirmed by all the people who knew her. Lemontey, who saw Madame Roland in Lyon, said that her eyes, her head and her hair were of remarkable beauty, that her delicate complexion was extraordinarily fresh. He recognized that she was very witty, and that she had a lot of common sense, piquant reason, and a naïve grace. "Her splendid conversation," he said, "ran unconsciously from her ivory teeth and pink lips. Her husband looked like her Quaker father."

Such was the woman who shut herself up during the first years of her marriage to collaborate in the "Art du Tourbier" and other works of the same character, and who isolated herself from all worldly agitation in the austere domain of La Platière, near Lyon.

The Revolution came. Madame Roland, from her distant observatory, had followed the stormy happenings with her passionate reason: the convocation of the States-General, the fall of the Bastille, the October days, the Federation . . . and so, when she came to Paris in 1791, she was quite ready, as much through her studies as through her knowledge of the events, to play a great part.

It was in her house that the Girondins met four times a week: Brissot, Pétion, Buzot, Condorcet, Barbaroux. When her husband became a minister, it was she who pulled the ropes behind the scenes and especially during the famous *patriotic* ministry. According to her own words, indeed, and without making any mystery of it, she played an important part in affairs; and she had a lot to do with the declaration of war.

Still young, beautiful, passionate, witty, surrounded by a great many celebrated men, a little like, by anticipation, a Madame Récamier, did that superior woman, the spouse of a sexagenarian, really remain the model wife, the clever woman whom we like to imagine? It is a grave question which has given rise to many controversies.

Of course, in moments of weakness she let escape significant admissions. "Married," said she, "with all the seriousness of reason, I found nothing to take me out of it. I devoted myself to reason with an entireness more enthusiastic than calculated. By dint of thinking only of the happiness of my partner, I saw that something was missing in mine. I never ceased seeing in my husband one of the most estimable men alive, but I often felt how much distance there was between us. If we had lived in solitude, I would have had some very painful moments."

Must we conclude that Madame Roland forgot her marriage vows? Not necessarily. At La Platière, of course, she had been very much besieged. Bosc, the naturalist, had declared himself but she calmed him down, and afterwards he became her sincere friend. She also had a weakness for Pascal des Issarts, but their relations remained platonic. The day was yet to come when her heart would take its revenge. Madame Roland fell madly in love with Buzot and wrote passionate letters to him. She confessed it to her husband, without hiding from him how great her passion was. Roland suffered and, curiously enough, his wife was hurt because he did not bear with equanimity his slight misfortune. But she remained faithful, — at least, so she says herself. It is certain, in any case, that in her prison she kept a "dear painting", a miniature of Buzot.

Madame Roland, who welcomed the Girondin meetings in her home, had too many dangerous acquaintances from the point of view of the Montagnards to avoid being included in her friends' fall. She was arrested with them and condemned to death.

Wearing a white dress which floated around her, she stood on the tumbril, which took her to her martyrdom, consoling and encouraging the other condemned. At that instant she really reached the sublime.

When she arrived at the scaffold erected near the statue of Liberty, that heroine from Corneille cried, "O Liberty! What crimes are committed in thy name!"

It was about three in the afternoon of November 9, 1793, when her head fell under the knife.

A life, a death, like that of Madame Roland, could scarcely be summed up better than by a phrase from Corneille, but the one Madame Roland used suits Charlotte Corday better. Not her life — since that virgin with the pure heart died at twenty-five — but the celebrated cause of her death.

Charlotte Corday d'Armont was twice Cornelienne; through her ancestry, since she was descended from the sister of the great Corneille, and through her soul, which did not belie her origin. "The sublime was her nature."

In the convent of the Abbaye-aux-Dames to which she had been sent upon the death of her mother, she gave herself up to the dreams that filled adolescent youth. She did not dream of the handsome knight or the Prince Charming who would come to free her, but of the proud heroes of her great granduncle. She was often caught declaiming verse from Horace or Cinna. Deprived of tenderness at an age when it is necessary to childhood, the little Charlotte retired within herself; she thought, she read much without any plan: Tacitus, Plutarch, Raynal and Jean Jacques Rousseau. "Her head was a hodgepodge of all kinds of reading."

It was worse when she left the convent. Her father, a poor gentleman who thought only of his library, had remarried and Charlotte went to one of her aunts in Caen. Poor, without any hope of getting married, this naturally dreamy and solitary girl was able to indulge excessively in her dreams and solitude. Her soul, it could be said, had modeled her face. This twenty-year-old beauty's expression was extremely grave and virile, but when she talked, her voice sounded very childish, suggesting a comparison between her and Joan of Arc, who always remained a little girl.

It has been said that she was in love with Barbaroux who, after the fall of the Girondins, took refuge at Caen and also with the Royalist Belzunce. The second hypothesis is an absurdity; the first is hardly more likely. It is hard to imagine Charlotte in love with the fat Barbaroux, and the fact that she went to him to get a letter of introduction to Minister Garat proves nothing. Be that as it may, the Revolution of May 31 and June 2, the proscription of the Gironde, the arrival of the exiles at Caen and their plan to persuade Normandy to rise, had carried to its height the exaltation of that young girl, fed only on lectures and dreams, to whom life as yet had brought no brake. She was present at the meetings of the exiles; she kept alive their smoldering fire and dreamed of becoming as great as those men who appeared to her to be heroes. She heard people talk of Marat, that "furious beast who was devouring all the Frenchmen", of Marat, the prime mover in all the crimes, the soul of all the plots. Soon her project was ripe: she would kill Marat.

The idea of sacrifice once born in her mind, she cherished it and henceforth it was her one and only thought. One day her aunt saw a Bible which she had left open and in which she had underlined these significant words: "Judith came out of the town in the marvellous beauty with which God had endowed her, to go to Hopophernes' tent." And one day she was found crying. "I am crying," she said, when she was asked why, "for the misfortunes of my country, my parent and yours. As long as Marat is alive, there will never be any security for the friends of law and humanity."

That idea of stabbing the false "friend of the people" became a monomania, but it would be wrong to suppose that Charlotte Corday obeyed her impulse blindly. Strange enough, for in a person who was the prey of a seemingly unbalanced imagination, she did everything cold-bloodedly. She was a somnambulist who went to her aim patiently, methodically, un-hesitatingly, but a somnambulist who could reason, as her departure proved.

On the morning of July 9, 1793, Charlotte took up her portfolio and her pencils, and told her aunt that she was going to look at the haymakers and do some drawings. She left the house and had hardly crossed the threshold when she met a small boy, Robert, the son of a workman who was one of the tenants. She gave the child her portfolio, kissed him and told him to be good. The boy, taken aback by her present, looked up at her and saw a tear coursing down the young girl's cheek. He was to remember that scene all his life. At the last moment, the woman in Charlotte had asserted itself, but for a moment only.

Indeed, resolutely pursuing her aim, Charlotte went to see her family, her sister, her father, without letting them guess anything. Then she started for Paris. An ironical chance decreed that she travel with some Montagnards, admirers of Marat, but she kept her project secret and even found the strength of mind to joke with them. At last, on July 11, about midday, she reached Paris. Tired out, she went to bed and slept peacefully, her conscience at ease, until the next day. She had no remorse, no fear, no hesitation. On the twelfth, she visited Duperret, Barbaroux's colleague, read Plutarch and went back to her lodging.

On the thirteenth, she asked where the Palais Royal was. She sought a knife maker and bought for two francs a kitchen knife with a black handle and sheath, which she hid carefully under her fichu. Then she took a cab and went straight to Marat, who lived at 20, Rue des Cordeliers, to-day Number 18 Rue de l'Ecole de Médicine. The Friend of the People was sick and, in spite of the decent appearance of the lady from the provinces who had come to see him, Catherine Evrard, Marat's companion, sent her away. Charlotte went back later, but did not succeed any better. A third time, about seven in the evening, she knocked again at Marat's door. A discussion started. Marat, who was in his bath, heard voices, asked what was the trouble, and ended by consenting to receive the visitor who had, she said, important secrets to disclose.

At last she was facing the terrible man, "the wicked beast." Marat, seated in his bathtub, covered with a dirty sheet and a board, was writing, only his head, his shoulders and his right arm out of the water. "His greasy hair, his yellow skin, his thin limbs and his big toadlike mouth," said Michelet, "hardly seemed human." The conversation began. Marat asked Charlotte for news of Normandy, for the names of the refugees in Caen. Coldly she gave them. "Fine," said Marat, "in a week they'll be guillotined." That sentence, as cutting as the knife, made Charlotte's heart jump. She pulled out her knife, raised her arm, and pushed the dagger up to its hilt into Marat's heart. This extremely violent blow crossed the lung, cut the arteries and went straight to the heart. The blood spurted. "Help, dear friend!" the Friend of the People cried weakly. Then he expired.

As for Charlotte, she was petrified and stood waiting near the window. People entered — Catherine Evrard first, then a porter, then the police. Outside, the mob was howling. To the accompaniment of cries for her death, the murderess was taken to the Abbaye. For one instant, in the midst of the outcry, she thought she would faint, but she recovered her self-possession. In prison, calm again, she wrote to her father a letter astonishing for its matter-of-factness.

Forgive me, dear father, — she said, — for having disposed of my life without your consent. I have avenged many innocent victims; I have prevented many disasters. The people, undeceived some day, will rejoice at having been freed from their tyrant. If I sought to persuade you that I was going to England, it was because I thought I would be able to keep my incognito, but I saw the impossibility of that. In any case, you'll find defenders in Caen.

Good-by, dear father, I beg you to forget me or rather to rejoice over my fate. You know your daughter. You know that she could not have had a reprehensible motive.

I kiss my sister whom I love with all my heart, and all our relatives.

Don't forget that verse from Corneille:
"Crime is shameful, not the scaffold."

Charlotte spent two days at the Abbaye. She wrote, she mended her clothes which had been torn by the mob and, with her own hands, made a cap in the fashion of her province. On the sixteenth, she was taken to the Conciergerie for her examination. It is worth reporting:

"What were the motives which made you assassinate Marat?"

"His crimes."

"What did you hope for by killing him?"

"I hoped to bring back peace to my country. I killed one man to save a hundred thousand. I was a Republican before the Revolution and I have never lacked energy."

"What do you call energy?"

"The ability to lay aside one's own interests, to sacrifice one's self for one's country."

"Who inspired you with so much hatred for Marat?"

"I did not need other people's hatred. I had enough of my own."

"The idea must have been suggested to you?"

"A plan one does not think of one's self is always badly executed."

"Do you think you have killed all the Marats?"

"With that one dead, the others may be frightened."

The witnesses testified. After some damaging testimony against her, the president asked her what she had to say.

"Nothing, except that I succeeded."

Her calm did not abandon her. Only once, however, she showed temper. Fouquier-Tinville called attention to the accuracy with which she had struck. He had the misfortune to add, "Apparently you had practiced a lot beforehand?"

Charlotte jumped up and, clinging to the bar of the tribunal, cried, "What a monster! He takes me for a murderess."

She had been given an official defender, Chauveau-Lagarde, who tried at first to minimize her responsibility. A look from the accused made him understand that he was on the wrong track, and he defended her then as she wanted to be defended, that is to say, without humiliating her, by admitting bravely premeditation. Charlotte thanked him gracefully and, after she had been condemned to death, "These gentlemen," said she, "have just told me that all my worldly goods have been confiscated. I owe something to my prison. I beg you to pay my debt." It was, to her mind, the best proof of gratitude she could give.

In her cell, she politely thanked the priest who offered her his ministrations. She remembered that a painter, during her trial, had tried to paint her, and she had him called so that he could finish the portrait. Half an hour went by. Then came the executioner, bringing the scissors, the red chemise.

"What! Already?" said Charlotte Corday, slightly upset. "Sir," she added, speaking to the painter Hauer, "I don't know how to thank you, I have only this to offer you. Keep it in remembrance of me." At the same time, with the scissors, she cut a curl of her long ash-blond hair and held it out to the artist.

As she climbed into the cart, a terrible storm burst, as if nature wished to participate in the madness of men. But, as they reached the Palais Royal, the weather became calm again and the sun shone. It was seven in the evening when the procession reached the scaffold. All the way Charlotte had kept her proud attitude and her calm; her face, haloed by the setting sun, was very majestic.

As she climbed the scaffold, the sight of the knife made her pale, but she went up the steps with a firm gait. The executioner tore away her fichu and her virgin modesty suffered. She shortened those sorrowful moments by thrusting her head forward . . . The executioner's helper, it is said, called Legros, took hold of her bleeding head and, showing it to the people, slapped it. A shiver of horror went through the mob. The head seemed to blush.

Charlotte Corday's death was one of the deaths which made a deep impression upon the people. Its effect was lasting. "Its effect was," said Michelet, "to make people love death." "She kills us," cried the imprisoned Vergniaud, "but she teaches us how to die." A religion was founded by Charlotte; the religion of the dagger. The tangible results of her act were the ruin of the Girondins and the glorification of Marat as a martyr. As for her, she left a complex impression in men's minds. "Angel of murder," Lamartine called her aptly. And the poet-historian expressed with a very arresting phrase the morality of the one act which was to immortalize that "red virgin." "In the presence of murder, History does not dare glorify; in the presence of heroism, History does not dare disparage."

Charlotte Corday, Madame Roland, Théroigne de Méricourt are the privileged of history, because, perhaps, although their virtues were not greater, their actions were more striking, posterity, rightly or wrongly, has raised to them brighter altars. But there were others. What devotion and what sublime sacrifices! What a flowering of intelligence and initiative! What exuberance of passion! What thirst for the ideal! There are, chosen haphazardly, Lucile Desmoulins, who died for her Camille; Madame Robert, who was the initiator of the famous petition of the Champ-de-Mars; Madame de Condorcet, with her Madonna-like face, the admirable companion of the great scientist and politician; Madame de Staël, daughter and admirer of Necker, with her heart full of love, whose great virtue was her great regard for her father, and whose gravest fault was the passion she showed for her mediocre lovers; so many others, Cazotte, Sombreuil, Cécile Renaud, "Robespierre's murderess", and even the ridiculous Catherine Théot, "mother of God." Grotesque or sublime, intelligent or stupid, clear-headed or mad, all had, at one time or another, their hour of celebrity and exerted their influence.

Should we be astonished by the influence of the sex called weak at the time of such tremendous events? Not at all. Robespierre, Danton, Desmoulins, Kléber, and many others belonged to the generation born when Rousseau held full sway, the Rousseau of "Emile", "a powerful generation born with the great thoughts of a wider love, conceived with a flame from heaven, in that sacred moment, much too short, when woman, through passion, catches a glimpse of the idea and worships it." Why should their wives and sisters have not been as they were, distinguished by the special sign upon their forehead, of which Michelet spoke, which set them apart from the children of the second half of the century? Why should they not have participated also in those "two sparks" which changed the whole situation: "Humanity and motherhood," whence came "a burning flow of love and fecund passion, a superhuman maternity."

The Revolution plunged the women much more than the men into an abyss of poverty and desolation. More sensitive, they felt its effects more intensely. With their marvelous instinct, they perceived more keenly still the miseries of the century and quite naturally they were led to seek for remedies. Who suffered more than they did from the upheaval, somberly accompanied by famine and privations of all kinds? Who was more cruelly wounded than the mothers and wives? From them, that savage energy which Marat opposed to the sterile talk of the assemblies. From them, the indomitable courage, the tenacity, those violent actions which, by a very natural contrast, are the prerogative of the weak.

They were weak, of course, by nature. But what force they gained from their weakness! They corrupted everything, they broke everything; for them there were no barriers strong enough. And there was no serious way of repressing them. "A government which executes women, executes itself," wrote Michelet, with the keen sense of the psychology of History, which is his most marvelous quality. "Nature which puts love and the propagation of the species above everything else has, on that account, put this mystery in women . . . They are very responsible, but not liable to punishment . . . As soon as we strike them, we strike ourselves . . . When they are young, they can't be punished. Why? Because they are young, lovely, happy, fecund. When they are old, they can't be punished. Why? Because they are old, that is to say, they have been mothers, they have remained sacred and have gray hair like your own mother. When they are pregnant, poor justice does not dare say a word . . . There is a power which defies law; if the law insists, all the worse for the law. It harms itself, it appears horrible, ungodly, the enemy of God !"

And this explains why the women of the Revolution have left an imperishable memory. Those terrible executions of young women, of lovers, wives, mothers, could only strike the imagination with horror and, when deserved, awoke compassion, pity, and wove for them immortal wreaths. They gained something else, too, not the least of their conquests. It was in the blood of those martyrs that the dawn of a new era started, that the rights of women, which are not yet recognized everywhere, but which will be, were founded, — those new rights which Olympe de Gouges summed up thus in a sublime sentence:

"They have the right to go on the platform, since they have the right to go to the scaffold."

SOLDIERS AND GENERALS

To struggle against all Europe with an army disorganized by emigration, by the treason of its chiefs, and by the lack of discipline of its soldiers, and not only to resist the enemy, but to win many splendid victories and to succeed in the most fruitful conquests, — such a miracle can only be explained by the patriotic enthusiasm which animated the improvised army of the Revolution. A magnificent spurt of youthful energy swept the whole nation, and from French soil came soldiers ready to fight to the death and generals able to lead them to victory.

To insure the national defense, men were needed, and the old royal army was insufficient. At first recourse was had to voluntary enlistment: by 1791 the appeals had begun; the declaration of war in April, 1792, multiplied them; the first disasters, the proclamation of "the country in danger", the tocsin, the cannon of alarm, the booming voice of Danton at the Champ-de-Mars, created a wave of enthusiasm. But these volunteers were not numerous enough, the spirit of discipline was not strong enough, to make them triumph; there was panic, flight in the face of the enemy, sedition, mutiny. When all Europe rose against France, conscription had to be used; on February 21, 1793, the Convention proclaimed the permanent conscription of unmarried men and childless widowers from eighteen to forty; they were to be called in turn, as they were needed. To say that all those called went with enthusiasm, that none tried to evade their duty, would be unduly optimistic. But once they had reached their regiments, these improvised soldiers fought well, especially when they were incorporated in the regular infantry regiments of the old army. The old troops gave the new recruits their own sense of duty and their own habits of order and discipline; the volunteers filled the old troops with their patriotic faith and their revolutionary enthusiasm.

It is in the notebooks, the letters, the memoirs left by some of those men that we must seek their real feelings: humble documents, devoid of all literary value, but precious evidence, because it is sincere and free from artifice.

Here is a volunteer of '91: Louis Belot. He enlisted at nineteen, not for glory, but "because he couldn't see his country threatened by the bands of scoundrels who owe their existence to her and who, after abandoning her, want to come back, arms in hand, to dictate new laws." He uses the phraseology of the times, pompous words; he is never tired of "branding the instruments of tyrants", the "vile aristocrats", but his spirit is as firm as those of the heroes of antiquity. "You are wrong to pity me," he wrote to his father. It is necessary to go through our apprenticeship and to buy our liberty with great trials, to enable us to keep it and to love it more and more"; and after a fierce fight, when his horse had been killed under him: "We are not discouraged. On the contrary, now is the time to show energy, courage, and republicanism. We swore to be free or to die and I can assure you that we won't be false to our allegiance."

The same feelings are expressed by many other volunteers, — the Dragoon Marquant, the artillery man Bricard. For ten years Bricard participated in all the campaigns and, in 1802, after he had become lieutenant of engineers, he asked for leave and came back to Paris to resume his trade of upholsterer.

One of the most typical is Sergeant Fricasse, an ordinary gardener at Château-Villain (Haute-Marne), but well-read enough and very fond of the gazettes. The misfortunes of France did not leave him indifferent and he wrote a very interesting diary of his campaigns. "How many times I have heard through the papers the news that our army had been repulsed and beaten everywhere! I was burning with impatience to see for myself all the things that I could not believe. You'll say it was innocence that made me speak that way, but I often said to myself: Is it possible that I only hear of misfortunes?" And when, on August 24, 1792, the National Guards of his district met to designate the men who were to be in the battalions, he decided, in spite of his shyness, to offer himself for the approval of his fellow citizens; and the latter, who showed so little enthusiasm to go themselves, applauded him at once. For eight years, Fricasse took part in all the campaigns with the Army of the North, with the Army of the Sambre and the

Meuse, with the armies of the Rhine and Moselle, with the Army of Italy: he was at the victory of Fleurus and the siege of Genoa. But the peasant did not yield to the soldier, and it was with joy that he laid down the arms he had used so well: he bewailed the wheat spoiled by the enemy, the potato seeds stolen by the hungry soldiers. But when he had to fight, he fought well, and his republican enthusiasm did not weaken: "Despite their agony, the wounded did not utter a sound; their faces were calm and serene, their last cry: Long live the Republic! . . . our warriors must be seen on the field of honor if we are to learn the difference between free men and slaves. The king's servants die, cursing the cruel ambition of their master; the defender of liberty blesses the blows which have struck him down. He feels that his blood is poured out only for freedom.

Less enthusiastic at the moment of their departure, even the most peaceful conscripts did not take long to catch the martial atmosphere and become good and heroic soldiers. Cognet was a student in Soissons when he was drafted in September, 1793. "Our hearts were sad," he wrote in his first letter, "at leaving our parents and our friends; but, little by little, the marching and the drums diverted us from our sorrow and encouraged the shyest." And, in fact, he was soon hardened. Better educated than most of his comrades, he judged men and events sanely: he approved of the amalgamation of the recruits with the seasoned soldiers, although that measure cost him his commission as second lieutenant; but he realized all that the young soldiers lacked, and which they could only acquire through practice: "Previously we have known life in common, but not military life at all. We are quite initiated now. The seasoned soldiers are pleased with our progress and assert that in a very short time we will be able to help them." Soon the student disappeared in the soldier. After a defeat, "The campaign is not over," he wrote; "we think only of vengeance and battle." Discharged and then recalled almost immediately, he was glad to rejoin his "so much longed-for company." But when the peace of Amiens gave him his freedom, he returned to his first vocation and this good soldier of the Republic became canon of the Cathedral of Soissons.

But all did not leave the uniform thus. From the ranks of those young soldiers came the leaders to replace those lost by emigration. And the generals who rose from the ranks by their civic virtues and their military talents quickly showed themselves worthy of the troops they were commanding. By their impatient enthusiasm, those young leaders, often younger than the men they commanded, upset the old traditions and the old maneuvers, changed all the conceptions of the time and gave birth to new strategy and new tactics. The Revolution took them from all classes and, diverse though their origins were, they were all alike in the warmth of their patriotism and their desire for glory. Lieutenants of the royal army like Desaix or Bonaparte, noncommissioned ex-soldiers like Hoche, Marceau, Jourdan, Kléber, simple bourgeois like Moreau, all proved themselves on the battlefields, as they fought the strategists of Old Europe.

Two youthful figures, two heroes whose premature death gave rise to a great deal of melancholy poetry, seem to incarnate the new army: Hoche and Marceau, both born of the people, both soldiers of the royal army, both brave, generous, attractive, both greatly admired by their contemporaries and by posterity.

Hoche was born in Versailles, almost a Paris gamin. At that time Versailles was a beehive, to which the Court brought the greatest brilliance in France. The town lived on the castle and, from the humblest to the greatest, its inhabitants were lost in the influence of the royal palace. Little Lazare Hoche's father was an ex-soldier, the keeper of the royal kennels, and the child, who had lost his mother when quite young, was brought up by his good aunt, a humble vegetable peddler. The boy helped her with her work, but he also went to school and was attentive and anxious to learn; an uncle of his, Abbé Merlière, had even given him a little smattering of Latin. But he had to live, and at fifteen he entered the king's stables as a supernumerary groom, a flattering position which enabled him to look after the royal horses, but which did not satisfy his eager imagination. Strong and fond of fighting, he dreamed of adventures and, on October 19, 1784, leaving the stables of the king, he joined a regiment which was going to India. At least he thought so, but the crimp had deceived him. Awful people those crimps: always well dressed, rosy-cheeked, freshly shaven and full of promises; but where were their promises after the unfortunates had signed up? Instead of going to India, Hoche was simply sent to the French guards. He made the best of a bad business and became a good soldier: first a grenadier, then a corporal. Between times, he finished his education, embroidering coats and digging gardens to get money to buy books. Still seeking adventures, he participated in fights and duels: one winter's day, in Montmartre, he crossed swords with a bully of the regiment and wounded him badly, but received on his own forehead a cut which gave a more bellicose appearance to his youthful face.

The Revolution filled him with enthusiasm, without making him lose his sense of duty: on July 14, he closed the gates of his barracks to the crowd demanding cannons. The French guards disbanded, and he became a sergeant of the official National Guard and, on October, 1789, helped to defend the castle at Versailles. In 1792, he became adjutant in the 104th Infantry and then, thanks to the influence of his ex-colonel — the Minister of War, Servan — lieutenant in the 58th. In September, 1792, he received his baptism of fire at the siege of Thionville. As a captain and then as aide-de-camp to General Le Veneur, he took part in the Belgian expedition. His general sent him to Paris to denounce Dumouriez' treason and during his stay he became friends with Marat, "the incorruptible defender of the sacred rights of the people." Hoche was ambitious to become an adjutant general and did everything he could to gain his promotion by petitions, the use of influence and appeals to the public in Marat's paper. On May 15, 1793, he obtained the rank he had desired so much. He had hardly got it when he almost spoiled his career. Although ambitious, he had a noble heart and could not stomach the arrest of his dear general Le Veneur; at the peril of his life, he cried: "It would be better if Coburg commanded our armies; our generals would be treated with more kindness than by these gentlemen!" His words were repeated, and he was brought before the Revolutionary Tribunal of the North; he came off well, and his arrest, by calling attention to him, helped his career. He was hardly free when he attacked Dunkirk and did so well that, on September 13, he was made a brigadier general. He justified this distinction by being the first to enter Furnes and by demanding the surrender of Nieuport, but he was soon to be sent to another field of action.

Hoche acted, but he also wrote; his reports to the Committee of Public Safety were noticed by Carnot, and his eulogistic letters to Robespierre flattered the tribune's vanity. Since he was in favor at court, Hoche was made Chief of Staff of the Army of Ardennes and then, on October 22, Commander of the Army of Moselle. It was there that he became famous. The Prussians and Austrians were encamped in the north of Alsace and had Landau very effectively blockaded. Hoche arrived, full of presumption, sure that the enemy could not hold out against him; he attacked Brunswick at Kaiserslautern, but failed in spite of his tenacity. His defeat was a profitable lesson to him. Carnot did not hold it against him.

"A defeat is not a crime," he wrote to Hoche, "when everything has been done to deserve victory. It is not through events that we judge men, but through their efforts and their courage; we admire those who do not despair of their country's salvation; we still have faith in you."

Hoche wanted his revenge and he had it. On December 22, his enthusiastic troops seized Froeschwiller and the neighboring villages. The day after this victory, the representatives Lacoste and Baudot confided to him the two armies of the Rhine and Moselle, to the great annoyance of Saint-Just, who would have preferred Pichegru. He made use of his advantage over the demoralized enemy; on December 26, the slopes of the Geisberg, covered with redoubts, were carried bravely and Hoche, triumphant, entered Wissembourg. On that eventful day the siege of Landau was raised, Alsace freed, and the enemy thrown back to the right bank of the Rhine.

While the troops were resting, Hoche married, on March 11, 1794, in Thionville, Anne-Marie Déchaux. A handsome man, tall, rather stiff, with very piercing black eyes, he had only one fault, — he used too often, in his correspondence or his proclamations, those curses which were supposed to belong to the real sans-culotte. His marriage and his later misfortunes improved his character; the ordeals he experienced ripened him and developed the qualities of kindness and straightforwardness which were in him and were to give to his virile figure the halo of the unjustly persecuted.

On March 10, Hoche was sent to the Army of Italy and he left with regret the troops with which he had accomplished such big things. But he had hardly reached Nice when he was arrested by order of the Committee and transferred to Paris. They believed him to be a traitor. Carnot reproached him for not having marched upon Trêves and pillaged the Palatinate; Saint-Just pursued him with his steady rancor and wanted to avenge his disappointed protégé Pichegru by ruining the victorious general. Imprisoned on April 11 (*Germinal* 22) at the Conciergerie, Hoche remained there until *Thermidor* 17, after the fall of Robespierre. His imprisonment was not in vain: thanks to the aristocrats in prison with him, his prejudices against the Old Régime, which he had detested without knowing it, decreased and his manners, which had remained slightly brutal, became more refined; he gave up the style of Père Duchesne and his swearing: henceforth Hoche was not only a hero, but a cultured man.

He had not long to wait for a new post. On *Thermidor* 26, he was given the command of the army on the coast of Cherbourg. A little later, concentrating three armies under his orders, he was made commander in chief of the operations against the Chouans. A new man was to emerge. Not only the soldier, the great "swordsman against the satellites of tyrants", but the good French citizen, unhappy because he had to shed the blood of his fellow citizens and resolved to do everything in his power to stop a fight between brothers: he was to remain before history as "the

Pacifier of Vendée." He tried first to win the chiefs
and signed with them the Treaty of La Jannaye
(February 15, 1795). A fleeting truce! They soon
started to fight again and Hoche had to act promptly
and vigorously against them, but he made a distinction
between the eternal insurgents and the peaceful
inhabitants. "I declare to the country folk," he said
in a proclamation, "whatever religion they may
profess, that the army which I have the honor to
command will protect by every means in its power the
safety of people and their property, the freedom of
religious worship and the peace of the ministers of
God when they observe the law, and instead of inciting to rebellion, preach peace and good will to men."
A clever move, for to leave their priests to the peasants of the West was a sure way of keeping them at
peace. And, when the émigrés, brought by the English, disembarked at Quiberon, they brought disaster upon themselves: Hoche wanted to spare the
prisoners but Tallien had them shot. Hunted down,
the last chiefs, Stofflet and Charette, were taken and
executed. Hoche continued to appeal for calm. "Do
you think that, greedy of blood, we will avenge murders by murders? Do you think that because I am
leading Republicans against those among you who are
armed I am going to murder and pillage? No, the real
Republicans do not commit cruel actions. The very
same soldiers from whom you flee want to give you
the kiss of peace. They are trying to deliver you
from tyranny, not to strangle you . . . Rebuild your
cottages, pray to God and plough your fields. You'll

find in us protectors as full of zeal as the brigands will find in us enemies bent on subduing them." In June, 1796, the West was definitely pacified.

Hoche was now able to turn once more to the enemies abroad. In July, 1796, he was made chief of the Army of Ireland which was to attack England over the seas. The fleet left Brest on December 15, but the vessel which carried Hoche was separated from the others by a tempest, and when they arrived at the designated meeting place, the squadron had already left Bantry Bay. They had to come back to escape from the English cruisers. On January 11, 1797, Hoche reached the island of Ré at last. The expedition was a failure.

At once he was put at the head of the Army of the Sambre and Meuse. On the nights of April 17 and 18, he crossed the Rhine and beat the Austrians at Neuwied, but just as he was ready to pursue his victorious march, he was stopped by the peace of Leoben, which Bonaparte had just signed.

Barras wanted to use him against the Royalists and called him to the War Ministry on the eve of *Fructidor*. Hoche was not built for politics and, suspected by his adversaries and disavowed by Barras, he retired without betraying the confidence placed in him. On September 8, he left for the Army of the Rhine and Moselle; but he had hardly reached his General Headquarters in Wetzlar, when, on September 19, he succumbed to pneumonia after a painful illness.

France learned with stupefaction of his premature death; poison was mentioned, for the people would not believe he had died from natural causes. The young hero was mourned as the conqueror of Geisberg, the pacifier of Vendée; later, in Saint Helena, Napoleon rendered him the greatest homage by saying, "His was one of the most magnificent military reputations of the Revolution . . . Hoche was a real warrior."

Marceau was still more attractive: this handsome hussar, with long hair like a young girl's, with soft and fearless eyes, is one of the purest figures of the army of the Revolution.

⟨He was a natural soldier. Born in Chartres in 1769, he volunteered when sixteen and served first in the regiment of Savoie-Carignan, then of Angoulême. He became enthusiastic about the Revolution: he was present at the fall of the Bastille, served in the National Guard of Paris, then of Chartres. He drilled his fellow citizens, he tried to fill them with his patriotic zeal; and so, in 1791, he was elected lieutenant colonel and made second in command of the First Battalion of the Volunteers from Eure-et-Loir. He was in Verdun when the Prussians appeared before it, and was against surrender; he fought heroically in the woods of the Argonne. But he wanted to leave his volunteers and to make his career in the regular army, and he asked for a post in the cavalry. He was made second lieutenant of infantry. He protested and, thanks to the recommendation of his compatriot Pétion, he was made lieutenant to the Cuirassier of the German Legion, a rather troublesome corps which was always denouncing its chiefs and never stopped intriguing. Marceau and the other officers were put in prison in Tours, on the order of the representative of the people. He only stayed there twenty days: on May 29 he was released, for things were in a bad way in the Vendée. On June 9 he was at the defeat of Saumur and acted heroically: during the fight, one of his persecutors, the representative Bourbotte, had his horse killed, and Marceau offered him his, saying, "It is better that a soldier like me should be made a prisoner than a representative of the people"; and as Bourbotte hesitated to accept this sacrifice, he left his horse and jumped behind a comrade. Bourbotte did not wish to be ungrateful: he acquainted the Convention with the wonderful conduct of the young man and had him made an adjutant general. His courage and his successes against the rebels soon brought him the grade of brigadier general, then major general. Commander in chief *ad interim*, he crushed the Vendée army at the Mans on December 13. During the battle, he had an opportunity to show his humanity: a girl sixteen years old, Angélique des Melliers, became separated from her mother in the rout; distracted, frightened at finding herself in the midst of Republicans, she threw herself at Marceau's feet. He kindly raised her up, gave orders to have her taken to a safe place and gave her a safe-conduct to protect her. Two days later, in Laval, he confided her to the care of an honest family. But the general had hardly gone when the representatives in mission, egged on by the fanatical Turreau, ordered, under threat of the most severe punishment, the denuncia-

tion of refugees. Angélique exhibited her safe-
conduct: the secretary clerk of the Revolutionary
Commission took it, under pretext of examining it, and
did not give it back. The unhappy Angélique was put in
Laval prison: she left it only on January 22 to appear
before the Revolutionary Commission and to go from
there to the scaffold. Before dying, she sent her small
gold watch to the young general who had tried to
save her. When Marceau received this sad present,
he was unable to master his indignation and his
tears.

At that time, he temporarily left the service.
With Kléber, he had, on December 23, achieved the
rout of the Vendée army at Savenay. But soon he had
to give back the chief command to the coarse Turreau and the numerous annoyances Marceau had to
suffer soon irritated him. He asked and obtained sick
leave. Moreover, this fratricidal war was repugnant
to him; he wrote to his sister, who had congratulated
him on his successes, "What! my dear sister, you con-
gratulate me on those two battles or rather those two
massacres, and you want leaves from my laurels!
Don't you know that they are spotted with blood,
with French blood? I will not go back to Vendée: it
grieves me too much to fight my compatriots. I
want to fight the foreigners. Only there is honor and
glory. I am asking for a post at the frontier, and I
hope that my friends will help me to get it."

Instead of spending his leave in Chartres as he had
intended to do, Marceau went to Rennes to visit a
friend, the Comte Leprêtre of Châteaugiron. He had

rendered a great service to the Count's son, Hippolyte, by taking him as his aide-de-camp, although he was under suspicion. He was admirably received and looked after by the Countess, and love soon brought together the daughter of the house, the young Agathe de Châteaugiron, and the charming general. The mother helped the budding love; the father, on the contrary, still filled with prejudices, refused to give in. Then the mother and daughter came to live at the Marais, near Argenteuil, in Seine-et-Oise, while waiting for the marriage to take place.

Meanwhile, Marceau had gone to the Army of the Ardennes. At Fleurus he had accomplished prodigies of valor, and Jourdan, in his report, had called him the "lion" of the army. A little later, after an audacious march, he took Coblentz, the General Headquarters of the émigrés, while the staff hastily fled. Put in charge of the administration of the province of Wiesbaden, he was beloved by every one because of his justice and kindness.

Soon the Army of the Sambre and Meuse, in which he was serving, was to know defeat. Marceau, in the rearguard, was entrusted with covering the retreat and he did it very successfully, holding the enemy in check. Besides, to console himself for that failure, happiness was waiting for him: leave of absence asked from the Directoire for his marriage with Agathe de Châteaugiron had been granted and, at the Marais, they were plunged in preparations for the event. But instead of the expected fiancé came the news of

his death. On September 19, Marceau, accompanied
by his aide-de-camp, Captain Souhait, had gone to
reconnoiter the pass of Altenkirchen. They had
hardly entered a small wood when a hussar of Kayser
passed before them, making his horse caracole.
Marceau stretched out his hand to show him to his
companion. That gesture was fatal: a Tyrolean
hunter, ambushed behind a tree, saw the braid shining
upon Marceau's sleeve and recognized an officer of
high rank; he aimed at him, fired, and the bullet,
going through Marceau's arm, lodged between his
ribs. The wound was fatal. Jourdan, his heart
bounding with rage, had to leave Marceau in the
village of Altenkirchen. The Austrian generals came
to see the young hero and tried to lighten his last
moments. In spite of excruciating pain, Marceau
kept his lucidity and his courage to the last: he died
on the twenty-first of September. His ashes were put
in an urn upon which was engraved: *"Hic cinis,
ubique nomen."* (His ashes are here, his name is
everywhere.) The Army of the Sambre and Meuse
put up a monument to him at the spot where, later,
the remains of Hoche were united with those of his
family. In the wood of Hochstbach, where he had
been wounded, Captain Souhait placed a marble
tablet recalling the death of the young general —
"mourned and regretted by the entire army, the enemy
and the inhabitants." Posterity ratified the praise
of his contemporaries. Due to his bravery and his
kindness, Marceau has remained one of the most

beautiful figures of the Revolution and we can only repeat Byron's judgment of him: "He kept his soul's purity, and therefore men mourned him."

Kléber was a violent contrast to Marceau: the latter a handsome man, gentle, modest, somewhat effeminate; the former a rough warrior, tall, stolid, with a powerful voice and a tempestuous spirit. Kléber was not an adolescent; he was a man thrown into the turmoil of the Revolution, a soldier who loved war and glory, a real Mars.

Kléber came from the people: he was born in Strasbourg in 1753, the son of a humble guard in the service of the town; his mother, who had been left a widow early, had remarried and was the wife of a master mason. The orphan studied a little with a priest, who was a friend of his, and soon left for Paris to study architecture under Chalgrin. Back in Strasbourg, he was mixed up in a brawl in a café, and defended two German gentlemen. One of them, the Count of Kaunitz, was the owner of a regiment of Walloon Infantry in Austria: he offered the young man his protection. Kléber accepted and entered the service of the emperor; in 1777 he became an ensign and in 1779 a second lieutenant. But he understood that since he was not of noble birth, he could never reach the higher ranks and in 1785, after more than seven years of service, he left the regiment. His colonel gave him a most eulogistic certificate: "Jean Baptiste Kléber has served with so much zeal and activity and has been so excellent, that he has earned

not only our esteem, but that of all his superiors,
his equals, and his inferiors."

Back in Alsace, he resumed his career as an archi-
tect. In 1789 he was a member of the National
Guard; his military talents drew the attention of his
compatriots to him and in 1792 the General Council
of the Upper Rhine had him made adjutant major to
the Fourth Battalion of volunteers of that department.
As second in command of a battalion commanded by
an old man, he soon became the real chief. When in
November, 1792, he joined the Army of the Rhine,
his enthusiasm shone forth in his letters; he never
tired of praising his men: "None of them think any
longer of leaving their flag. A few sick ones, yes, a
few sick ones, have begged me to let them go with
the battalion, offering to follow on foot, if only I will
take charge of them." He reached the front just as
the situation was becoming tense. Mainz was besieged by the Prussians, and Kléber, caught in the
fort, distinguished himself during the siege. His
athletic figure, his lion's mane, awed his subordinates; his courage, his self-possession, his good
nature, made him beloved by all; he fascinated his
subordinates and obtained from them what he liked.
He was a past master in night raids, which allowed
him to make prisoners; one evening he captured some
Prussians dancing at the inn and made his excuses to
the ladies for troubling the party. The representatives
of the people, Reubell and Merlin, made him adjutant general, then brigadier general and put him in
charge of the defense of the outposts. He multiplied

his enterprises and got the better of the enemy in stealing cattle, hay, straw, wine. During the whole of June, he carried on this skirmishing upon the left bank of the Rhine. Whenever the enemy opened a trench he would make a forceful sortie, throw panic into the Prussian ranks and upset the work begun, taking all their ammunition, which he would later use against them. Vain efforts! On July 23 Mainz capitulated. Kléber almost lost his life because he had shown such great courage. On July 30 he was arrested at Sarre-louis, with two other generals. Luckily, the two representatives, Merlin and Reubell, were compromised with them; they hastened to the Convention, pleaded their cause and justified the garrison; Kléber was released.

Since Mainz' garrison could not fight against the Allies for a year, Kléber was sent into the West against the Vendée. He was a brigadier general, serving under Rossignol, in the Army of the Côtes de la Rochelle. His début was unlucky: he was wounded at Torfou, and his exuberant courage could not keep his troops from being beaten, but some days later he took his revenge at Saint-Symphorien. Sent to the Army of the West, he won the victories of La Tremblaie and of Cholet (October 17, 1793); and the same day he was made a major general. Then he crushed the Vendée: with Marceau he was victorious at the Mans and at Savenay, but, like Marceau, he hated civil war. Again he faced the enemy, first with the Army of the Ardennes, then with the Army of the Sambre and Meuse; at Fleurus, he commanded the left wing and accomplished prodigies of valor. With the Army of the Rhine, he reappeared before Mainz, but besieging it, not besieged.

In 1796, he helped Jourdan with the most brilliant success: a victor at Altenkirchen, he took Frankfort and entered Namberg. He had been offered several times the chief command but he had always refused. He was forty-four years old and thought of rest; he left the army to live in peace while writing his memoirs, but he did not enjoy his retirement long: the country needed him, and perhaps he himself was longing for the battlefield. In January, 1798, he was given a division of the Army of England and Bonaparte took him to Egypt. They had hardly disembarked when he rushed at the head of his troops to the walls of Alexandria and fell, struck by a bullet upon his forehead. His head was hard and the wound was not deadly; but Kléber was unable to follow his comrades and as he was bored in Alexandria he asked to be recalled to France. Instead, Bonaparte took him to Cairo and then to Syria. Kléber took Jaffa and Haifa and upon the Biblical slopes of the Thabor won a brilliant victory from the Turks. But Saint-Jean d'Acre resisted and Egypt had to be reached again; Kléber covered the retreat magnificently. And so, when Bonaparte left Africa furtively, he left the command of the army to Kléber. When he received the letter which gave such a burden to him, Kléber burst into a fit of anger; he thought he was abandoned, betrayed. But his bad humor did not last long; he did not think of refusing the task which had been confided to him, although he had no faith in the future of French domination in Egypt and merely wished to make the best of a bad situation. While collecting all the documents which were to be used in writing the great "Description of Egypt", he negotiated with the English commodore, Sydney Smith, and he signed with him the Treaty of El Arich (January 20, 1800): the French Army was to leave Egypt, but was to be repatriated in France. Evacuation had already begun when Kléber received a letter from the English admiral Keith, notifying him that he refused to ratify the treaty and inviting him to surrender. "Soldiers," cried Kléber, after reading the letter to his troops, "the only answer to such insolence is victory!" And two days later he crushed the Turks at Heliopolis. He won the alliance of Murad-Bey, his most dangerous adversary, and then returned to Cairo, where a revolt had already begun. The troops regained confidence when they saw how they were commanded: Kléber himself began to enjoy his conquests and installed himself in Egypt; he might even have conquered it for France. But on June 14, 1800, he came back from Gizeh to Cairo to lunch with his friend, the chief of staff, General Damas. Just as he left the house, a young fanatic Mussulman struck him several times with a dagger. Kléber died almost at once and his loss was fatal to the French army; he was the only man capable of keeping it in Africa.

Thus, at forty-seven, perished this great Alsatian with the martial air, the stentorian voice, this hero of a hundred battles, whom his soldiers had nicknamed "Mars in uniform" and of whom Napoleon said, "Kléber was wonderful in battle . . . He towered under fire."

Moreau was of better extraction. The son of a barrister of Rennes, he was destined to follow the law and to take his father's place. But the young bourgeois was hot-headed: at seventeen he enlisted, and his father had to use all his influence to have him sent back to the University. In 1788, at twenty-five, he was made Provost of the Law School, but he did not lose his love of war. The following year, at the time of the troubles in Brittany, he was at the head of the students of Rennes: the nobles, angered by Necker and by his innovations, set their valets and partisans against the students who were defending the rights of the Tiers. But from all the towns of Brittany people came to help the students: the nobles were attacked, pushed back to the Assembly Room and obliged to flee. It was Moreau's first victory.

Such a début proved him capable to be the commander of a company in the National Guard. In September, 1791, he was made lieutenant colonel of the First Battalion of volunteers from Ile-et-Vilaine and in 1792 he was in the Army of the North, first with Dumouriez, then with Jourdan. In April, 1794, he was made major general, under Pichegru's orders; he won the victory of Tourcoing, then took Ypres, Bruges and Ostend. On July 28, during an expedition against the island of Cadzand, he threw himself into the water and saved a captain of grenadiers who was drowning. While he was covering himself with glory, he heard of the death of his father who had been condemned by the Revolutionary Tribunal of Brest and executed on July 31; he only sought vengeance by serving his country as best he could.

His reputation was established in 1796. After commanding the Army of the North, he went to the Army of the Rhine and Moselle, and he had under him Desaix and Gouvion Saint-Cyr. Carnot had conceived a very audacious plan: three armies were to march on Vienna, the Army of Italy through the path of Tarvis, the Army of the Sambre and Meuse through the valley of the Main, the Army of the Rhine and Moselle through the Neckar and Danube. Moreau fulfilled splendidly the task given to him: he crossed the Rhine during the night of the twenty-third, vanquished the Austrians at Reistadt, entered Stuttgart and crossed the Danube. He was in Bavaria; but Jourdan, who was to have joined him, was beaten at Würzburg and the Archduke Charles was able to turn against him. Moreau then managed that marvelous retreat which has remained celebrated in military annals: he came back through the southern part of the Black Forest, beat the Austrians at Bibe-rach and brought back all his flags, all his cannon and all his prisoners. Moreau was not an inspired general: he did not have the broad views and flashing improvisations of Bonaparte, but he was an admirable tactician, — cold, thoughtful, leaving nothing to chance, and beating the enemy according to the rules. The following year he thought he would take his revenge; but he had hardly crossed the Rhine when the peace of Leoben stopped him.

A short disgrace halted his career for a moment. In Pichegru's correspondence he found the proofs of the latter's treason, but he was slow in letting the Directoire know about it. His attitude was considered suspicious and as a result he had to keep away from active service: after *Fructidor*, he was put on the retired list. But France was threatened anew: the situation was grave in Italy. Moreau received the heavy burden of uniting the remnants of the armies of Scherer and Championnet and stopping the Russian advance. Beaten at Cassano by Souvorov, he succeeded in saving his thirty thousand men from the clutch of a hundred thousand Russians. Joubert came to replace him and Moreau humbly accepted service under the orders of his young rival. At Novi, at the beginning of the action, Joubert received a fatal wound and Moreau, by one of his excellent retreats, succeeded in saving the army and bringing it back to Genoa.

When he returned to Paris, Sieyès wanted to put him in charge of the *coup d'état* he was contemplating. Moreau hesitated but, during their interview, the news of the return of Bonaparte became known; he turned then to the ex-Abbé: "That's your man," he said; "he'll carry out your *coup d'état* much better than I."

Moreau's reputation was much greater than his popularity; outside the armies, he was shy and undecided. Bonaparte dominated him easily, and Moreau helped the enterprise, but as the second in command. On *Brumaire* 18, he accepted the not very attractive rôle of jailer: it was he who watched in their Luxembourg apartments the directors Gohier and Moulin, who had refused to retire. His reward was the chief command of the Army of the Rhine, the best in France: a hundred thousand tried men.

The First Consul had to deal carefully with him and really to negotiate for the conduct of the armies. However, Moreau crossed the Rhine and, at Stokach, took from the Austrians seven thousand prisoners and nine cannons. He went on with his prudent march, entering Bavaria and chasing the enemy before him. On December 3, 1800, he won from the Archduke Charles the decisive victory of Hohenlinden which opened the road to Vienna to him; on December 25, Austria, vanquished, signed the armistice of Steyer.

Up till then Moreau's jealousy of Bonaparte had not shown, but his marriage was to unloose it. In November, 1800, Josephine arranged for him to marry her friend, Mademoiselle Hulot, a Creole like herself. Ambitious and vain, the latter was jealous of Josephine, and in every possible way she excited envy in her husband. Madame Hulot built a small "temple to glory" at Orsay, in honor of her son-in-law, the victor at Hohenlinden. Moreau retired to Grosbois, which became the center of a sulky opposition to

Bonaparte, and which deserved the name "Club Moreau"; he refused the title of marshal and the Legion of Honor and all the malcontents turned their eyes towards him. But the consular police were watching him. It became known that he had had an interview with Pichegru who had come back secretly to France to conspire against the First Consul: that was sufficient ground for his arrest. Before his judges, he protested his innocence of any complicity in the plot directed against Napoleon, but he could not deny his relations with Pichegru. On June 10, 1804, he was condemned to two years' imprisonment. Napoleon, now emperor, commuted this sentence to banishment. Moreau went to Spain and then to America where, on his property in Morristown, New Jersey, he led the existence of a gentleman farmer. He never lost his interest in European affairs: the retreat from Russia awoke his hopes and his desire for vengeance prompted him to listen to the tsar's proposals. On July 26, 1813, he arrived in Sweden and went quickly to the Russian General Headquarters. In his clairvoyant hatred, he advised the Allies to "avoid open battle, to refuse to fight Napoleon and to crush his lieutenants: deadly tactics which, followed to the letter, brought about France's defeat. On August 27, at the battle of Dresden, a French shell wounded his right knee and removed his left calf. Six days later, Moreau died at Lahn, in Bohemia, in the midst of the enemies of his country: a great general but a bad citizen, who had been unable to secure from the love of his country the strength to overcome his personal jealousy and to smother his resentment.

Desaix of Veygouz belonged to that petty provincial nobility who, better than the great lords of the Court, kept the virtues of their class, and whose titles did not prevent them from knowing the difficulties of living: the nursery for officers who served the king and France obscurely, who poured out their blood upon the battlefields and who, when old, came back to their native heaths, to live on small pensions without ever having had the satisfaction of reaching the higher ranks.

He was born in Auvergne, that country of a modest race, but strong, tenacious and courageous. His father, who lived poorly by cultivating his land, had him entered in 1776, at the age of eight, as a scholar in the Military School of Effiat; he left it in 1783, a second lieutenant to the regiment of Brittany. At the time of the Revolution, he became aide-de-camp to General de Broglie and, after the magnificent defence of Worms, he was made adjutant general, then brigadier general and finally on October 20, 1793, major general. His military talent and his perfect republicanism made people overlook his noble origin; always fearless and modest, he was adored by his men. He directed the right wing of the Army of the Sambre and Meuse and then, after Pichegru's departure, he commanded temporarily, against his wishes, the Army of the Rhine and Moselle. It was with joy that he received Moreau and took orders from him. He executed with intelligence and courage the instructions of the commanding general; he participated in the expedition to Bavaria and, in the glorious retreat, defended the entrance to the bridge of Kehl against all attacks. During his stay in Germany, the population learned to love him and it was a German who spoke thus of him: "Among those generous men of the army of the Rhine, Desaix is remarkable, amiable and talented." He was also praised by one of the principal Austrian generals: "He treats the inhabitants with kindness and nobly resists any proposals of pillage. God bless his memory!"

When peace had been signed, Desaix asked and obtained a mission in Italy. He wanted to meet Bonaparte, whose extraordinary exploits had struck his fancy. Bonaparte welcomed him cordially and a mutual affection sprang up which henceforth united them till death. Desaix devoted himself to Napoleon's fortunes and the latter found in him the most faithful, devoted, disinterested lieutenant. He took part in the expedition to Egypt. After the first battles and the entrance into Cairo, Bonaparte put him in charge of the pursuit of Murad-Bey, the chief of the Mamelukes. Desaix conquered Upper Egypt and his kindness and his justice to the natives earned for him the nickname of the "Just Sultan." After the treaty of El Arich, he hastened to come back to France. He was arrested in Livorno for a short while, but was released and immediately upon his arrival in Marseilles, he hastened to join the First Consul in Italy. Bonaparte also was no less impatient than he was, for he had sent him this urgent message: "At last you have come; good news for the Republic, but more especially for me, for I give you all the esteem and affection which my heart, now very old and knowing men too well, has for no one else . . . Come as quickly as you can to join me, wherever I am."

On June 14, 1800, on Marengo plain, the French armies were falling back. Bonaparte, deprived of several of his divisions, had let himself be caught by the enemy: the fifteen French cannons were crushed by a hundred Austrian. Vainly the Consul talked to his soldiers and comforted them, but he could not prevent them from giving in under the formidable push of their adversaries: defeat was near. Suddenly, about five in the evening, fresh troops arrived; it was Desaix who, sent to Genoa, had gathered an army and cannons and marched back with them. "The battle is lost, but we have time to win another one." Desaix, forming his division into columns, threw himself upon the left wing of the Austrians and cut it off from the rest of the army. The enemy troops ran away in disorder. It was victory, but a very dear victory. Desaix, a bullet through his heart, died in the midst of his triumph.

The First Consul mourned his friend. "Ah!" he said, "if I had been able to kiss him after the battle, how beautiful this day would have been!" He not only had several statues of Desaix put up in different towns in France, but gave him a worthy tomb; on the Grand Saint-Bernard, in a magnificent setting of snowy mountains, rests the one who, disclaiming the nobility of his birth, desired to be great only by the nobility of his heart.

It was also a provincial noble, a noble from Corsica, the young General Bonaparte, who arrived in Nice on March 26, 1796, to take the command of the Army of Italy. Who knew him? What had he done? A general from the streets! A protégé of Barras! All his subordinates — Masséna, Augereau, Serrurier, Laharpe, Joubert — tried generals, taller than he by a head, had decided not to let him impose himself upon them; and they spoke loudly and they made their sabers ring. But the pale young man had hardly come into contact with them before he had conquered: they were won, subjugated. In a few days order reigned again in the army and hope in the hearts of the soldiers.

On April 11, the Army of Italy began the campaign. The eagle had begun its flight over Europe, soaring over the battlefields of the most diverse countries only to fall nineteen years later, on the mournful plain of Waterloo.

LEADERS OF THE MOB

To some extent the history of the Revolution is the history of the popular uprisings. With each of the "days" a new phase begins: July 14, October 5 and 6, August 10, May 31 — the dates of the insurrections in the slums — are landmarks in those heroic years. But the people, miserable and irritated as they were, did not rise of themselves. To excite and to direct their anger, to give an aim to their manifestations, required leadership: perhaps of their own accord, perhaps in accordance with well-thought-out plans, leaders went into the crowded streets of the slums and, through the force of their eloquence, cleverly directed the ignorant and vulgar mob, making of it a blind and formidable instrument to serve the cause they had embraced. Perhaps those obscure leaders influenced events even more than the orators who, at the tribune of the Assembly, figured as heads of the parties, for when the chiefs seemed to hesitate, their humble collaborators often compelled them to act. History does not know them; buried in the mass of the people, they are not easily distinguishable, and their influence is more suspected than proven. It was to their own interest to remain hidden, for, in case of failure, they could disappear and escape pursuit, free to begin all over again a little later. Only a few of them are known; some, like Danton or Marat, rose to the highest positions; others, after being momentarily in the limelight, either perished in some catastrophe or other, or fell back into obscurity.

Strangely enough not one of them was, properly speaking, "a man of the people." They all belonged to the lower middle class, which was irritated by the contempt of its superiors and which, although too close to the people to inspire them with envy, enjoyed the prestige of superior education. They were clerks like Maillard or Hanriot, journalists like Hébert or Chaumette, merchants like Santerre or Legendre. And although their actions may have been reprehensible, they were really sincere men, for they sought, not their own profit, but the triumph of the Revolution and the happiness of the people.

Maillard, the "Septembrisor", the son of a merchant from Gournay, had come to Paris in 1778, when fifteen years old, to join his brother, one of the doorkeepers of the Châtelet. He took part in all the revolutionary days. On July 14, he played a rôle rather hard to define; some pretend that he imperilled his life by accepting the capitulation of the besieged. On October 5, he was in the first line: the howling mob of women forced open the doors of the Hôtel de Ville and wanted to burn the archives. Maillard interfered; he harangued the shrews, dissuaded them, assumed their leadership and took them to Versailles; the next day he came back in one of the Court's carriages and received the compliments of the town.

He reappeared in September, 1792. Bands of stranglers were rushing to the prisons, into which suspects had been crammed. The advance of the Prussians, the fall of Verdun, the proclamation of the "Country in Danger" had upset the nerves of the mob, and they firmly believed that the prisoners were only awaiting the departure of the patriots to the frontiers before starting to strangle women and children. And the awful butchery began: federates from Marseilles, Parisian *sectionnaires* — a handful of men — for four days killed ceaselessly, encouraged by the watchful Committee of the Commune, while the Assembly, mute and terrorized, dared not hinder them. Maillard reigned over the prison of the Abbaye, where he had formed a tribunal. By order of the Commune? On his own authority? No one knew. In black evening clothes, his hair powdered, his hat upon his head, he sat with the register of prisoners in front of him. The prisoners were called in turn; a few questions were asked; Maillard decreed, "To the Force", and the prisoner, pushed outside, was killed on the spot. Sometimes the president was humane and the prisoner was set free to the cries of "Long Live the Nation!" It was certain that the survivors owed their rescue to the "Tribunal" instituted by Maillard. For three days this tubercular fanatic of thirty presided over his sinister court; his work finished, he went elsewhere.

Unlike the others, he did not try to be forgotten: he was proud of the part he had played. He organized a revolutionary police to ferret out the suspects, the game for the guillotine, earning thus his nickname of "the knocker." He took part in the riot of

May 31. It was his last victory. Fabre d'Eglantine attacked him violently, accusing him and his band of brigandage. On October 11, 1793, he was arrested. A month later he was released, but not for long. On December 17, he was arrested again, but he did not go back to prison; for they left him in his house, worn out and spitting blood. He still had the strength to write a pamphlet against Fabre: "The veil has fallen and the calumniator is revealed." On April 15, 1794, in his own words, "He gave back to Nature the commission of life it had confided to his keeping."

Fournier, the American, was another "September-brisor." According to Madame Roland, his pale, sinister, moustached face and his three belts of pistols succeeded in frightening many people. The son of a weaver of Auvergne, he had gone to seek his fortune in San Domingo, where he had started a distillery. Ruined by a fire, he went back to France in 1785 and threw himself, body and soul, into the Revolution. He took an important part in the fall of the Bastille, in the march to Versailles, in the affair of the Champ-de-Mars and, on August 10, 1792, in the attack on the Tuileries. In September, Fournier, the American, was at the head of a band which went to Orleans to get some prisoners whom the High Court was too slow in judging. There was some choice game in that bag: two ex-ministers of Louis XVI, De Lessart and Franqueville d'Abancourt, the Duc de Brissac, the Bishop of Mende . . . On September 9, the column reached Versailles, where the prisoners were to be incarcerated in the Ménagerie. A hostile mob filled the streets and uttered threats of death: the railing of the Orangerie opened but only to admit the soldiers in the escort, separating the unfortunates from their defenders. And then came the butchery, a hideous massacre, in spite of the generous efforts of the Mayor of Versailles, Hyacinthe Richaud, who almost lost his life in consequence. A few minutes later, their bloody heads were stuck on the railings of the Orangerie, and Fournier's men, drunk with slaughter, invaded the prisons of the town and killed the political prisoners.

In spite of his services, Fournier became suspect to the revolutionary government. Marat did not hesitate to accuse him, and Marat's accusations were formidable. "I denounce," he said, "a man called Fournier, who has been present at all the rebellions, the same who, at the affair of the Champ-de-Mars, aimed at La Fayette's heart and remained unpunished, while the patriots were slaughtered. I ask a decree of accusation against him."

Fournier was arrested and remained in prison from December 12, 1793, to September 22, 1794, and then, after a first release, from March 9, 1795, to the armistice of *Brumaire*, *An* IV (October 26, 1795). But the police watched him. When, after the attempt of the Rue Saint-Nicaise, Fouché deported without trial a great number of ex-Jacobins, Fournier, crossing the Atlantic again, was among those that went to Guiana. He came back in 1809 to Auxerre, where he was again closely watched. But he could not remain quiet. In

July, 1811, accused of fomenting a riot, he was incarcerated in the Chateau d'If. The emperor's fall set him free, but the Bourbons imprisoned him again as a "Septembrisor" from November 1, 1815, to August 16, 1816. He was put in the prison of the Force, which had been the scene of some of the most dreadful massacres. Definitely freed, the adventurer, who could not resign himself to oblivion, wrote many libels and secret memoirs; he died finally in Paris, almost an octogenarian, on July 27, 1825.

Hanriot, although of much lower origin, was a more important personage: this clerk of *octroi* was the son of a poor farmer of Nanterre. Although employed by the farmer generals, he shared the popular hatred against "the wall around Paris." And on July 12, 1790, instead of defending the pavilion of the *octroi* which had been left in his charge, he gave it up to an incendiary mob. He was arrested for that and remained in Bicetre's prison until the end of 1790, when Marat intervened to secure his release. Then in his district of the Jardin des Plantes, which became the section of the *sans-culottes*, he became very influential and was put at the head of the battalion for his district. His popularity secured him the chief command of the Parisian National Guard, after Santerre's departure for the Vendée. In that capacity, he played the leading part on May 31 and June 2. He demanded the arrest of the Girondins. On the thirty-first he failed and only obtained the suppression of the Committee of Twelve. Two days later, when the Convention refused to give up the threatened deputies and, led by its president, Hérault de Séchelles, tried to leave the Tuileries, Hanriot, upon his horse, stopped the procession. His troops were massed behind him, with ready cannons and lighted fuses. Vainly Hérault tried to persuade him: "The people did not rise to hear talk; they want the twenty-four culprits," and, as Hérault insisted, "Gunners, to your guns!" cried Hanriot in a stentorian voice. Defeated and despised, the Convention resumed its sessions and gave up the desired victims.

Such a success assured a triumphant election for Hanriot. On July 1, he was given his post permanently, and Marat called him "The Country's Savior." He tried to deserve that title and, during the winter of 1793-1794, he succeeded in keeping order without bloodshed, in spite of the suffering caused by famine. He was compromised for a while by the Hébertists, but was saved by Robespierre's protection and henceforth became the docile instrument, the tool of the latter.

He appeared for the last time on *Thermidor* 9. The evidence about the part he played on that day is incomplete, confused and contradictory. The Thermidorians claim that he was drunk, a false accusation, but it is certain that he failed to show self-possession and judgment. Taken unawares, he did not have his enthusiasm of June 2.

When he learned of Robespierre's arrest, Hanriot jumped upon his horse and hastened to the Tuileries to rescue the prisoners. He had counted too much on his prestige. When he entered the room of the Committee of Public Safety almost alone, it was he who was seized by the gendarmes of the Convention and tied up, — an unlucky adventure, which disorganized Robespierre's defence! Hanriot would have remained in the Tuileries, if at about eight in the evening, the vice-president of the Revolutionary Tribunal, Coffinhal, an energetic and resolute man, had not come with two hundred gunners to set him free. At that moment Hanriot could have easily invaded the Convention and ended it all. He dared not. Discouraged by his first failure, he hastened to take refuge in the Hôtel de Ville, where he remained inactive. When the Convention troops invaded the big hall, he disappeared. Next he was found, wounded, hidden in an outhouse of the Hôtel de Ville. What had happened? Had he resisted? Had he tried to escape? Had Coffinhal angrily thrown him out of the window? All those explanations have been given. That same evening Hanriot, still stupefied, was taken to the guillotine in the Place de la Revolution.

Other agitators preferred the pen to action. The Revolution, by establishing the freedom of the press, had brought forth a swarm of newspapers and journalists; amongst these, some acquired sufficient prestige in the eyes of the public to become, in a way, the director of its conscience and to play an important part in politics. Such were, among others, Hébert and Chaumette.

A man with a sinister face, smoking a long pipe,

holding in one hand one of the revolvers from his belt and in the other an enormous hatchet, above a kneeling priest, — this was the vulgar caricature which headed the paper, *Le Père Duchesne*. This "Père Duchesne" was a dealer in stoves, a terrible braggart, with filthy words in his mouth, who claimed ceaselessly heads for the executioner. The mob loved his coarseness, and this ignoble sheet, in which oaths took the place of wit, calumnies the place of discussion, had a circulation, at times, of six hundred thousand copies and was distributed generously to the armies. One would picture the editor of such a paper as an illiterate giant, brutal and uncouth; but he was a small, slight, very well dressed man, with delicate features. Behind Père Duchesne's mask was Jacques-René Hébert, assistant prosecutor of the Paris Commune.

He was a bourgeois: his father, a master jeweler of Alençon, had been in that town the leading judge, alderman and lieutenant of the bourgeoise, belonging to what was called "the belfry nobility." However, young Hébert had a stormy youth: ruined by a long lawsuit which ended in defeat, he had to leave his native town and seek his fortune in Paris. He had trouble in supporting himself there. For a while he was ticket collector at the Théâtre des Variétés Amusantes; then, when discharged, he walked the streets, eating when he could, living from day to day, until the Revolution caught him up. He fought with his pen, by writing pamphlets: the first, in 1790, was "The Magic Lantern or The Curse of the Aristocrats."

But he was not often seen where there was any fighting: that braggart was a coward who barked but did not bite. On July 17, he was at the Champ-de-Mars, and was so greatly frightened by hearing the bullets whistle around his head that henceforth he nursed a violent hatred of Bailly and La Fayette.

In 1791 he married an ex-nun, Françoise Goupil. They were an extraordinary household, for the wife, who had remained pious, preached the teachings of Christ, "the first of the *sans-culottes*," to the Jacobin women, while her husband worked at deChristianization.

On August 10, he became a member of the Insurrectional Commune; he did not take part in the September massacres, but he approved of them in a pamphlet. On the following December 22, he was elected assistant prosecutor of the Paris Commune.

From then on his activities were doubled: he sat at the Hôtel de Ville, in the great hall of the Commune. Well combed, well powdered, his neat appearance contrasting with the uncouthness of the prosecutor, Anaxagoras Chaumette, nevertheless he was the idol of the lively mob which sat in the tribune. He talked coarsely to all who appeared before him, and his vulgarity was applauded, for he was the editor of *Père Duchesne*, the journalist who was a real *sans-culotte*, the defender and the apologist of the common people.

He aspired to be Marat's successor. "Marat, I'll profit by your lessons, yes, . . . cherished shadow, inspire me. I swear I'll face daggers and poison and always follow your example. Everlasting war with the conspirators, with the plotters, with the rogues! That's my motto. . . . 'It was also mine,' said his spirit as it left me. 'Keep your word.' Yes, . . . I will keep it."

He had few political ideas and only one passion: hatred; only one idea: the guillotine. He pursued his adversaries relentlessly. When his pipe had been smoked thrice over, he said a reputation must fall, and a head went under the knife.

First it was the royal family. He insulted the vanquished: Louis XVI was "a rhinoceros foaming with rage"; Marie Antoinette, "Madame Veto" or "the Austrian harridan"; sweet Madame Elisabeth, "fat Babet"; the royal children, "the young wolves" or "the young baboons." He recommended their murder. "Let the little serpent and his sister be thrown upon a desert island. I do not know any other way of getting rid of them, and yet we must do it any price. And what is a child, when it is a question of the safety of the Republic?" Marie Antoinette he hated especially, and he asked ceaselessly for her death. He hoped that "in a few days, Samson would play ball with the head of the Austrian she-wolf." During the trial of the queen, he acted abominably. He dared accuse her, with revolting details, of having debauched her son, and the child, unaware of what he was doing and terrorized by his guardians, confirmed Hébert's accusations. Asked to reply, Marie Antoinette cried: "If I do not answer, it is because Nature refuses to believe such an accusation against a mother. I appeal to all present!" The whole room shook with sympathy and the *tricoteuses*, the lechers of the guillotine, almost applauded the queen. After the execution, Hébert returned triumphant "after seeing with his own eyes the head of the female Veto separated from her strumpet neck."

Once the queen was dead, it was the Girondin's turn. Hébert gave them no respite. Their trial, in his opinion, was lasting too long. "Must we make so much fuss over cutting short the lives of scoundrels whom the people have already condemned?" With sadistic pleasure, he was present at their martyrdom, happy to see them "playing at hot cockles in the Place de la Revolution!"

All pity, all scruples, seemed criminal to him. "Where would we be without the holy guillotine?" The Revolutionary Tribunal itself was too slow, too circumspect for him. It should act more quickly and pour forth ever-increasing torrents of blood. "Let us form a revolutionary tribunal in the public squares! . . . The jury and the judges will not be lawyers. The guillotine will be near the tribunal, and the knife will be raised and shining, ready to behead the guilty or any judge who dares pardon . . ." As leader of the Club des Cordeliers, to which Danton went no longer, Hébert saw his influence increase. He gave his name to the most advanced party. The Hébertists unloosed the Terror, the movement towards de-Christianization; they were in favor of war to the death, of demagogic measures against merchants whom they accused of monopoly. But they met strong adversaries: the Indulgents, with Danton and Camille Desmoulins, and Robespierre himself, was irritated by their exaggerations.

Believing himself sure of the help of the Parisian people, Hébert did not worry over his opposition and multiplied his attacks. "I'll have no more mercy upon the carrot dealer than upon the big merchants because, . . . I see there is a league of all sellers against all buyers, and I find as much bad faith in the small shops as in the big ones." Incautious words, for his threats made Hébert disliked even by the small people at the moment he chose to fight his adversaries in the open! He thought the time had come for his partisans to seize the power, and he denounced violently the inertia of the committees. Vainly Collot d'Herbois tried to arbitrate between the two clubs: the Jacobins, who were for Robespierre, the Cordeliers, for Hébert. After a semblance of reconciliation, the violent succeeded. But the call to insurrection failed and the Hébertists were arrested without any difficulties. On *Germinal* 1, *An* II (March 1, 1794), they appeared before the Revolutionary Tribunal; on the fourth, they were executed.

Hébert's death was gruesome; he fainted before the Tribunal; he had hallucinations during his last night. In his turn Hébert, who had insulted his victims, knew the insults of the mob who had worshipped him. They hooted, using his own words: "Are you to-day, Père Duchesne, to watch the aristocrats take their medicine? It's your turn to play at hot cockles, to look through the small window!" He collapsed in front of the guillotine; he had to be carried, almost unconscious, to the fatal scaffold.

Chaumette, his chief, was to follow him shortly after, with no more courage. This prosecutor of the Commune was a curious figure, all contrasts, a naïve yet clever peasant, a hypocrite yet sincere in his revolutionary enthusiasm, capable of taking the initiative courageously, yet ready to crumple abjectly when threatened. He was the son of a humble shoemaker from Nevers. At the height of the Revolution, he boasted of his plebeian origin, but previously he had been ashamed of it. He had tried to alter his birth certificate, to make his honest father a jeweler! He had studied at the college in Nevers, but had been dismissed from it. At thirteen, in 1776, he became a cabin boy and later, a pilot's apprentice. He did not remain in the navy and, back in Nevers in 1782, he had studied anatomy and been interested in botany. In 1784, he was a surgeon in Moulins. Then his taste for roving seized him again: he went to Marseilles and tried vainly to embark for the Antilles. In 1786, he accompanied an English doctor, S. Tluck, in his travels through France as both pupil and secretary. After that, he settled in Nevers; but while continuing his study of physics, he began to take an interest in politics. He contributed to the local papers, published in Avignon, which were fighting against the existing régime.

Then the Revolution, that goal of all ambitious people, attracted him irresistibly. From the beginning, he was eager to take part, but it was not until September, 1790, that he reached the only scene he thought worthy of him.

Like Hébert, he had difficulties at the beginning and had to live in devious ways. But he wanted to be known; he wanted to get on. He prated in the clubs, in the Cordeliers, in the section of the Théâtre Français; in the Jacobins he was not afraid to attack the masters of the day: Mirabeau, Lameth, Bailly. If he is to be believed, they tried to buy his silence; he denounced their offer to the Cordeliers, and he was saved. A post as contributor to the paper, *Les Révolutions de Paris*, whose principal writer, Loustallot, had just died, was offered him. He accepted and in articles that were often anonymous he used the flight to Varennes to install the Republic, and his name was one of the first on the petition of the Champ-de-Mars. Sought for a while, after the firing of July 17, he succeeded in hiding and in reorganizing the scattered Girondin Club.

In 1792, he continued his republican propaganda and played an important part in the preparations of August 10. As a member of the Insurrectional Commune, he did not take part in the attack on the Castle, but had all the Royalist papers seized at the post office and solemnly burned. It was less dangerous! In the evening, he was at the Hôtel de Ville, presiding over the General Council of the Commune. On the following day, he was one of the commissaries whose duty it was to see that all the "bad citizens", "the aristocrats", "the traitors" were jailed, a prelude to the sinister happenings of September. But during the massacres, he was in Normandy, engaged in overseeing the conscription of sixty thousand men. On his return, he started fighting Minister Roland. On December 12, he was elected General Prosecutor of the Paris Commune; his exaltation shone in all the jottings in his intimate notebook: "I am showered with blessings and cheers . . . Louis Capet! Louis Capet! I doubt that, when you were king, you had so much pleasure as I . . . "

To the president who, when receiving him, asked his name and surname, he answered: "During the Old Régime, my name was Pierre-Gaspard, because my godfather believed in saints; but since the Revolution, I have taken the name of a saint who was hanged for his republican principles. That's why I am now called Anaxagoras Chaumette."

His great period had begun as prosecutor of the Commune. It was he who represented the Parisians, brought their complaints before the Convention and insured public order with more power than the mayor, the insignificant Chambon or the good Pache. At the Hôtel de Ville, he pontificated in endless homilies to the people, eager to hear him. The unemployed workmen listened to him delightedly. He adopted the dress of a real *sans-culotte:* long hair, badly combed; a big, rumpled collar; a kerchief negligently tied, and clogs. With a voice raucous and cracked from liquor, he preached virtue; he prosecuted loose women and forbade the sale of obscene writings. And yet, in spite of his Puritan exterior, this rigorist had unspeakable morals; though he practiced unnatural vice, he did not blush to say, "Without morals, the Republic will crumble . . . Paris is the sewer of morals. This depraved town must be regenerated!"

There was the same contradiction between his protestations of humanity and his conduct towards his adversaries. He trampled with rage over the vanquished Girondins. "No more quarter, no more pity for traitors. If we do not forestall them, they'll forestall us. Let us put between us the barrier of Eternity!" He was ruthless to Marie Antoinette. It was he who brought to the General Council the odious accusations which Hébert had the audacity to repeat before the full session of the Tribunal. More than that, he did not hesitate, when he felt threatened, to betray his friends like a coward and to slander them hypocritically for his own protection.

That coward dreamed of deChristianizing France. There was in him something of the spoiled priest, and most of his speeches were reversed sermons. He wanted to replace the traditional religion by lay fêtes. "We shall have fêtes, of course, but secular ones. We shall celebrate wives and mothers, and especially mothers who feed their children. We shall have civic fêtes. On August 10, we shall have a meeting, and the people will be our God. There must be no other." To accomplish his purpose, Catholicism had to be overthrown, and Chaumette unloosened the anti-religious feeling. In October, he forbade the ministers of different religions to exercise their ministry outside their places of worship. On November 7, he asked that a date should be kept in the new calendar for the cult of Reason. Two days

later, with ridiculous, naïve fatuity, he had the
Commune decree that "his anti-ecclesiastical edicts
should be translated into Italian and sent to the Pope
to apprise him of his errors!" Gobel, the constitutional Bishop of Paris, shaking with fear, came to be
unfrocked at the bar of the Assembly. Chaumette
at once caused the Assembly to decree that, "to
celebrate the triumph that Reason had won in that
session over the prejudices of eighteen centuries", a
civil ceremony should be celebrated "before the
image of that divinity, in the building formerly the
metropolitan church." It took place on *Brumaire*
20 (November 10, 1793), that famous fête in which
Reason was represented by a dancer from the Opéra,
Mademoiselle Maillard, dressed in white, draped in
the tricolor, and wearing a red cap. And Chaumette,
leading the Opéra goddess before the Convention,
caused the latter to decide that Notre Dame would be
consecrated to the new cult. Two days later, the
statues on the big porch were destroyed, that ever-
to-be regretted vandalism which deprived us of one of
the masterpieces of Gothic architecture. The movement of deChristianization did not stop there. In
Paris, as in the provinces, Liberties and Reasons
abounded, very earthly goddesses, with a very mixed
following. Grotesque scenes took place: one citizen,
Barucaud, went to the Hôtel de Ville with his wife
and children, asking to be debaptised and unmarried,
so that they might be reunited in a republican marriage. Solemnly, the General Council of the Commune decided that his name henceforth would be

Châlier (the name of the Jacobin mayor of Lyon executed by the Royalists); his wife, Atrié and his children, Aristide, Régulus, Porai and Eponème!

This anti-religious propaganda was Chaumette's greatest mistake. Robespierre, who had tolerated it until then, was heartsick by these pseudo-philosophical masquerades, the deist in him hating those atheistic manifestations, and the politician fearing an uprising of the people who had remained Christian. Chaumette achieved his ruin by opposing the committees. On December 1, the Commune decided to add two members to each of the forty-eight revolutionary committees: it was the forerunner of a new "day", but the edict was nullified by the Convention, and Chaumette, frightened, backed down. He was too cautious to dare even to follow the Hébertists in their rebellion; he hesitated, contradicted himself, gave way. A vain recantation: he was arrested a few days after they were and accused of atheism. He was not in the "Hébertist batch" but was included "in the prison conspiracy", with ex-Bishop Gobel and the widows of Hébert and Camille Desmoulins. He was executed on April 13, 1794, without even redeeming by a firm attitude towards death the meannesses of his life. "Flat on his belly he pleaded," said Michelet, a terrible expression which branded for eternity the cowardice of the Prosecutor of the Paris Commune.

A fortune well spent is a sure means of popularity: merchants, kind to the poor, easily become the leaders of their district. Like the Roman patricians, they have a poor clientele devoted to them. The butcher Legendre and the brewer Santerre are examples.

Legendre was the son of a butcher of Versailles. Like Chaumette, he had spent a part of his youth at sea. Back in France after ten years, he had become a butcher in Paris, in the Rue des Boucheries-Saint-Germain. He had a large business, but he was good-natured, loving to oblige people and was more anxious to be popular than to make a fortune. He ended by ruining himself and by having only his salary as a deputy.

Butchers have played a part in all the Parisian revolutions. Legendre carried on the tradition of his fifteenth-century forbears. He took part in all the manifestations; in July, 1789, he was one of those who carried the busts of Necker and the Duke of Orleans in triumph; he led the crowd to the Invalides to get arms; he went to the assault of the Bastille. Loving eloquence, he frequented the clubs. He became a member of the Jacobins and contributed to the founding of the Cordeliers. His idol was Danton, whom he admired ingenuously; he became blindly attached to him, just as in the fifteenth century he would have followed Caboche. He was compromised at the time of the shooting affray of the Champ-de-Mars, but succeeded in hiding himself and giving shelter to the outlawed Marat. On June 20, on August 10, he was again encouraging the outskirts of Paris to the assault of royalism.

At the Convention, to which he was elected by Paris, he sat on the benches of the Montagne, beside Danton, and voted the king's death. In February, 1793, during a mission in Lyon, he was on the side of Châlier and the Jacobins against the local moderates. In favor of conciliation at first, he soon became, following Danton's lead, a violent adversary of the Girondins. He loved grand, eloquent manifestations, wild gestures. On June 2, he shouted to Lanjuinais, shaking his fist at him, "Come down or I'll brain you!", which brought him the reply, "Have a decree passed to show I am an ox, and then you can slaughter me." On the platform, that uneducated man was able to make the public listen to him by his vehemence and sincerity; modest, he sincerely admired his better educated colleagues, but in spite of some haphazard metaphors, he had a natural eloquence which made every one listen to him and appreciate him.

The drama of his life was his denial of Danton. On *Germinal* 11 (March 31) when he heard of the arrest of his friend and master, Legendre generously devoted himself to saving him; he asked that the accused should be brought before the Convention. "I believe Danton to be as loyal as I am . . . I can only say this of the man who, in 1792, caused France to rise through the energetic measures he took to move the people . . . The enemy was at the gates of Paris: Danton came, and his ideas saved the country."

But Robespierre wanted his prey; by a clever and vehement speech he won the Convention to his side:

"To-day, we shall see if the Convention knows how to destroy an idol, which has been rotten for a long time," and, turning to Legendre, "I say that any one who trembles now is guilty, because innocence has never feared public supervision."

Faced by that threat, Legendre collapsed. "Little does Robespierre know me if he does not think me capable of sacrificing an individual to liberty." And, frozen with fright, still thinking he felt the incorruptible's eyes fixed upon him, he ceaselessly denied his friend: his wife died of her fright. But the remorse of his betrayal kept haunting him. He was divided between his desire to avenge Danton and his fear of the guillotine. On *Thermidor* 9, at the beginning of the session, he remained quiet: it was only when Robespierre had left the hall, when he was freed from that paralyzing presence, that he found courage again and secured the decree of outlawry.

Then, to make up for his fright, Legendre fought the Jacobins with a vengeance. He was one of the chiefs of the Thermidorian reaction and took part in the closing of the famous club. On *Germinal* 12 and *Prairial* 1, when the Convention was invaded by the hungry bands from the outskirts, it was he who gathered the golden youth, the *muscadins*, and freed the Assembly by beating back the invaders with clubs. His anti-Jacobin fury, in spite of himself, encouraged the progress of royalism. When he saw that, he wanted to react, but it was too late. In the Council of the Ancients, of which he had become a member, his part was humble: he died soon afterwards, on *Frimaire* 23, *An* VI (December 17, 1797), bequeathing his body to medicine, so that after his death he could be of some use to humanity.

Santerre was the "Father" or the "King of the Faubourg." The son of a brewer from Cambrai, who had settled in the Faubourg Saint-Antoine, he had received a good education. Rich, elegant, fond of riding, he was one of those who introduced in France the horse races in the English fashion, and he was on good terms with the Duke of Orleans on that account. His generosity was great, and the poor people of the Faubourg were always sure of his help: in the days of unemployment, he tried to employ the greatest possible number of workmen. His popularity led to his playing a prominent part in the first days of the Revolution. On July 13, 1789, he was unanimously made commander of the Tenth Battalion of the National Guard, and the next day he courageously took part in the fall of the Bastille. On October 5 he was in Versailles with La Fayette to defend the Castle. During the winter of 1789-1790, he tried to provide food and fuel for all the inhabitants of his district. After the massacre of the Champ-de-Mars, he was denounced as a leader of the people, and he had to hide himself a while. Soon he reappeared and, on June 20, 1792, it was he who led to the Assembly, then to the Tuileries, the long column of the people of the Faubourg. He managed to maintain a semblance of order in that mob and to prevent any shedding of blood. On August 10, the insurrectional Commune gave him a leader's part. He was placed, after the assassination of the Royalist Mandat, at the head of the Parisian National Guard. If he did not take a direct part in the attack on the Castle, he was given the task of watching over the royal family, and it was he who escorted them to the Temple. During the September massacres, he could not be found: he was at Versailles, busy inspecting the local troops! On January 21, 1793, he commanded the contingent of National Guards which accompanied Louis XVI. The king tried to utter a few words: the drums prevented him. Was it Santerre who cut short the words of the dying man? Posterity accuses him; perhaps it was the fault of General Berruyer, who commanded the infantry.

Days of trial were soon to begin for Santerre. He was made General of Division, and went to Orleans to organize the Parisian volunteers who were to march against the Vendée. Badly armed, badly equipped, badly disciplined, those improvised troops were beaten in all encounters, and Santerre, suspected of Orleanism, was arrested in Rennes and incarcerated in the prison of the Carmes. He was only freed on *Thermidor* 15, after Robespierre's fall. Coming out of prison, he found his affairs in the greatest disorder: his second wife had taken back her dowry and ruined his firm. He had to sell his brewery, and he lived in straitened circumstances, if not poverty.

A man full of resources does not let himself be downed by misfortune: lucky speculations in national property soon enabled him to build up another fortune. But his luck turned; he participated in some unfortunate business ventures and again he was completely ruined. At the end of his life, he had only his pension as a retired general, which was given to him by the Consulate. He died at the age of fifty-seven, in 1809.

For a long time he had had no influence. On *Brumaire* 18, the rumor was current that he had been seen in the streets, trying to rouse the people. Bonaparte, questioning Director Moulin, his relative, told him, "If Santerre shows himself, I'll give orders to have him followed and killed." Moulin, his illusions lost, had answered, "Santerre couldn't gather four men around him." And it was true: the people had turned away from its old idols. Those who had not been gathered by death were sinking slowly into oblivion.

SECONDARY FIGURES

THE ten years of the French Revolution were marked by the most formidable disturbances of modern times; a whole society crumbled, while one after the other new social strata rose to power; one by one, the chiefs of the different parties were struck by proscription. It is, therefore, not astonishing that an enormous number of great men should have been used up. In addition to the principal protagonists, a multitude of talent was revealed which, in less troubled times, would have had the spotlight and, which although lost in the glamor of the stars, nevertheless had considerable influence. The staff of each party was rapidly eliminated through exile or death, and when the principal figures disappeared, there remained only the seething appetites: the dwarfs fighting over the giants' remains.

The first to espouse the cause of the Revolution, the first to try to insure the triumph of reforms, were the constitutional Royalists. With Mirabeau — sometimes even against him — they wished to reconcile their respect for monarchy and their love of liberty. Sieyès, La Fayette, Bailly, the theorist, the fighter, the administrator, were the most important.

Sieyès was one of those priests without vocation, of whom there were so many at the end of the eighteenth century. Coming from a good middle-class family of Provence, he entered the church and sought fortune far from his own home. He became Canon of Tréguier, and then, in 1784, vicar-general and chancellor to the Bishop of Chartres. In that important position, he secured experience in public affairs. He was a member of the Provincial Assembly of Orleans in 1787, and his reputation was already well enough established for his colleagues to choose him as president of the Intermediary Commission of that Assembly, which had to settle current affairs between sittings. A philosopher, an atheist, he never confessed or preached, and he welcomed joyfully the preliminaries of the Revolution; he wrote several pamphlets against Minister Brienne, one of which, at least, was very popular; its title was a whole programme: "What is the *Tiers-Etat?* Everything. What has it been until now in the political order? Nothing. What does it want? To become something." The author became popular over night, and was sent to the States-General by the *Tiers-Etat* of Paris.

From the very first, his rôle was considerable, and he was looked upon as an oracle. And the theorist proved himself a clever tactician: it was he who, on June 12, brought about the vote which caused the privileged orders to join the *Tiers*, it was he who, on the seventeenth, persuaded the *Tiers* to transform itself into a National Assembly; it was he again who drew up the Oath of the *Jeu de Paume*. He loved solemnity: On June 23, as the deputies were hesitating, even after Mirabeau's eloquent address and

Dreux-Brézé's retreat: "You are to-day," he said, "what you were yesterday: let us deliberate." And the decrees of the preceding days were upheld.

A mediocre orator, he rarely took the platform: Mirabeau knew his weakness and pretended to be sorry for him. "Abbé Sieyès' silence," he said, without secret irony, "is a public calamity." Sieyès, who did not draw attention to himself, saw his popularity waning. He compromised it, too, by favoring the repurchase of the tithes and by crying bitterly, "They want to be free, and they don't know how to be just!" Though he regained his popularity by his hostility to the royal veto, Sieyès understood that he could never supplant the brilliant orators in the public favor, and he adopted that sphinxlike attitude, which made people believe he was profound, and which he kept throughout his career. He pontificated more than he directed. President of the Assembly in June, 1790, a member of the Directoire of the Department of Paris in 1791, he could easily have been constitutional bishop of the capital, but he refused, for he wanted to break all ties with the Church.

During the legislative he was very careful of his reputation and retired to the country. Sent to the Convention by three departments, he decided for the Sarthe. At the beginning he played a very small part: he voted for the king's death without comment; he sat in the ranks of the *Plaine*, but carefully avoided compromising himself; and if he acted, it was secretly. He escaped the proscription of June 2, for although he was known by every one to be the adviser of the Gironde, there was no evidence against him. Robespierre called him the "Mole of the Revolution." "Abbé Sieyès shuns the lights," he said, "but he never ceases his activity in the underground passages of the National Assembly; he directs and embroils everything. He raises some earth and disappears; he creates factions, starts them going, eggs them on against each other, and stands aside to profit afterwards, if circumstances are suitable." The two men hated and feared each other; both affected pontifical attitudes, both wanted to be moral dictators. So when Sieyès had Lakanal present a plan of national instruction, Robespierre refused it in a terrible and contemptuous manner: "Citizens, you have been deceived, that work is not by the one who offers it to you." Sieyès understood and remained silent; he is said to have uttered the following words, and although he denied saying them, they are typical of his prudence: "What did you do during the Terror? — I lived!"

When Robespierre was overthrown, he raised his head. His party was in power, and he could have governed if he liked, but he affected a detached skepticism. In the midst of the most stormy debates, he looked into all the corners of the room with his lorgnette. A member of the Committee of Public Safety, he was not present often, and, though he was a Doctor of Political Science, he did not even take part in the drawing up of the constitution of *An* III. He had been made a member of the Committee on Preparation: he refused to sit on it. The oracle remained silent, preferring not to risk again his reputation of infallibility. He confined himself to proposing a constitutional jury, independent of the two Chambers, and as his idea was not accepted, he despised and slowly undermined that constitution which was not his.

Nineteen departments sent him to the Council of Five Hundred: it was almost a plebiscite in his favor. He refused to be a member of the Directoire when they wanted him; always according to his prudent tactics, he would not compromise himself. He would keep his prestige intact. He even had the halo of martyrdom: a madman, Abbé Poulle, came to his house to kill him and only succeeded in breaking his wrist with a shot from his pistol! A regicide, and as such, threatened by the Royalists, Sieyès was in favor of *Fructidor*. But the *coup d'état's* atmosphere, the ambiguous combinations, the underhand dealings about elections were compromising; it was better to go away. And Sieyès accepted the ambassadorship to Berlin (May 10, 1798); about the same time, another ambitious man also left the directorial muddle to seek fame in Egypt. Sieyès, more prudent, preferred diplomacy to war. He was familiar with diplomacy; he had already negotiated the treaty of La Haye with Holland.

In Berlin, while succeeding in keeping Prussia neutral, he did not lose sight of the course of events in France, where his friends were working for him. Reubell had hardly been put out of the Directoire when Sieyès was elected in his place. This time he

accepted and all of France had confidence in him, for
it seemed as if the philosopher knew all the secrets of
good government. In the Directoire he acted: two
embarrassing colleagues were put aside and replaced
by two nullities devoted to him: Barras, frightened,
gave him a free hand. But to assure the success of his
plan to strike the decisive blow to Jacobinism, which
was looming up again, a sword was necessary. He
thought he had found it in Joubert, a young general,
good-looking, brave and unscrupulous: let him be
winner in Italy and, proud of his prestige, he would
drive the talkers away. Catastrophe! On August
15, 1799, Joubert was killed at Novi. Like Diogenes,
Sieyès looked around for a man: he thought of Moreau,
who eluded the honor, when a rumor spread: Bonaparte had disembarked at Fréjus. There was the man
he was looking for: and Sieyès, with Bonaparte's aid,
thought out the *coup d'état* of *Brumaire*. On the
nineteenth, in the evening, the deputies scattered;
they were both made provisional consuls and got
the mediocre Ducos to assist them.

The ex-Abbé and general were now face to face, but
the tool was to be the principal actor; the man of
the sword had no trouble in eliminating the duped
philosopher. At last that famous Constitution, which
had been developed in Sieyès' head and which was to
make France's happiness, was going to be promulgated. Alas! The most beautiful projects are those
which never come to maturity, and Sieyès foggy
ideas were brutally cleared by the solid good sense of
Bonaparte. When the philosopher proposed to him a

kind of pyramid, having for its base the people, and at the top a pro-consul whose sole task would be to designate the members of councils from the lists of notables, Bonaparte answered that he did not want to be "a pig fattened by the millions!" Sieyès offered a new proposition: two consuls, one for peace, the other for war; a new refusal from Bonaparte who, leaving the philosopher alone upon his Mount Sinai, dictated the Constitution himself. Henceforth, Sieyès' political importance was at an end. He was not even a permanent consul. He had only to enjoy peacefully his reputation and the profits it brought him, and secretly to invent new political systems which would never see the light of day. He was given the property of Crosne, he was senator, academician, count of the empire. Louis XVIII exiled him as a regicide; but he had the supreme cleverness to survive the Restoration and he came back to Paris to die, over eighty years old, in 1836.

La Fayette's vanity was as great as Sieyès': noble, rich, courageous, with the halo of a brilliant reputation, he thought himself a statesman, and thus caused his own ruin. All through his long career La Fayette was the perfect type of liberal, full of good intentions, but very short-sighted, incapable of learning from experience.

He belonged to the very best nobility. Since his father had been killed at the Battle of Minden, in 1759, two years after his birth, he could follow no other career but the army. At sixteen he was a second lieutenant in the regiment of Noailles. Already very rich in his own right, he married Adrienne-Françoise de Noailles, one of the best matches in France. But he had a taste for adventure: when the American colonies rebelled against England and proclaimed their independence, the young man's imagination was fired by their ideas of liberty. Cunningly, to avoid the opposition of his family-in-law and the Court, he disguised himself and succeeded in sailing from Bordeaux on April 26, 1777. On June 15, he was at Georgetown. The rebels received the young messenger from Europe with enthusiasm and gave him the rank of major general. He did his best to justify their confidence by his services and his courage; he was wounded before Philadelphia and became a great friend of George Washington. In 1779 he came back to France to plead in favor of his comrades in arms, obtained help for them and joined them again in the spring of 1780. On his return he assisted in the defeat of Cornwallis, who had contemptuously nicknamed him "the boy", and the surrender of Yorktown. When the independence of the United States was assured, he came back to France. He was celebrated, popular; the king made him a colonel; the Americans, in 1784, gave him a triumphant reception; the sovereigns of Prussia and Austria received him with great consideration.

Then began the second part of his career: in America he had breathed the intoxicating air of liberty and he was ready to fight to give France institutions in harmony with the new principles. At the Assembly of the Notables, in 1787, to the great astonishment of the Comte d'Artois, he demanded the suppression of the *lettres de cachet* and the consolidation of the States-General. He was the soul of the opposition to the edicts of Minister Brienne, and the king punished him by relieving him of his command. So, in 1789, he was elected deputy to the States-General by the nobility of Riom. Eager for popularity, he imagined that he was called to play in France the part of his friend Washington, and his first steps were to assure the public applause: on July 8, he demanded the recall of the troops massed around Paris; on the eleventh, he read at the tribune a proposed Declaration of the Rights of Man, which brought great applause. The day after the fall of the Bastille, the Parisian electors made him commander of the recently formed National Guard: he had armed force in his hands, his ambition was satisfied, he thought he was the man of the hour.

His illusion did not last long: factions divided the Assembly and La Fayette was powerless against them. While Mirabeau could move the Assembly with his powerful eloquence, La Fayette, who was not an orator, had to confine himself to secret negotiations: he sought in vain to reconcile the Right and the Left, and his failure should have shown him how fragile his popularity was. His powerlessness showed much more on October 5: he could not prevent the women's departure for Versailles and had to follow them with the National Guard: he succeeded in saving Marie Antoinette's life by showing himself on the balcony with her. But he had only followed the events; he had not directed them.

He tried then to approach the Court and to foist himself upon the government. With Mirabeau, or against him? The question is very important, for they were jealous and despised each other: Mirabeau called La Fayette Gilles-Caesar or Cromwell-Grandisson; La Fayette felt an instinctive repugnance for the gay adventurer. A sincere alliance between them could never have existed, in spite of the king's efforts to reconcile them. However, La Fayette's prestige was still very considerable; July 14, 1790, was his apotheosis. Medals were struck with his image; he was carried in triumph. The federates kissed his hands, his boots, and even his horse!

The decline came very quickly. Frightened by the military uprisings, he desired to act very harshly: in the Nancy affair, he succeeded in persuading the Assembly to use repression. But the Swiss of Château-vieux found defenders in the people who, little by little, veered away from the marquis. He had known how to get the help of the bourgeois, but he did not know how to reach the people; he was a liberal, not a democrat. As a founder with Bailly and Sieyès of the Society of 1789, he forsook the Jacobins where the violent orators dominated; the break was soon to come.

The king's flight made him lose standing; the affair of the Champ-de-Mars made him odious. Duped by Louis XVI, at the time of the flight to Varennes, he is supposed to have been an accomplice. At the Champ-de-Mars, he ordered the firing which killed so many innocent bystanders and which created a deep rift between him and the men of the Revolution.

He resigned his command of the National Guard and retired to Auvergne, but the peril from without drew him out of his retreat and restored his hope of playing a great part. Success was not forthcoming: the invasion of Belgium failed, while in Paris the Jacobins shook the throne before overthrowing it. Indignant over June 20, La Fayette hastened to save the king. At the bar of the Assembly, he made a violent speech against the Jacobins and tried to utilize a review of the National Guard to force them to close the club. But the queen, who hated La Fayette more than she hated the men of the Left, warned Mayor Pétion, and the review was countermanded. La Fayette, discouraged, joined his army; he had compromised himself uselessly: to the Jacobins he was henceforth "an enemy of the country, a rogue and an imbecile, the greatest of scoundrels", and to the reactionaries "an intriguer and a knave."

Once more, after August 10, he tried to save the throne. With the aid of the municipality of Sedan, he imprisoned the Convention commissaries, but his army did not follow him; he then went over to the enemy with part of his staff. The Austrians treated him as a prisoner of war and, in cowardly revenge, kept him in captivity in the fort of Ollmutz. In spite of the efforts of the United States, he was only freed upon the orders of the victorious Directoire, when he went to Holland and did not return to France until after *Brumaire*. Bonaparte, who did not love metaphysicians, kept him inactive, and during the whole of the Consulate and the Empire, he had to confine himself to a discreet and powerless opposition. During the Hundred Days, he seemed to be nearer to the emperor, but only to crush him more effectively: as vice-president of the Chamber of Deputies, he secured from Napoleon his abdication by threatening him with dethronement. Under the Restoration, he was one of the chiefs of the liberal opposition; he voted against the laws of exception; became affiliated with the Charbonnerie, and led the fight against the Polignac Ministry.

In July, 1830, he was absent from Paris, but hastened there when he heard about the Revolution. Acclaimed as commander of the National Guard, as in 1789, he disappointed the hopes of his partisans, as in '89. While the proclamation of the Republic was awaited, he enthroned Louis-Philippe at the Hôtel de Ville and saluted a popular throne surrounded by republican institutions. Eternal illusions, as soon dispelled as had been those of '89: La Fayette opposed Louis-Philippe as he opposed Louis XVI, Napoleon and Charles X. He died in 1834, an impenitent liberal, popular despite his indecision and his quick changes, a typical knight of freedom, who remained naïve till his death, but deserving of sympathy because of his sincerity, which the very clever and calculating exploiters around him knew how to use for their own ends.

Bailly was less clever and less happy: that man of science lost through politics his popularity and his life.

At first, however, he was successful in everything. Born in Paris, his father, Jean Sylvain Bailly, the keeper of the galleries of the king, had been brought up in the Louvre, and was to keep all his life long a taste for order and pomp. When quite young he wrote bad tragedies in verse, but it was while looking at the sky from the windows of the palace that he discovered his vocation, and from a bad poet changed to a good astronomer. The study of planets was to make his fortune: at twenty-seven the Academy of Science admitted him; he wrote varied academic studies and a remarkable History of Astronomy. He became a member of the French Academy in 1783, and of the Academy of Inscriptions in 1785; honors poured upon him; he was a happy man.

The Revolution came to upset his quiet happiness. At first it loaded him with honors. The Parisian electors, flattered at counting among them a member of so many learned societies, named him secretary of their Assembly, then a deputy of Paris, the first on the list. On June 3 he was chosen dean of the Communes. In that capacity he played a very important part in the tragic days that followed; he was a grave and dignified president. His long face and his long nose gave him a solemn air, which pleased the public. On June 13 he went to Marly to take to the king a memoir from the *Tiers-Etat;* on the twentieth, standing upon a table in the Salle du Jeu de Paume, he was the first to take the famous oath; on the twenty-third he received with dignity the Marquis de Dreux-Brézé, but his honest answer was put in the shade by the impetuous improvisation of Mirabeau. After the fall of the Bastille the Parisian electors elected him Mayor of Paris, and it was in that capacity that he received Louis XVI on July 17. "Sire," he said, offering the keys, "they are the same keys that were presented to Henri IV; he had reconquered his people: here, the people reconquered their king," and he made the king accept the tricolored cockade which had been established.

But the happy days were at an end for Bailly: that position as mayor, which had seemed to fulfill his desires, was to cause his ruin. He loved grandeur, and his enemies, Marat, Camille Desmoulins, reproached him bitterly for his coach, his valets and his armed escort. They were soon to have other things against him: on July 17, 1791, frightened by the crowd which hovered around the altar to the country, he had martial law proclaimed and went to the Champ-de-Mars with La Fayette, a red flag unfurled. The blood poured on that day was to fall later upon his own head. Four months later, he resigned his position as mayor and, giving up politics, he started to travel. But the Revolution had not forgotten him: he was arrested in Melun towards the end of July, 1793. The Revolutionary Tribunal sent him to the guillotine on *Brumaire* 28, *An* II (November 18, 1793). The warrant decreed that he would be beheaded on the Champ-de-Mars, but the people would not allow that sacred spot to be desecrated. During the preliminaries, a fine rain fell continuously, and the old astronomer could not help shivering.

"You are trembling, Bailly," some one shouted jeeringly.

"Yes, my friend," he answered gently, "but from the cold."

A powerful orator, a clever politician, Mirabeau's rival, Barnave was the only one of the Feuillant deputies who has left a name. Though he died at thirty-nine, he had already lived too long. The Revolution, which he had helped to loose, devoured him.

He was born at Grenoble on October 22, 1761. The son of a Protestant barrister, destined for the bar himself, when still quite young he knew oratorical success. The political agitation which upset his province in 1788 placed him in a prominent position; he wrote a pamphlet against the nobility and participated in the Assembly of Vizille, that prologue to the Revolution. Sent by the *Tiers* to the States-General, he was noticed from the first day; in spite of his youth, he was asked to draft the first address of the *Tiers* to the king. He was one of the founders of the Jacobin Society, whose rules he drew up. His oratorical enthusiasm, egged on by the sarcasms of the Right, carried him sometimes to a violence of language which went beyond his thoughts. Irritated by the complaints which the massacre of Toulon and Berthier aroused, he cried, "Was that shed blood so pure?" The whole of the Right rose indignantly and sarcasms poured upon him. In the restaurants, the aristocrats, instead of asking for underdone chops, asked for "chops à la Barnave."

And yet his power as an orator grew every day. Unlike most of his colleagues, who read or recited their speeches, Barnave improvised with marvelous ease. His clear, sober eloquence, purposely cold ("There is no divinity in him," said Mirabeau), could rise to the heights to defend those great ideas of humanity, tolerance and liberty; he carried conviction more by the truth of his reasoning than by great flights of eloquence. Only one orator was greater — Mirabeau — and their rivalry became stronger every day. While Mirabeau was on friendly terms with the Court, Barnave became bolder and bolder. The culminating point of that struggle was, from May 16 to May 23, 1790, the debate upon the authority for peace and war: the two orators showed all the resources of their eloquence. Barnave was pressing, bitter, sharp, but Mirabeau surpassed himself. He won: after his last rebuttal the Assembly refused to let his rival speak.

Barnave was to know in his turn that Tarpeian rock which Mirabeau had evoked in his improvisation. Already shaken when he had helped the interests of the white landlords in the Antilles, his popularity was soon to sink in the Varennes affair.

Over the road from Châlons to Paris drove the royal coach, accompanied by insults and cries of hatred. At the hamlet of La Cave, between Epernay and Château-Thierry, it met the commissaries of the Assembly: Latour-Maubourg, Pétion and Barnave; the three of them climbed into the heavy vehicle in which the royal family was already crowded. It was overwhelmingly warm: Louis XVI, stupefied, did not seem to hear the threats and sarcasms; the queen was suffering, but remained impervious. Barnave looked at her, and in his heart was born a new feeling of admiration and pity for that courageous woman whom fate was crushing and whom he wished to save.

And Barnave was friendly to the Court. Through chivalry, he took upon himself the rôle of adviser which Mirabeau and La Fayette had assumed for their own interest. He became the defender of royalty in the Assembly, and he saved the king in spite of Robespierre, by urging that he should not be prosecuted for his attempt to escape. The firing on the Champ-de-Mars hastened his evolution: he broke with the Jacobins who were too republican for him, and founded the Club of Feuillants to which most of the deputies followed him. During the last two months of the Constituent Assembly the triumvirate — Barnave, Duport, Alexandre de Lameth — governed: the Constitution was amended in favor of the monarchy and threats of war were postponed. A wise policy, but he did not have the time to carry it through.

The decree forbidding the Constituents to be reelected sent Barnave back to private life. He went to Grenoble as early as January, 1792: his policy had failed, and the Feuillants were slowly being ousted from power. The papers found in the Tuileries after August 10 proved his relations with the Court, and a warrant for his arrest was issued on August 29, 1792. He suffered a long imprisonment. On *Frimaire* 7, *An* II (November 27, 1793), the Revolutionary Tribunal condemned him to death. As he mounted the scaffold, he stamped his feet upon the floor of the guillotine, crying out, "This, then, is the price I pay for my services to Liberty!" It was the second generation of great men of the Revolution which was disappearing in that way; soon the Girondins were to follow.

On the brilliant general staff of the Gironde, there was no chief: if Vergniaud was the orator, Brissot was the statesman, and Condorcet the thinker.

Brissot was not a man for the platform; he was a journalist, a propagandist, but a journalist who knew his trade, a propagandist who knew what he was talking about. When quite young, he had tried to acquire an encyclopedic culture. His father, an honest caterer of Chartres, and well-to-do, although possessor of a numerous family — Jacques Pierre was his thirteenth child — had him educated at the College of Chartres. Entering the office of a good lawyer, the young man studied law and devoured the wonderful library of his chief. At twenty-four, in 1778, he wrote a "Theory of Criminal Law" which Voltaire read in manuscript and which he honored with a letter of praise. He learned English and studied English political life and its institutions. As a contributor to the *Courier de l'Europe*, he went to London, where he followed, with the most active sympathy, the parliamentary life so different from that of France. He read a great deal and watched events even more: he wrote a "Tableau de l'Angleterre" and a "Tableau de l'Inde"; he wished to start a *Journal du Lycée de Londres*, and he returned to France to get money. It was an unlucky move. He had hardly arrived when he was sent to the Bastille for having distributed in England a pamphlet against the ministry. He came out after a while, but he was ruined, and he had dragged down with him an associate. Later, this was to give rise to all the slanders against Brissot, that honest man who was accused of being a thief, although he actually lived in poverty, always in debt and often deprived of the necessities of life.

His failure did not discourage him: he went on with his studies and his work with a prodigious activity of mind. He was enthusiastic about American freedom and made it known to the French by his "Examen du voyage du Marquis de Chastellure dans l'Amérique du Nord", and more especially by his book "De la France et des Etats-Unis." In 1788 he went to Holland and then to the United States: doubtless he would have settled there if the Revolution had not recalled him. He arrived, well armed for the fight; at that time no one, except Mirabeau, possessed a wider knowledge than he of the affairs of Europe and the New World.

Back in France, Brissot immediately threw himself into the thick of things, publishing on April 1, 1789, the prospectus of the *Patriote Français*, but his paper, suppressed at once by order of the Council, only reappeared on July 28, 1789. From the first days of the Revolution, Brissot was famous; the keys of the Bastille were handed to him on the day of its fall. After the triumph of the people, he was elected a member of the Parisian section of the Assembly. He was one of the first to join the Jacobin Club and he became one of their most successful orators; he made the acquaintance of Robespierre and they seemed to work well together. All the oppressed found a defender in him: to aid the Negroes, he had founded, as early as 1788, the Société des Amis des Noirs. He was very advanced politically, of republican and even socialistic tendencies.

The flight to Varennes brought him into prominence. He asked for the deposition, he gave a very eloquent picture of Europe divided, powerless, incapable of a serious effort against revolutionary France and, carried away by his eagerness, he drew up the petition of the Champ-de-Mars, which was to have such bloody results.

He was a candidate in Paris for election to the Legislative. The Court, which hated him, put on his tracks a vile pamphleteer, Morande, a well-known calumniator who dragged him in the mud and invented the verb *brissoter*, meaning "to steal." In vain; he was elected, although with difficulty.

At the Legislative, he looked further than the frontiers and was soon to be Foreign Minister for the Gironde. He encouraged war with all his might: according to him, the offensive was without danger, and the Court would be unmasked. On April 20, he triumphed. But Robespierre, a partisan of peace, had become his deadly enemy and undermined his popularity in the Jacobin Club, to which he had been too busy to come since he had been on the Diplomatic Committee. When he reappeared in the Club, on April 25, 1792, to answer the attacks against him and to justify his policy, he was greeted with insults. It was worse on July 26, when he fought against the deposition of the king as untimely: his courageous speech was received with invectives, the tribunes hissed him and even threw things at him, as he went back to his seat; he was accused of wanting to save the king, when he was only thinking of saving France.

Paris disowned him, but Eureet Loir remained faithful; he arrived at the Convention soured, disillusioned. The Republic was established; now calm had to be reëstablished. And during the trial of Louis XVI he was in favor of appealing to the people. If he voted death, it was on condition that the sentence should not be executed until the Constitution had been ratified by the people. He had no sympathy for the king, but was statesman enough to be unwilling to arouse a formidable coalition against France. Until March, 1793, he played a very important part in the Diplomatic Committee, but from that time on he had to defend himself against more and more virulent attacks. Then, on May 22, he published a booklet, "To my constituents", which was a violent attack on the Club of Jacobins, urging that it be closed and the municipality dismissed. The Montagnards answered by May 31 and June 2. Brissot tried to escape to Switzerland, but was arrested in Moulins and brought back to Paris. Before the Revolutionary Tribunal, he was honored by the armchair offered to the most important prisoner. His defence was clever and eloquent, but what were eloquence and sincerity worth against prejudiced judges? He was taken to the scaffold on October 31, 1793. Miss Williams, his friend, saw him pass. "Brissot was serious and thoughtful, and at times an air of discontent clouded his brow, but it was evident that he mourned for the fate of his country rather than his own."

Neither an orator, nor a man of action, Condorcet nevertheless had considerable influence. This thinker, the heir to the Encyclopedists, appeared to many as a beacon and a guide, until the day when unbridled passions calumniated that honest man and finally killed him.

Condorcet belonged to the nobility he was to fight. Against the wishes of his family, he did not enter the army, but was attracted by mathematics. At twenty-two, in 1765, he presented to the Academy of Sciences an "Essai sur le Calcul Intégral", which was remarkable. At twenty-six he became a member of the Academy of Sciences. A new task was awaiting him there: the continuation and completion of Fontenelle's *Eloges* of the dead scientists, — an enormous and difficult task, to which he consecrated himself with scrupulous conscientiousness and in which he showed the extent of his knowledge. His friendship with d'Alembert, his affection for Turgot, led him into new fields. He took the part of the minister reformer and tried to help him with his pen. He became a polemist. His "Reflections on the Commerce in Wheat" were followed by many pamphlets suitable to the occasion:

he defended the Negroes and the Protestants; he was interested in financial and political questions. Soon his name became known by the mass of the public.

And yet he was not in the States-General, for his modesty had prevented him from seeking a place there. He was only in the Parisian municipality elected in September, 1789, but he influenced the writing of the statements which the Commune sent to the Assembly. As a scientist, he was interested in the uniform system of weights and measures, and came to the Assembly to promise the help of the Academy of Sciences for the establishment of the meter; as a journalist he made the public acquainted with his ideas on national education.

Until June 20, 1791, Condorcet remained a constitutional Royalist. The flight to Varennes made a Republican of him; he broke with his friends, abandoned his duties as inspector of the National Treasury and campaigned in favor of the Republic; the reaction which followed the shooting of the Champ-de-Mars did not make him change.

His firm attitude gained popular favor for him: in September, 1791, Paris sent him to the Legislative. He rarely appeared in the tribune: his voice was weak, his delivery monotonous and intentionally cold. Nevertheless, he was always welcomed with great enthusiasm, so great was the respect he commanded. His influence, which was especially great on the committees, spread over all branches of national activity, especially to popular instruction, which he wanted to organize. Hostile to royalty and to the

Church, he approved all revolutionary measures, and August 10 fulfilled all the wishes of one of the first Republicans.

Sent to the Convention by the Department of Aisne, his attitude to the trial of the king astonished his contemporaries: he recognized that the king had to be tried, but he denied that the Convention was competent; he thought the king guilty, but was in favor of the most severe punishment next to death; he could not make up his mind about the question of reprieve. His philosophical scruples were bitterly denounced as hypocrisy by both Royalists and Montagnards. But his influence remained great: naïvely he thought, with many of his colleagues, that other people were ready to espouse the cause of the Revolution and to rise against their tyrants, and he drew up addresses to the Spaniards, to the Batavians, to the Germans, to all the people! This philanthropist lost in politics, encouraged the war of propaganda, the most dangerous and the longest of all.

He was the author of a plan for a constitution, which he read to the Assembly on February 15 and 16, 1793, without being able to have it approved on the spot. The love he had for his work led him to his ruin. On June 2 when the Girondins were exiled, Condorcet remained free. But, to calm the departments in revolt, Hérault de Séchelles and Saint-Just improvised a constitution which the Convention adopted on June 24. Imprudently Condorcet dared, in an "Address to the French Citizens", to attack the work of his young colleagues and to show their

imperfections. Unforgivable blasphemy! Denounced
to the Convention by the ex-Capucin Chabot, Condorcet was declared under arrest. But he had been
able to escape, and he found refuge with an heroic
woman, Mme. Vernet, who for eight months hid
him in her house, number 21, Rue Servandoni. One
does not know which to admire most: the quiet courage of that woman, who daily risked her freedom and
her life to save an outlaw, or the freedom of mind of
the philosopher who, hunted, obliged to hide from
all eyes, yet found time to write in his retreat his
"Esquisse ou Prospectus d'un Tableau historique des
Progrès de l'esprit Humain", a serene profession of
faith in the perfectibility of the human race.

But Condorcet did not wish to compromise his
benefactress any longer. In spite of her watch over
him, he was able to escape. He left Paris and, with
steps made shaky from a long confinement, he reached
Fontenay-aux-Roses where the house of his friend
Sirard was to be opened. The door was shut! Then
Condorcet wandered about the country and slept in a
quarry. Dying of hunger, he entered an inn at Clamart; his ways made him a suspect; his scholar's
innocence achieved his ruin.

"How many eggs in your omelet?"

"A dozen," replied the hungry one.

That was enough to denounce him. He was arrested
and taken to the prison of Bourg-la-Reine. On the
morning of March 29, 1794, he was found dead,
lying face downward. Hunger? Weariness? Poison?
It was only some days later that the name of the

celebrated man who had died obscurely, became known.

Quite different from the Girondins, orators or journalists, the Montagnards were especially men of action. The great stars occupied the tribune and drew notice upon themselves, but a whole set of workers acted in the background and, through their energy, succeeded in saving France. The most illustrious of those workers was Carnot, a great and austere figure, a man of duty first of all.

The mere name of Lazare Carnot evokes the gigantic efforts which France made to organize armies and to overthrow the danger of invasion. It was that silent one who accomplished the colossal labor of organizing the weakening military forces and sending to the frontiers those soldiers who were soon to be triumphant.

That Bourguignon was a man of arms. After studying at the Engineering School of Mézières, in 1783, he had entered the army and been made a captain at thirty. He had been garrisoned in the forts of the North, Calais, Havre, Arras. In that last town, when he was elected in 1787 a member of the local academy, he had become a colleague of the barrister Robespierre. He welcomed the Revolution with joy, as he had had to suffer unjustly. In 1789, he had been imprisoned in Bethune, for having, on a technical question, disagreed with his superiors.

In 1791, he presided at Aire-sur-la-Lys over the Société des Amis de la Constitution, and that same year the Pas-de-Calais sent him to the Legislative.

His début was not very happy. He was suspected of treason because he favored the destruction of the fort of Arras: he cleared himself easily and this honest and modest worker soon regained the favor of his colleagues. He was given missions to the camp of Soissons and to the Army of the Rhine. At the Convention, to which the Pas-de-Calais sent him again, he voted the king's death; but, soon leaving pure politics, he confined himself to technical matters. He was a member of the War and the Diplomatic committees; he was sent as commissary to the Army of the North and, luckier than his colleagues, was not abandoned to the enemy at the time of Dumouriez' betrayal. A member of the Committee of Public Safety, he took charge of military supplies and the movement of the armies: it was he who thought out the plans of campaign and who saw that they were carried through. He was not content to work sixteen hours a day at his desk; he knew how to appear in person: at Wattignies he was seen, a gun in his hand, charging at the head of his troops, beside the commander in chief, Jourdan. Colossal labor, soon to be rewarded! Fourteen armies were raised and they repelled the invasion! Yet, in spite of so many eminent services, Carnot was threatened by the very heart of the Committee of Public Safety itself. Robespierre had taken a dislike to him and Saint-Just, whose military plans he had vetoed on several occasions hated him: there were violent altercations between the proud young representative and his older and more experienced colleagues. And so, on *Thermidor* 9, although he was not among the more active plotters, Carnot did not interfere with them. With Robespierre gone, Carnot went on with his work of reconstruction: he shared in the creation of the Ecole Polytechnique, the Conservatoire des Arts et Métiers, the metric system and the Institute, which he entered himself. The Thermidorian reaction placed him in danger for a short while: Tallien, the former slaughterer, wanted to have him exiled as a Jacobin and might have succeeded if an indignant member had not cried, "But Carnot organized the victory!"

After organizing victory, he wanted to organize peace — too wise to prolong disastrous convulsions, too honest not to be indignant at the rule of rogues. As a member of the Conseil des Anciens, and then of the Directoire, he turned to the moderates and refused to be associated in the *coup d'état* directed against national sovereignty. Barras, not able to make an accomplice of him, treated him as an enemy; on *Fructidor* 18 he was exiled. But his adversaries, in spite of their desire to do so, could not send him to die to Guiana; he succeeded in escaping to Switzerland. He came back after *Brumaire* 18 to be, for a time, minister of war for Bonaparte. But their temperaments were opposed: Carnot served his country, not the ambition of one man. At the Tribunal, he was the steadiest and firmest adversary of budding Caesarism; he was opposed to the Legion of Honor, to the Consulate for life; he even had the courage to be opposed to the establishment of the empire. "Whatever services," he declared, "a citizen has rendered his country, there are limits which honor as well as reason impose to national gratitude. If that citizen has restored public liberty, will it be a reward to offer him the sacrifice of that same liberty? I vote against the proposition."

When the empire was proclaimed, he went into retreat. He came out of it during the somber days of 1814, when France was threatened anew. Napoleon asked him to defend Anvers and he showed himself worthy of the emperor's confidence. During the Hundred Days he believed in Napoleon's sincerity and accepted the post of Minister of the Interior. After Waterloo, when all had abandoned the vanquished and when Fouché was preparing his betrayal, he was almost alone in fighting against the second abdication and in advising resistance to the death. It was because he saw France behind the emperor and understood that to abandon one was to deliver the other to its enemies.

The restored Bourbons sent that great citizen, that great honest man, to die in exile in Magdeburg.

After Robespierre's fall, the heroic period of the Revolution was at an end. The men in power, the Thermidorians, were corrupt ex-terrorists who had become reactionaries or cowards, delighted at having escaped the dangers which had threatened them. Barras was typical of those "rotten bellies", who used the Revolution to feather their own nests and who only thought of enjoying in peace the pleasures of power. He was one of those misled aristocrats who brought to the new society some of the elegance and many of the vices of the Old Régime.

Viscount Paul François de Barras was an army man, an officer in the regiment of Languedoc. Born of a noble family in Provence, he had had an adventurous youth, and a scandalous love affair with a relative of the Bishop of Viviers had caused him to be sent to the Ile-de-France. He was shipwrecked at the Maldives, then rescued and reached Pondichéry just in time to be made a prisoner. Coming back to France after a second campaign, he had led a life of makeshifts and intrigues, and struck up an acquaintance with the Comtesse de la Mothe-Valois, the doubtful heroine of the "Affair of the Necklace." When the Revolution burst, his affairs were in very bad shape. He welcomed enthusiastically the first revolutionary movements, was at the fall of the Bastille, and then went to his native province to proselytize. His patriotic zeal, his affiliation with the Société of the Jacobins, gained him the office of Head Juror to the National Court of Orleans, then deputy of the war to the Convention.

He voted the king's death and sat among the Montagnards. Sent in mission to the Army of Italy, he was at the siege of Toulon, and after its fall formed with his colleagues, Saliceti, Ricord, Fréron, the bloody commission which decimated the guilty town by its shooting. He accompanied Fréron to Marseilles and seconded the zeal of his implacable colleague: the inhabitants were persecuted without regard to party, the statues were destroyed, the town even lost its name to become the-Town-without-a-name. Such excesses irritated the Committee of Public Safety, and the two proconsuls were recalled. Disappointed because they were not received as conquerors, irritated and uneasy at feeling themselves watched and threatened by Robespierre, they plotted his fall in secret. On *Thermidor* 9, Barras played a prominent part without appearing at the Tribune: he was a man of action, not of words. Towards the evening, he formed a small army with the sectionists faithful to the Convention and marched at their head upon the Hôtel de Ville, where Robespierre and his friends were sitting. On that tragic night, when the bravest and the most audacious lost their heads, Barras appeared as the Man of Destiny.

He governed for three days: as commander in chief of the armed force of Paris, he saw to the execution of the Robespierrists and bragged about saving the other victims that were to have gone to the scaffold. He retired on the twelfth, but remained one of the chiefs of the Thermidorian reaction, hostile to the Jacobins, hostile to the Royalists. When they lifted their heads, it was still to Barras, the man of arms, that the frightened Convention looked. On *Vendémiaire* 12, he was again commander of the Parisian Army: he took for his aide a young general on leave, Napoleon Bonaparte, and they broke the Royalist rising without any difficulty. Barras rewarded his lieutenant by securing for him, a little later, the command of the Army of Italy. Barras choosing Bonaparte! It was Destiny once again.

When the Convention was dissolved, Barras became a director and remained one till the end. He incarnated the régime marvelously: audacity and corruption. In the midst of public poverty, he flaunted an insolent luxury and, remembering his origin, he acted as a mighty lord. A handsome man, he wore easily the sumptuous costume designed by David. He loved to receive, and in his drawing-rooms at the Luxembourg there was a very motley society: beside the "Merveilleuses", Madame Tallien, Madame Hamelin, the citizeness Bonaparte and other belles as beautiful and as little clad as the goddesses of Olympus, were financiers, army contractors, speculators, detectives, army men of the *coup d'état*, renegade erring noblemen: a disreputable society, as corrupted as the master of the house himself, who incarnated elegant vice in his person. Barras had beautiful properties in the neighborhood of Paris, bought for a song; his house in Suresnes, his magnificent castle in Grosbois, where he had taken the place of the Comte de Provence. He went there in a coach drawn by milk-white horses, with a pomp worthy of a king of France. It was there that, more at ease, he went on with his orgies.

Very amiable with all, quite a good fellow when his interests were not in jeopardy, he had no scruples, neither in his private nor in his political life. His policy was simple: to last. He struck to the right, to the left, brutally, savagely, like a threatened animal, but the misfortunes of the country left him cold. In 1797 the danger came from the Royalists; he appealed to the soldiers to fight them and Augereau "*Fructidorised*" deputies and directors. In 1798 the danger came from the Jacobins: in *Floréal*, the most dangerous were eliminated; in 1799 the danger was in the Directoire itself: Barras got rid of the two most dangerous ones. But that see-sawing could not last long; a serious rival appeared: Sieyès, whose reputation put in the shade that of the too famous director. Then Barras wanted to be sure of the future and he began negotiations with the pretender, the future Louis XVIII, but too slowly, for Sieyès, on his side, acted quickly. Bonaparte arrived in time to help him and *Brumaire* 18 saw the collapse of the Directoire. Barras was duped in a clever manner: certain approaches had been made and he thought he knew everything, when everything had been done without him. His life of debauch had weakened his intelligence and slackened his energy. On *Brumaire* 18 he was expecting Bonaparte to dinner! Talleyrand and Bruix came, carrying a letter of dismissal: resigned, and without doubt consoled by an enormous sum, Barras signed and retired to Grosbois.

His political career was ended. After offering him several positions in vain, Napoleon mistrusted him and sent him to Brussels, to Marseilles, then to Rome. In return, the Bourbons did not worry him; they even consulted him, and he was able to die in peace in his property in Chaillot, on January 29, 1829. Alexandre Dumas tells that he was present at a dinner at Barras', who was then old and crippled, and saw him eating only bread dipped into the blood of a whole leg of mutton. A symbolical scene: the blood spilt during the Revolution had, on the whole, helped to fatten the Barrases!